Cisco ACI Cookbook

Accelerating application deployment and IT processes

Stuart Fordham

BIRMINGHAM - MUMBAI

Cisco ACI Cookbook

Copyright © 2017 Packt Publishing

All rights reserved. No part of this book may be reproduced, stored in a retrieval system, or transmitted in any form or by any means, without the prior written permission of the publisher, except in the case of brief quotations embedded in critical articles or reviews.

Every effort has been made in the preparation of this book to ensure the accuracy of the information presented. However, the information contained in this book is sold without warranty, either express or implied. Neither the author, nor Packt Publishing, and its dealers and distributors will be held liable for any damages caused or alleged to be caused directly or indirectly by this book.

Packt Publishing has endeavored to provide trademark information about all of the companies and products mentioned in this book by the appropriate use of capitals. However, Packt Publishing cannot guarantee the accuracy of this information.

First published: May 2017

Production reference: 1190517

Published by Packt Publishing Ltd.
Livery Place
35 Livery Street
Birmingham
B3 2PB, UK.
ISBN 978-1-78712-921-4

www.packtpub.com

Credits

Author
Stuart Fordham

Reviewers
Muhammad Rafi
Vijay AR

Commissioning Editor
Pratik Shah

Acquisition Editor
Meeta Rajani

Content Development Editor
Sweeny Dias

Technical Editor
Mohit Hassija

Copy Editor
Madhusudan Uchil

Project Coordinator
Virginia Dias

Proofreader
Safis Editing

Indexer
Mariammal Chettiyar

Graphics
Kirk D'Penha

Production Coordinator
Melwyn Dsa

About the Author

Stuart Fordham is a networking engineer who focuses on security and DevOps. He is CCIE #49337 (Routing and Switching), along with other qualifications such as CCDP, CEH, RHCSA, and MCSE. He has also been a Cisco Champion for 2017 and has authored a series of networking books. He is the network manager for a leading global Communication-as-a-Service company and has worked for hedge funds, the government, and the National Health Service.

First and foremost, I would like to thank my lovely wife. Without her encouragement and inspirational guidance (like saying "You'd be an idiot if you didn't write it"), I would have never written this book.

Secondly, I would like to thank Michael Yandulov and Louie Liang for helping me out while writing this book. I would also like to thank the two people who helped them help me. A big thanks goes to my good buddies Muhammad Rafi and Vijay AR for their invaluable help in editing this book.

Finally, I'd like to thank the team at Packt Publishing for giving me the opportunity to write this book and their support while doing so.

About the Reviewers

Muhammad Rafi, CCIE #49281, is an IP design consultant with one of the UK's largest mobile network operators. He has been in the field of IT and networking for more than 7 years and has worked on several small-to-medium sized network design deployment projects. His entire educational background is related to IT; he holds a BS in electronics engineering from SSUET Karachi and a master's in telecommunication and computer network engineering from London South Bank University, London. Apart from holding a BS, MS, and CCIE, he also possesses certifications from VMware, Microsoft, Citrix, and several others. As technology is changing rapidly, he is never going to stop learning and having bigger dreams, as everyone else does. You can follow him on LinkedIn.

> *I would like to first thank the Almighty God for all his blessings upon me and then my super mom and dad, because they really worked hard on me in the early days of my education and made me the person I am today. Also, I also want to give special thank to my beautiful wife and my two little boys for their sacrifices and moral support whilst working and building up my career in IT. Last but not least, all of my teachers, colleagues, and friends, who really helped me with their support during the whole journey and still do.*

Vijay AR is a cloud architect at OneCloud Consulting with over 10 years of expertise in designing and building solutions for complex enterprise projects across infrastructure, virtualization, and cloud computing. He is also a certified trainer for VMware, Cisco, Microsoft, and NetApp, responsible for training and consulting for both partners and internal teams. He specializes in converged-infrastructure, cloud-computing, and data-center solutions.

www.PacktPub.com

For support files and downloads related to your book, please visit www.PacktPub.com.

Did you know that Packt offers eBook versions of every book published, with PDF and ePub files available? You can upgrade to the eBook version at www.PacktPub.com and as a print book customer, you are entitled to a discount on the eBook copy. Get in touch with us at service@packtpub.com for more details.

At www.PacktPub.com, you can also read a collection of free technical articles, sign up for a range of free newsletters and receive exclusive discounts and offers on Packt books and eBooks.

https://www.packtpub.com/mapt

Get the most in-demand software skills with Mapt. Mapt gives you full access to all Packt books and video courses, as well as industry-leading tools to help you plan your personal development and advance your career.

Why subscribe?

- Fully searchable across every book published by Packt
- Copy and paste, print, and bookmark content
- On demand and accessible via a web browser

Customer Feedback

Thanks for purchasing this Packt book. At Packt, quality is at the heart of our editorial process. To help us improve, please leave us an honest review on this book's Amazon page at https://www.amazon.com/dp/1787129217.

If you'd like to join our team of regular reviewers, you can e-mail us at customerreviews@packtpub.com. We award our regular reviewers with free eBooks and videos in exchange for their valuable feedback. Help us be relentless in improving our products!

Table of Contents

Preface   1
Chapter 1: Understanding Components and the ACI Fabric   7
   Introduction   7
   Understanding ACI and the APIC   10
   An overview of the ACI fabric   14
      ACI hardware   14
      Understanding third-party integration   18
   Converting Cisco from Nexus NX-OS mode to ACI mode   20
      Uploading the ACI image   21
         How to do it...   21
            Method 1 - Using SCP to copy the ACI image from the APIC   21
            Method 2 - Using SCP to copy the ACI image from another SCP server   22
            Method 3 - Using a USB drive to copy the ACI image   22
      Upgrading the image   22
         How to do it...   22
      Logging in   22
         How to do it...   22
      Reverting to NX-OS mode   23
   ACI fabric overlay   24
   An introduction to the GUI   29
      System menu   30
      Tenants menu   36
      Fabric menu   37
      VM Networking   41
      L4-L7 Services   41
      Admin   42
      Operations   42
Chapter 2: Configuring Policies and Tenants   45
   Introduction   46
   Creating fabric policies   47
      How to do it...   48
      How it works...   59
   Creating access policies   60
      How to do it...   60
      How it works...   68

There's more...	70
Creating tenants	**77**
How to do it...	78
How it works...	78
Configuring bridge domains	**79**
How to do it...	80
How it works...	86
Configuring contexts	**88**
How to do it...	89
How it works...	92
There's more...	94
Creating application network profiles	**95**
How to do it...	97
Creating endpoint groups	**98**
How to do it...	99
How it works...	101
Using contracts between tenants	**102**
How to do it...	102
How it works...	115
Creating filters	**115**
How to do it...	116
Creating contracts within tenants	**118**
How to do it...	118
Creating management contracts	**121**
How to do it...	121
How it works...	123
Chapter 3: Hypervisor Integration (and Other Third Parties)	**125**
Introduction	**125**
Installing device packages	**128**
How to do it…	128
How it works…	130
There's more...	131
Creating VMM domains and integrating VMWare	**131**
How to do it…	132
There's more…	142
Associating vCenter domains with a tenant	**143**
How to do it…	143
How it works...	146
Deploying the AVS	**147**

How to do it…	147
How it works…	149
There's more…	150
Discovering VMWare endpoints	150
How to do it…	150
How it works…	151
Adding virtual machines to a tenant	152
How to do it...	153
How it works...	154
Tracking ACI endpoints	154
How to do it…	155
How it works…	155
There's more…	156
Integrating with A10	156
How to do it...	157
How it works...	168
There's more...	168
Deploying the ASAv	169
How to do it...	169
How it works...	171
There's more...	172
Integrating with OpenStack	172
How to do it...	172
How it works...	173
There's more...	173
Integrating with F5	174
Getting ready	174
How to do it...	174
There's more...	183
Integrating with Citrix NetScaler	183
Getting ready	183
How to do it...	183
There's more...	184
Chapter 4: Routing in ACI	**185**
Introduction	185
Creating a DHCP relay	186
How to do it…	186
Creating a DHCP relay using the Common tenant	187
Creating a global DHCP relay	191

How it works…	196
There's more...	196
Utilizing DNS	196
How to do it...	197
How it works...	201
There's more...	201
Routing with BGP	201
How to do it...	202
Configuring a layer-3 outside interface for tenant networks	210
How to do it…	210
Creating routed interfaces	210
Configuring an external SVI	213
Configuring routed sub-interfaces	215
Associating a bridge domain with an external network	215
How to do it…	216
Using route reflectors	219
How to do it...	220
How it works...	223
Routing with OSPF	223
How to do it...	223
Routing with EIGRP	230
How to do it...	230
Using IPv6 within ACI	233
How to do it...	233
How it works...	234
Setting up multicast for ACI tenants	236
How to do it...	236
How it works...	236
Configuring multicast on the bridge domain and interfaces	238
How it works...	238
How it works...	238
There's more...	239
ACI transit routing and route peering	240
How to do it...	241
How it works...	242
There's more...	243
Chapter 5: ACI Security	**245**
Introduction	245
AAA and multiple tenant support	245

Understanding ACI role-based access control (RBAC)	246
Creating local users	247
How to do it...	247
How it works...	249
Creating security domains	250
How to do it...	250
Limiting users to tenants	254
How to do it...	254
Connecting to a RADIUS server	256
How to do it...	256
How it works...	261
Connecting to an LDAP server	265
How to do it...	266
Connecting to a TACACS+ server	268
How to do it...	268

Chapter 6: Implementing Quality of Service in ACI — 269

Introduction	269
Preserving existing CoS settings	270
How to do it...	270
How it works...	271
There's more...	271
Configuring user-defined classes	271
How to do it...	272
How it works...	273
There's more...	274
Creating a basic QoS configuration	274
How to do it...	274
How it works...	276
There's more...	277
Verifying QoS	277
How to do it...	278

Chapter 7: Network Programmability with ACI — 279

Introduction	279
Browsing the object store using the Object Store Browser	280
How to do it...	280
Programming the ACI through REST	286
Getting ready	286
How to do it...	286

Authenticating through REST and XML	287
How to do it...	287
How it works...	288
Creating a tenant using REST and XML	289
How to do it...	289
How it works...	289
Deleting a tenant using REST and XML	290
How to do it...	291
How it works...	291
Creating an APN and an EPG using REST and XML	291
How to do it...	292
How it works...	292
Creating an application profile and EPG using REST	293
How to do it...	293
How it works...	294
Authenticating through REST and JSON	294
How to do it...	294
How it works...	295
Creating a tenant using REST and JSON	296
How to do it...	296
How it works...	296
Using the Python SDK	297
Getting ready	297
How to do it...	298
Logging into the APIC using Cobra	298
How to do it...	298
Creating a tenant using the SDK	299
How to do it...	299
Chapter 8: Monitoring ACI	**301**
Introduction	301
Finding faults	302
How to do it...	303
There's more...	305
Viewing events	306
How to do it...	306
Tenant events	306
Fabric events	306
AAA events	308
Navigating the audit logs	308

How to do it...	308
Setting up Call Home	**311**
How to do it...	311
How it works...	318
There's more...	319
Configuring SNMP	**324**
Getting ready	324
How to do it...	325
How it works...	330
There's more...	330
Configuring Syslog	**332**
How to do it...	332
How it works...	333
Configuring NetFlow	**333**
How to do it...	333
There's more...	334

Chapter 9: Troubleshooting ACI — 335

Introduction	**335**
Layer 2 troubleshooting	**336**
How to do it...	336
FEX troubleshooting	**338**
How to do it...	338
There's more...	339
SSL troubleshooting	**339**
How to do it...	339
There's more...	340
Switch diagnostics	**341**
How to do it...	341
How it works...	344
APIC troubleshooting	**345**
How to do it...	345
There's more...	348
Upgrading the ACI software	**349**
Getting ready	349
How to do it...	351
There's more...	351
VMM troubleshooting	**356**
How to do it...	356
Routing verifications	**359**

How to do it...	359
Troubleshooting external connectivity	359
How to do it...	360
Multicast troubleshooting	361
How to do it...	361
QoS troubleshooting	362
How to do it...	362
There's more...	364
Chapter 10: An End-to-End Example Using the NX-OS CLI	367
Introduction	368
Background	368
Before you start...	368
Setting up in-band and out-of-band access to the nodes	369
How to do it...	369
How it works...	370
Creating the security domain	371
How to do it...	371
Creating the VLAN domain	372
How to do it...	372
How it works...	372
Creating the VMWare domain	373
How to do it...	373
How it works...	374
Creating the tenant	375
How to do it...	375
How it works...	376
Creating the VRF	376
How to do it...	376
How it works...	377
Creating the bridge domains	377
How to do it...	378
How it works...	378
Creating the applications and EPGs	379
How to do it...	380
How it works...	380
Creating the contract	382
How to do it...	382
How it works...	383
Creating an L4-L7 device	385

How to do it...	385
How it works...	389
There's more...	389
Creating service templates	389
How to do it...	390
How it works...	394
Setting up the client VMs	397
How to do it...	397
Index	**401**

Preface

Welcome to the Cisco ACI cookbook! Through a series of easy-to-follow recipes, you will learn how ACI can solve a number of data-center challenges and how to create tenants, implement policies, integrate virtualization technologies, perform routing, secure your ACI Fabric, and troubleshoot and monitor it.

What this book covers

Chapter 1, *Understanding Components and the ACI Fabric*, covers the issues that ACI can overcome and the building blocks of the ACI fabric and walks you through the interface of the controller.

Chapter 2, *Configuring Policies and Tenants*, begins our journey of creating an environment for our tenants and applying policies to them.

Chapter 3, *Hypervisor Integration (and Other Third Parties)*, builds on the foundation of our fabric and extends it, using VMWare and third-party devices.

Chapter 4, *Routing in ACI*, shows how we will unleash our ACI fabric to the rest of the network using IPv4, IPv6, and multicast.

Chapter 5, *ACI Security*, secures our fabric by implementing centralized role-based security.

Chapter 6, *Implementing Quality of Service in ACI*, walks us through prioritizing our traffic through the fabric.

Chapter 7, *Network Programmability with ACI*, explores the ways in which we can control our fabric through APIs.

Chapter 8, *Monitoring ACI*, shows us how to stay on top of any issues as they arise.

Chapter 9, *Troubleshooting ACI*, walks us through a bottom-up troubleshooting approach.

Chapter 10, *An End-to-End Example Using the NX-OS CLI*, brings everything we have covered into one complete scenario.

What you need for this book

All you need is a computer with Internet access, some time, and some coffee.

The majority of the recipes in this book can be performed using the free Cisco Devnet sandboxes, which are browser based.

Who this book is for

This book is meant for network engineers looking to learn about ACI.

A basic understanding of routing protocols, SNMP, and NetFlow is recommended.

Sections

In this book, you will find several headings that appear frequently (Getting ready, How to do it, How it works, There's more, and See also).

To give clear instructions on how to complete a recipe, we use these sections as follows:

Getting ready

This section tells you what to expect in the recipe, and describes how to set up any software or any preliminary settings required for the recipe.

How to do it…

This section contains the steps required to follow the recipe.

How it works…

This section usually consists of a detailed explanation of what happened in the previous section.

There's more…

This section consists of additional information about the recipe in order to make the reader more knowledgeable about the recipe.

See also

This section provides helpful links to other useful information for the recipe.

Conventions

In this book, you will find a number of text styles that distinguish between different kinds of information. Here are some examples of these styles and an explanation of their meaning.

Code words in text, database table names, folder names, filenames, file extensions, pathnames, dummy URLs, user input, and Twitter handles are shown as follows: "Create a new user for JIRA in the database and grant the user access to the `jiradb` database we just created using the following command:"

A block of code is set as follows:

```
<Contextpath="/jira"docBase="${catalina.home}
/atlassian- jira" reloadable="false" useHttpOnly="true">
```

Any command-line input or output is written as follows:

```
mysql -u root -p
```

New terms and **important words** are shown in bold. Words that you see on the screen, for example, in menus or dialog boxes, appear in the text like this: "Select **System info** from the **Administration** panel."

Warnings or important notes appear in a box like this.

Tips and tricks appear like this.

[3]

Reader feedback

Feedback from our readers is always welcome. Let us know what you think about this book-what you liked or disliked. Reader feedback is important for us as it helps us develop titles that you will really get the most out of.

To send us general feedback, simply e-mail feedback@packtpub.com, and mention the book's title in the subject of your message.

If there is a topic that you have expertise in and you are interested in either writing or contributing to a book, see our author guide at www.packtpub.com/authors.

Customer support

Now that you are the proud owner of a Packt book, we have a number of things to help you to get the most from your purchase.

Downloading the color images of this book

We also provide you with a PDF file that has color images of the screenshots/diagrams used in this book. The color images will help you better understand the changes in the output. You can download this file from https://www.packtpub.com/sites/default/files/downloads/CiscoACICookbook_ColorImages.pdf.

Errata

Although we have taken every care to ensure the accuracy of our content, mistakes do happen. If you find a mistake in one of our books-maybe a mistake in the text or the code-we would be grateful if you could report this to us. By doing so, you can save other readers from frustration and help us improve subsequent versions of this book. If you find any errata, please report them by visiting http://www.packtpub.com/submit-errata, selecting your book, clicking on the **Errata Submission Form** link, and entering the details of your errata. Once your errata are verified, your submission will be accepted and the errata will be uploaded to our website or added to any list of existing errata under the Errata section of that title.

To view the previously submitted errata, go to https://www.packtpub.com/books/content/support and enter the name of the book in the search field. The required information will appear under the **Errata** section.

Piracy

Piracy of copyrighted material on the Internet is an ongoing problem across all media. At Packt, we take the protection of our copyright and licenses very seriously. If you come across any illegal copies of our works in any form on the Internet, please provide us with the location address or website name immediately so that we can pursue a remedy.

Please contact us at `copyright@packtpub.com` with a link to the suspected pirated material.

We appreciate your help in protecting our authors and our ability to bring you valuable content.

Questions

If you have a problem with any aspect of this book, you can contact us at `questions@packtpub.com`, and we will do our best to address the problem.

1
Understanding Components and the ACI Fabric

In this chapter, we will cover the following:

- Understanding ACI and the APIC
- An overview of the ACI fabric
- Converting Cisco Nexus from NX-OS mode to ACI mode
- ACI fabric overlay
- An introduction to the GUI

Introduction

Cisco's **Application Centric Infrastructure** (**ACI**) is a big evolutionary step in data center networking, not because it adds programmability to the network--this has been a rising trend over the last few years--but because of the increased compatibility between vendors. This is where the real benefits are.

We can see the start of this evolutionary step with Cisco's FlexPod (an amalgam of Cisco UCS, VMWare hypervisors, and NetApp storage). Here we see properly validated designs that span more than one vendor. This in itself was a big step; after all, it makes sense for a vendor to try and encourage the end user to purchase their equipment instead of their competitors'. This is done for two reasons: compatibility between devices and the vendor's financial success.

Understanding Components and the ACI Fabric

So, what of networks where one vendor can supply all of the equipment, from the networking to the storage and compute elements? It is actually quite rare to find an environment comprising one single vendor in the real world; most networks (and I am including virtualization platforms and storage within this term) have equipment from more than one vendor, because when you are looking for the best performance, you go with the big names (VMWare for virtualization, NetApp for storage, and so on) because they have longevity in the industry and the knowledge and support options that are required. The network becomes heterogeneous, because it needs to be in order to fulfill user, application, and business demands.

The downside to this is that we lose some degree of compatibility. There are industry-standard protocols that provide some level of compatibility back, such as **SNMP (Simple Network Management Protocol)**, Syslog, and **LLDP (Link Layer Discovery Protocol)**, that can facilitate alerting, logging, and communication between devices, but ACI takes this all one step further, taking the heterogeneous data center network and making it, well, homogenous. Through ACI, the data center can be configured rapidly as the application demands, and this includes physical and virtual network elements from multiple vendors. All of this can be performed through one GUI.

Before we dive in, let's take a few moments to understand what ACI is all about, dispelling some of the myths along the way.

Myth: ACI is too expensive

ACI is not cheap to purchase; it is engineered for the data center, so it commands data center prices. Even the most basic of starter kits has a list price of $250,000. While a quarter of a million dollars is enough to get you started in the world of ACI, it is probably out of reach of most people. Even trying to sell ACI, as a "this could revolutionize our business" proposal, within most companies would be difficult. Despite the fact that most companies do not pay list price, ACI represents a huge risk, and for a number of reasons.

ACI is in its infancy, so adoption will be slow. The companies that have the easily available financial resources to dive into it are, most likely, the same kind of businesses that are not typically early adopters. Established companies that have the cash have more accountability to stakeholders, shareholders, and the public, so they are less likely to rush into investing six-figure sums than the eager startup company, to whom $250,000 represents a massive proportion of their available funds.

Nevertheless, as ACI becomes more prevalent, its adoption rate will increase, despite the cost (which can always be negotiated).

Myth: SDN (and ACI) will replace the engineer

The idea of **software-defined networking (SDN)** has caused quite a stir in the networking industry as engineers question whether having a programmable network will mean that the developer slowly takes their place. So, we have some degree of fear when it comes to ACI, yet SDN and ACI only represent a small portion of the market. As the infrastructure scales up and out, SDN makes more sense. In smaller deployments, the costs outweigh the benefits, yet SDN (and ACI) will never replace the network engineer. The developer does not speak the language of networks in the same way, that a traditional network engineer does not talk in development code. The two will remain separate entities in their little silos-- ACI offers a bridge between the two, but both roles remain safe.

So as much as ACI is expensive, data center-specific, and occasionally perceived as a threat to the traditional network engineer, why should you look at it favorably?

This is SDN, the Cisco way

ACI allows the network administrator and application developers to work closer together. Applications change; networks change. Both have life cycles of varying length, and ACI allows these life cycles to coexist with each other and complement each other. Both teams can work together to achieve a common goal.

ACI reduces the complexity of the network with respect to deployment, management, and monitoring, and does this through a common policy framework. Applications can be deployed rapidly, and the administrative overhead on the network is significantly reduced. It is, therefore, application-centric and can facilitate services at layer 4 to 7 to enhance the application life cycle.

Through ACI, we can automate and program the network. We have a singular platform with which to provision the network. We can bring in, with ease, services such as virtualization (VMWare and Hyper-V), firewalls, load balancers, and a whole range of infrastructure that would previously have meant many hours being spent configuring and reconfiguring as the demands of the application changed.

This automation is performed through policies. Policies are centrally configured on **APICs (Application Policy Infrastructure Controllers)**, which are (usually) clustered.

The APIC is where we will start.

Understanding ACI and the APIC

ACI is for the data center. It is a fabric (which is just a fancy name for the layout of the components) that can span data centers using OTV or similar overlay technologies, but it is not for the WAN. We can implement a similar level of programmability on our WAN links through **APIC-EM (Application Policy Infrastructure Controller Enterprise Module)**, which uses ISR or ASR series routers along with the APIC-EM virtual machine to control and program them. APIC and APIC-EM are very similar; just the object of their focus is different. APIC-EM is outside the scope of this book, as we will be looking at data center technologies.

The APIC is our frontend. Through this, we can create and manage our policies, manage the fabric, create tenants, and troubleshoot. Most importantly, the APIC is not associated with the data path. If we lose the APIC for any reason, the fabric will continue to forward the traffic.

To give you the technical elevator pitch, ACI uses a number of APIs (application programming interfaces) such as REST (Representational State Transfer) using languages such as JSON (JavaScript Object Notation), and XML (eXtensible Markup Language), as well as the CLI and the GUI to manage the fabric, and other protocols such as OpFlex to supply the policies to the network devices. The first set (those that manage the fabric) are referred to as **northbound** protocols. Northbound protocols allow lower-level network components talk to higher-level ones. OpFlex (which we will discuss later in this chapter) is a **southbound** protocol. Southbound protocols (such as OpFlex and OpenFlow, which is another protocol you will hear in relation to SDN) allow the controllers to push policies down to the nodes (the switches).

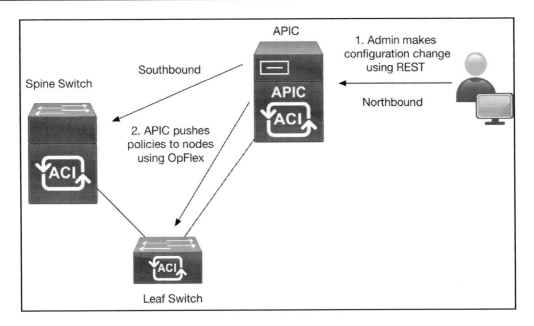

Figure 1

This is a very brief introduction to the *how*. Now let's look at the *why*. What does ACI give us that the traditional network does not?

In a multi-tenant environment, we have defined goals. The primary purpose is that one tenant remains separate from another. We can achieve this in a number of ways.

We could have each of the tenants in their own **DMZ (demilitarized zone)**, with firewall policies to permit or restrict traffic as required. We could use VLANs to provide a logical separation between tenants. This approach has two drawbacks.

It places a greater onus on the firewall to direct traffic, which is fine for northbound traffic (traffic leaving the data center) but is not suitable when the majority of the traffic is east-west bound (traffic between applications within the data center; see Figure 2).

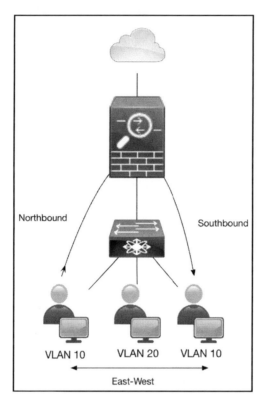

Figure 2

We could use switches to provide layer-3 routing and use access lists to control and restrict traffic; these are well designed for that purpose.

Also, in using VLANs, we are restricted to a maximum of 4,096 potential tenants (due to the 12-bit VLAN ID).

An alternative would be to use **VRFs (virtual routing and forwarding)**. VRFs are self-contained routing tables, isolated from each other unless we instruct the router or switch to share the routes by exporting and importing **route targets (RTs)**. This approach is much better for traffic isolation, but when we need to use shared services, such as an Internet pipe, VRFs can become much harder to keep secure.

One way around this would be to use route leaking. Instead of having a separate VRF for the Internet, this is kept in the global routing table and then leaked to both tenants. This maintains the security of the tenants, and as we are using VRFs instead of VLANs, we have a service that we can offer to more than 4,096 potential customers. However, we also have a much bigger administrative overhead. For each new tenant, we need more manual configuration, which increases our chances of human error.

ACI allows us to mitigate all of these issues.

By default, ACI tenants are completely separated from each other. To get them talking to each other, we need to create contracts, which specify what network resources they can and cannot see. There are no manual steps required to keep them separate from each other, and we can offer Internet access rapidly during the creation of the tenant. We also aren't bound by the 4,096 VLAN limit. Communication is through VXLAN, which raises the ceiling of potential segments (per fabric) to 16 million (by using a 24-bit segment ID).

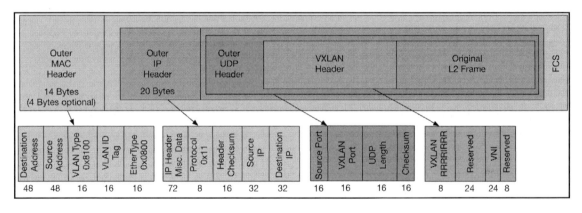

Figure 3

VXLAN is an overlay mechanism that encapsulates layer-2 frames within layer-4 UDP packets, also known as MAC-in-UDP (Figure 3). Through this, we can achieve layer-2 communication across a layer-3 network. Apart from the fact that through VXLAN, tenants can be placed anywhere in the data center and that the number of endpoints far outnumbers the traditional VLAN approach, the biggest benefit of VXLAN is that we are no longer bound by the Spanning Tree Protocol. With STP, the redundant paths in the network are blocked (until needed). VXLAN, by contrast, uses layer-3 routing, which enables it to use **equal-cost multipathing** (**ECMP**) and link aggregation technologies to make use of all the available links, with recovery (in the event of a link failure) in the region of 125 microseconds.

With VXLAN, we have endpoints, referred to as **VXLAN Tunnel Endpoints (VTEPs)**, and these can be physical or virtual switch ports. **Head-End Replication (HER)** is used to forward broadcast, unknown destination address, and multicast traffic, which is referred to (quite amusingly) as BUM traffic.

This 16M limit with VXLAN is more theoretical, however. Truthfully speaking, we have a limit of around 1M entries in terms of MAC addresses, IPv4 addresses, and IPv6 addresses due to the size of the TCAM (**ternary content-addressable memory**). The TCAM is high-speed memory, used to speed up the reading of routing tables and performing matches against access control lists. The amount of available TCAM became a worry back in 2014 when the BGP routing table first exceeded 512 thousand routes, which was the maximum number supported by many of the Internet routers. The likelihood of having 1M entries within the fabric is also pretty rare, but even at 1M entries, ACI remains scalable in that the spine switches let the leaf switches know about only the routes and endpoints they need to know about. If you are lucky enough to be scaling at this kind of magnitude, however, it would be time to invest in more hardware and split the load onto separate fabrics. Still, a data center with thousands of physical hosts is very achievable.

An overview of the ACI fabric

A **fabric** is a fancy term for how the computing, network, and software components of a data center are laid out. The name itself comes from the crisscrossing of the network, much like an item of weaved clothing. The ACI fabric is relatively simplistic. It employs a two-tier design made of **spine** and **leaf** switches, but very particular switches.

ACI hardware

In Figure 4, we can see a typical deployment with two spines and three leaves. The Nexus 9500 modular switches are deployed at the top of the topology and act as spines, which in a traditional three-tiered network design would be the aggregation or core switches. Line cards are used to provide the **ASICs (application-specific integrated circuitry)** required for ACI. There are different line cards available, so make sure you are not purchasing a card that is NX-OS mode only.

The next component is the leaf switches. These are the Nexus 9300-series switches.

The spines connect to the leaves through 40 GE ports, but the spines and leaves are never connected (spine to spine or leaf to leaf).

Chapter 1

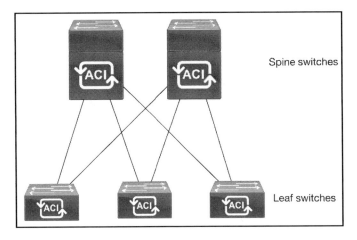

Figure 4

We can also extend the network, offering greater port density through Nexus 2000-series fabric extenders:

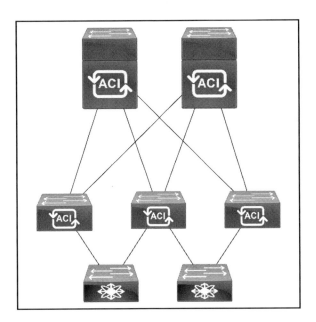

Figure 5

We can also add storage directly to the leaves themselves:

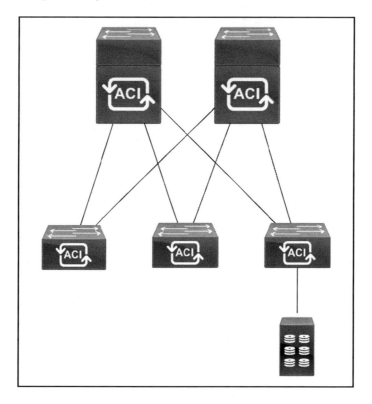

Figure 6

Alternatively, we could use another pair of switches, such as Cisco Nexus 5000-series switches, which would connect to the leaf switches:

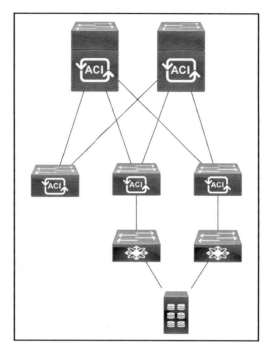

Figure 7

The APIC controllers connect to the leaf switches.

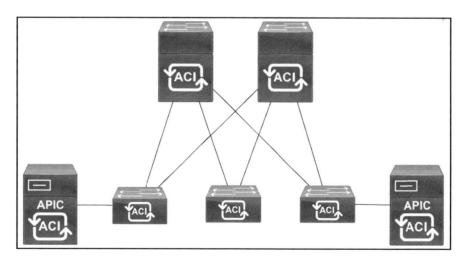

Figure 8

The APIC controllers are completely separate from the day-to-day running of ACI. We need them to push new policies. They do not play a part in the functioning of the ACI fabric's data plane, however--only in the control plane.

The control plane is what we learn, such as routing information. The data plane is the movement of packets based upon information in the control plane.

If we lose one controller, then our tenants' traffic still flows. If we lose all our controllers, then our tenants' traffic still flows; we are just unable to push new policies until the controllers are reinstated into the network.

ACI best practice states that we should have a minimum of three controllers. Having three controllers offers high availability; it offers physical redundancy as well as database redundancy. Why not just two controllers, though? Three controllers (well, just an odd number greater than one) work better in a split-brain scenario (one controller disagreeing with another). In such an event, the majority would rule. The controllers use LLDP to find each other, which is part of the process discussed in the ACI fabric overlay section later on in this chapter. We will look at how to use multiple controllers in the troubleshooting section, as the majority of this book uses a much simpler design with just one controller, one spine, and two leaf switches, as seen when we look at the fabric menu later on in this chapter.

Understanding third-party integration

One of the most attractive reasons to deploy ACI is the ease of integration with other Cisco products (such as the ASAv firewall) and third-party systems.

This integration is performed through **OpFlex**. OpFlex is an open standards-based southbound protocol, designed to facilitate multi-vendor integration in both data center and cloud networks. OpFlex is important as it distinguishes ACI from other SDN models, which have integration but do not support the full feature set. The easiest way to try and explain this would be to look at it in the context of SNMP.

SNMP (Simple Network Management Protocol) allows monitoring network hardware, and all devices support the most basic **MIB (Management Information Base)** of `iso.org.dod.internet.mgmt`, so at the most basic level, you can pull out data such as interfaces and IP addresses. We are getting data but at the lowest common denominator. We need extra information, by way of specific MIBs, to be able to monitor our firewall's VPN tunnels or the nodes in our load balancers. OpFlex gives us all the information, but the data is not bound to any particular format. It is a declarative model, which benefits any interested party. This declarative model is based on promise theory.

Promise theory, developed by Mark Burgess in the 1990s, sets ACI apart from other SDN implementations. They use imperative control, in which we have a controlling system, and the system being controlled is relieved of the burden of doing the thinking. While this does offer more autonomy to the controller, it can also create a bottleneck within the system. ACI, however, uses a declarative model. This model states what should happen but not how it should be done (leaving that up to the node being controlled). The node then makes a promise to achieve the desired state and, importantly, communicates back to the controller the success or failure of the task, along with the reason why. The controller is no longer a bottleneck in the system, and the commands are simpler; instead of separate commands to implement the same function on different vendor equipment, we have one command set understandable by both vendors' equipment. This is the benefit of open standards.

Even with open standards, though, there can be some ulterior motive. It is all well and good having the next best thing for integrating different technologies, but when this is designed for those technologies to run under one particular company's product, there can be some hesitation. However, there is a large backing from several renowned companies, such as Microsoft, IBM, Citrix, Red Hat, F5, SunGard Availability Services, and Canonical. So why has OpFlex gathered such a wide backing?

With the *traditional* SDN model, there is a bottleneck: the SDN controller. As we scale out, there is an impact on both performance and resilience. We also lose simplicity and agility; we still need to make sure that all the components are monitored and safeguarded, which invariably means bolting on *more* technology to achieve this.

OpFlex takes a different approach. A common language ensures that we do not need to add any extras that are not part of the original design. There is still complexity, but it is moved toward the edges of the network, and we maintain resilience, scalability, and simplicity. If we lose all of the controllers, then the network continues to operate--we may not be able to make policy changes until we restore the controllers, but the tenant's data still flows, uninterrupted.

The protocol itself uses XML or JSON as the transmission medium. It allows us to see each node as a **managed object** (**MO**). Each MO consists of the following:

- Properties
- Child relations
- Parent relations
- MO relations
- Statistics
- Faults
- Health

While the ins and outs of these are beyond the scope of this book, you can read about them more in the IETF drafts. The first one in 2014 (`https://tools.ietf.org/html/draft-smith-opflex-00`) listed all these seven items, but subsequent drafts--the most recent being October 27, 2016 (`https://tools.ietf.org/html/draft-smith-opflex-03`)--compress the last four items into one, labeled *observables*.

What all this means is that for third-parties, OpFlex means greater integration across SDN platforms. If and when OpFlex does become a truly open standard, different vendors, equipment will be able to speak the same language using a simple JSON file.

Converting Cisco from Nexus NX-OS mode to ACI mode

To use ACI, we need to make sure that we are running our switches in ACI mode. We can check which version we are running by using the `show version` command:

```
BIOS: version 08.06
NXOS: version 6.1(2)I3(3)
BIOS compile time: 12/03/2014
NXOS image file name is: bootflash:///n9000-dk9.6.1.2.I3.3.bin
NXOS compile time: 12/05/2014 10:50:20 [12/05/2014 2:25]
```

We can tell that we are running an NX-OS mode switch as the image filename begins with `n9000`. ACI image filenames begin with `aci-n9000`.

The following instructions are for NX-OS release 6.1(2)I3(3) and later, and ACI image version 11.0(2x) or later. There are slight differences with earlier releases, so it is best to make sure you are on these releases before attempting the switch from NX-OS mode to ACI mode.

Check whether your hardware is supported: look in the release notes for Cisco Nexus 9000 Series ACI-mode switches.

Remove or turn off any unsupported module (`poweroff module <module>` command). If you do not do this step, the software will use a recovery/retry mechanism before powering down the unsupported module, which can cause delays.

If you have a dual-supervisor system, then confirm that the standby supervisor module is in the ha-standby state using the `show module` command.

Use it like this: `show install all impact epld <epld-image-name>`. This will check that the switch does not require any EPLD image upgrade. **EPLD** stands for **electronic programmable logic device**, and these enhance hardware functionality or resolve known issues. EPLD upgrades are quite infrequent, but they should not be overlooked.

Uploading the ACI image

We have a number of ways of performing the upgrade. We can use SCP to copy the image from the APIC to the switch, upgrade from another SCP server, or copy it directly from a USB port. We will look at all three methods, and are assuming that the Nexus switch has already been introduced into the network and has connectivity.

A word of warning when using USB drives, though: smaller is better. Taking a 1 TB drive loaded with all your favorite Nexus images and expecting it to work will only leave you hunting around for a 2 GB drive that has sat in a drawer gathering dust for a few years. This is due to the level of file system support. Older IOS versions only supported FAT16, which has a file size limit of 2 GB, while newer ones support FAT32 (such as IOS 15.1). Sometimes, it is easier to play it safe and go with FAT16.

How to do it...

Method 1 - Using SCP to copy the ACI image from the APIC

1. Enable SCP on the Nexus switch:

   ```
   switch(config)# features scp-server
   ```

2. Copy the image from the APIC server to the Nexus switch using the CLI:

   ```
   scp -r /firmware/fwrepos/fwrepo/<switch-image-name>
   admin@switch-ip-address:switch-image
   ```

Understanding Components and the ACI Fabric

Method 2 - Using SCP to copy the ACI image from another SCP server

1. Copy the file from the SCP server using the switch's command line:

   ```
   Switch# copy scp: bootflash:
   ```

You will be prompted for the details of the SCP server and filenames.

Method 3 - Using a USB drive to copy the ACI image

We can copy an image from a USB drive to bootflash, using the `dir` command first so that we can cut and paste the filename in the `copy` command:

```
Switch# dir usb1:
(or dir usb2: depending on which USB slot you have plugged the drive into)
Switch# copy usb1:<ACI-image-name> bootflash:
```

If we have a dual-supervisor system, we have an additional step, which is to copy the ACI image to the standby supervisor module:

```
Switch(config)# copy bootflash:aci-image bootflast://sup-standby/
```

Upgrading the image

The next step is to upgrade the image.

How to do it...

In the following code, we first turn off NX-OS mode. We then make sure that the first change survives a reboot. In the third line, we boot the supervisor modules using the ACI image specified. Lastly, we perform a reload of the switch.

```
Switch(config)# no boot nxos
Switch(config)# copy running-config startup-config
Switch(config)# boot aci bootflash:aci-image-name
Switch(config)# reload
```

Logging in

Once the switch has rebooted with the new image, we can log in.

How to do it...

We log in using the username `admin` and the password specified during setup. Notice that the fabric discovery process has been started at this point. It may be some minutes before the services start and we are able to access the switch via the console.

```
User Access Verification
(none) login: admin
************************************************************************
**
    Fabric discovery in progress, show commands are not fully functional
    Logout and Login after discovery to continue to use show commands.
************************************************************************
**
(none)#
```

Reverting to NX-OS mode

If, for any reason, you need to revert to NX-OS mode from ACI mode, then follow these steps:

1. Reload the switch:

   ```
   admin@apic1:aci> reload
   ```

2. Access the bootloader:

   Ctrl+]
   ```
   loader>
   ```

3. Boot using the NX-OS image:

   ```
   loader> boot nxos-image-name
   ```

This can take a little while (usually under half an hour) while the filesystem is reformatted to make subsequent reloads faster.

As you can see, from the previous code, the switch performs a fabric discovery. We will look at this in the next section.

ACI fabric overlay

ACI uses **inter-fabric messaging** (**IFM**) to communicate between the different nodes. IFM uses TCP packets, which are secured by 1024-bit SSL encryption, and the keys are stored on secure storage. The **Cisco Manufacturing Certificate Authority** (**CMCA**) signs the keys.

Issues with IFM can prevent fabric nodes communicating and from joining the fabric. We will cover this in greater depth in the SSL Troubleshooting recipe in Chapter 9, *Troubleshooting ACI*, but we can look at the output of the checks on a healthy system:

```
apic1# netstat -ant | grep :12
tcp        0      0 10.0.0.1:12151          0.0.0.0:*               LISTEN
tcp        0      0 10.0.0.1:12215          0.0.0.0:*               LISTEN
tcp        0      0 10.0.0.1:12471          0.0.0.0:*               LISTEN
tcp        0      0 10.0.0.1:12279          0.0.0.0:*               LISTEN
<truncated>
tcp        0      0 10.0.0.1:12567          10.0.248.29:49187       ESTABLISHED
tcp        0      0 10.0.0.1:12343          10.0.248.30:45965       ESTABLISHED
tcp        0      0 10.0.0.1:12343          10.0.248.31:47784       ESTABLISHED
tcp        0      0 10.0.0.1:12343          10.0.248.29:49942       ESTABLISHED
tcp        0      0 10.0.0.1:12343          10.0.248.30:42946       ESTABLISHED
tcp        0      0 10.0.0.1:50820          10.0.248.31:12439       ESTABLISHED
apic1# openssl s_client -state -connect 10.0.0.1:12151
CONNECTED(00000003)
SSL_connect:before/connect initialization
SSL_connect:SSLv2/v3 write client hello A
SSL_connect:SSLv3 read server hello A
depth=1 O = Cisco Systems, CN = Cisco Manufacturing CA
verify error:num=19:self signed certificate in certificate chain
verify return:0
SSL_connect:SSLv3 read server certificate A
SSL_connect:SSLv3 read server key exchange A
SSL_connect:SSLv3 read server certificate request A
SSL_connect:SSLv3 read server done A
SSL_connect:SSLv3 write client certificate A
SSL_connect:SSLv3 write client key exchange A
SSL_connect:SSLv3 write change cipher spec A
SSL_connect:SSLv3 write finished A
SSL_connect:SSLv3 flush data
SSL3 alert read:fatal:handshake failure
SSL_connect:failed in SSLv3 read server session ticket A
139682023904936:error:14094410:SSL routines:SSL3_READ_BYTES:sslv3 alert handshake failure:s3_pkt.c:1300:SSL alert number 40
139682023904936:error:140790E5:SSL routines:SSL23_WRITE:ssl handshake failure:s23_lib.c:177:
---
Certificate chain
```

```
    0 s:/CN=serialNumber=PID:APIC-SERVER-L1 SN:TEP-1-1, CN=TEP-1-1
       i:/O=Cisco Systems/CN=Cisco Manufacturing CA
    1 s:/O=Cisco Systems/CN=Cisco Manufacturing CA
       i:/O=Cisco Systems/CN=Cisco Manufacturing CA
    ---
    Server certificate
    -----BEGIN CERTIFICATE-----
    <runcated>
    -----END CERTIFICATE-----
    subject=/CN=serialNumber=PID:APIC-SERVER-L1 SN:TEP-1-1, CN=TEP-1-1
    issuer=/O=Cisco Systems/CN=Cisco Manufacturing CA
    ---
    No client certificate CA names sent
    ---
    SSL handshake has read 2171 bytes and written 210 bytes
    ---
    New, TLSv1/SSLv3, Cipher is DHE-RSA-AES256-GCM-SHA384
    Server public key is 2048 bit
    Secure Renegotiation IS supported
    Compression: zlib compression
    Expansion: NONE
    SSL-Session:
        Protocol  : TLSv1.2
        Cipher    : DHE-RSA-AES256-GCM-SHA384
        Session-ID:
        Session-ID-ctx:
        Master-Key: 419BF5E19D0A02AA0D40BDF380E8E959A4F27371A87EFAD1B
        Key-Arg   : None
        PSK identity: None
        PSK identity hint: None
        SRP username: None
        Compression: 1 (zlib compression)
        Start Time: 1481059783
        Timeout   : 300 (sec)
        Verify return code: 19 (self signed certificate in certificate chain)
    ---
    apic1#
```

IFM is essential in the success of the discovery process. A fabric node is only considered *active* when the APIC and the node can exchange heartbeats through IFM. Going forward, though, we still need IFM once we have active nodes, as it is also used by the APIC to push policies to the fabric leaf nodes.

Understanding Components and the ACI Fabric

The fabric discovery process has three stages and uses IFM, **LLDP (Link Layer Discovery Protocol)**, **DHCP (Dynamic Host Configuration Protocol)**, and **TEPs (tunnel endpoints)**:

1. **Stage 1**: A second discovery brings in any spines connected to initial "seed" leaf.
2. **Stage 2**: The leaf node that is directly connected to APIC is discovered.
3. **Stage 3**: In this stage, we have the discovery of other leaf nodes and other APICs in the cluster.

The process can be visualized as follows:

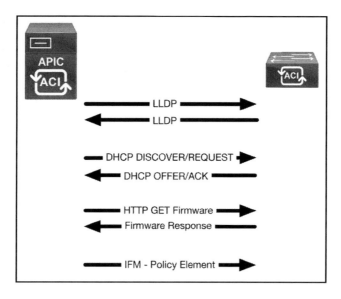

Figure 9

The node can transition through a number of different states during the discovery process:

- **Unknown:** Node discovered but no node ID policy configured
- **Undiscovered:** Node ID configured but not yet discovered
- **Discovering:** Node discovered but no IP address assigned
- **Unsupported:** Node is not a supported model
- **Disabled:** Node has been decommissioned
- **Inactive:** No IP connectivity
- **Active:** Node is active

Chapter 1

Using the `acidiag fnvread` command, you can see the current state. In the following command output, the leaf node is in the `unknown` state (note that I have removed the final column in the output, which was `LastUpdMsg`, the value of which was 0):

```
apic1# acidiag fnvread
ID  Pod ID Name        Serial Number     IP Address      Role            State
-------------------------------------------------------------------------------
 0      0              TEP-1-101         0.0.0.0         unknown         unknown
Total 1 nodes
apic1#
```

During fabric registration and initialization, a port may transition to an *out-of-service* state. In this state, the only traffic permitted is DHCP and CDP or LLDP. There can be a number of reasons why we would transition to this state, but these are generally due to human error, such as cabling or LLDP not being enabled; again, these are covered in the *Layer-2 troubleshooting* recipe in `Chapter 9`, *Troubleshooting ACI*.

There are a couple of ways in which we can check the health of our controllers and nodes. We can use the CLI to check LLDP (`show lldp neighbors`), or we can use the GUI (**System | Controllers | Node | Cluster as Seen by Node**):

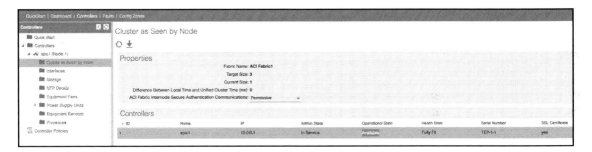

Figure 10

[27]

Understanding Components and the ACI Fabric

This shows us the APIC, and we can look at our leaf nodes from the **Fabric** menu. In the code output from `acidiag fnvread`, we saw a node named `TEP-1-101`. This is a leaf node, as we can see from the GUI (**Fabric** | **Inventory** | **Fabric Membership**):

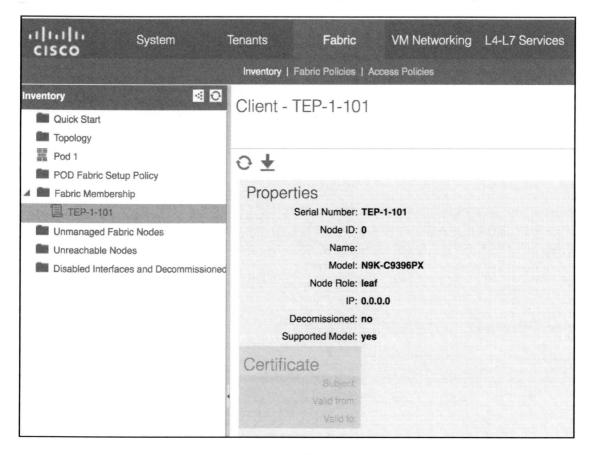

Figure 11

We will look at the GUI in the next section.

An introduction to the GUI

On accessing the APIC, we are presented with the login page. It can take a few minutes for the system to fully initialize before we can log in.

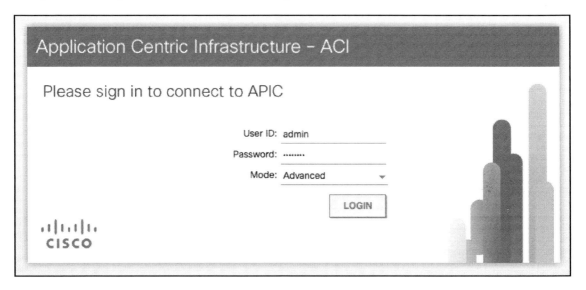

Figure 12

Once we have successfully logged in, we are shown the **System** page. We have the main menu at the top, and each menu item has a submenu.

Understanding Components and the ACI Fabric

Here, we can see the **System** menu, with its submenu showing **Quickstart**, **Dashboard**, **Controllers**, **Faults**, and **Config Zones**:

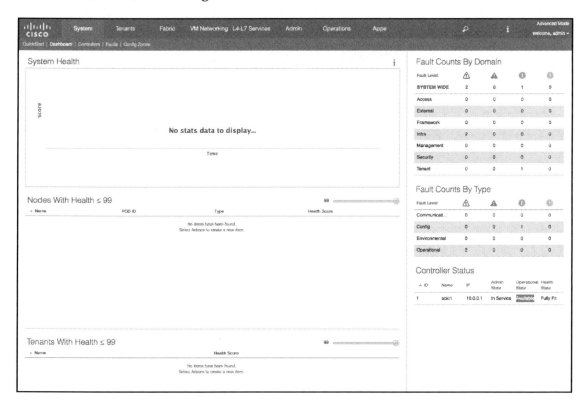

Figure 13

System menu

The system page shows us the health of the system, separated into the overall system health and nodes and tenants with under 99% health. Faults counts are listed on the right-hand side, by domain, and by type. We can see the controller status in the bottom right-hand corner.

Chapter 1

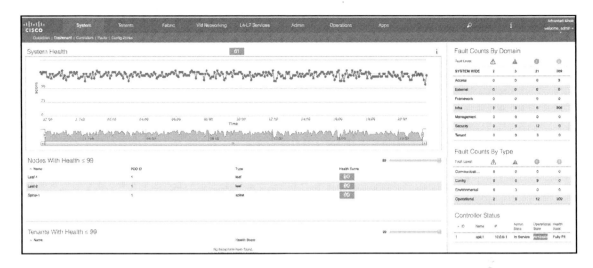

Figure 14

Moving on to the **Controllers** submenu we can see the screen from the previous section.

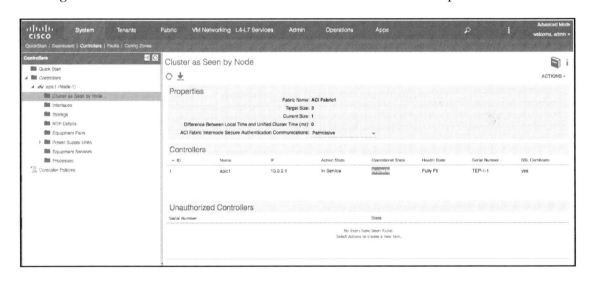

Figure 15

Understanding Components and the ACI Fabric

We have one controller (`apic1`); its IP address is `10.0.0.1`, it is in service and available, and the health state is **Fully Fit**. If we click on any of the column headings, we can sort them by ascending or descending order, which is useful if you have a large number of controllers.

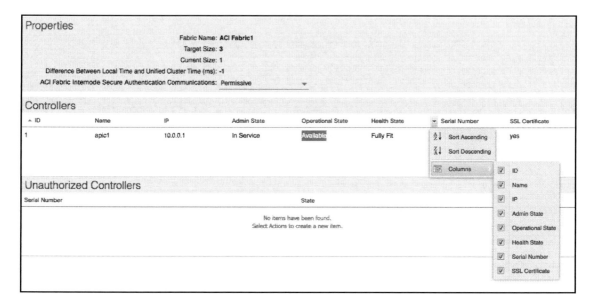

Figure 16

We can see the interfaces present on our controller (`apic1`) from the **Interfaces** menu on the left-hand side:

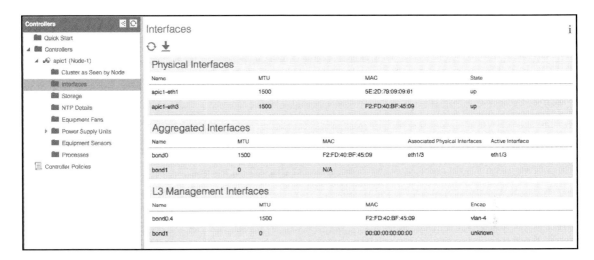

Figure 17

We can keep track of how much storage we have used from the **Storage** menu option, and again, this is sortable by clicking on the column heading:

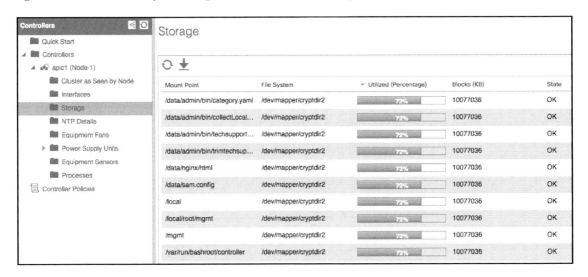

Figure 18

Understanding Components and the ACI Fabric

You will notice that the screen flickers every few seconds as it refreshes.

Also, in this section, we can see stats on our NTP servers, our fans and power supply units, and the equipment sensors (which in the simulator are all empty). Under **Processes**, we can see how much memory we are currently using from the **Stats** option:

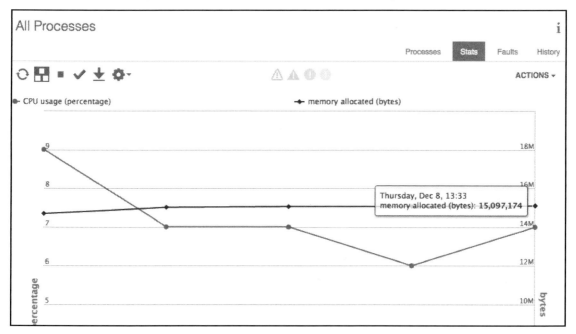

Figure 19

Chapter 1

We can also check on the CPU usage from the same window:

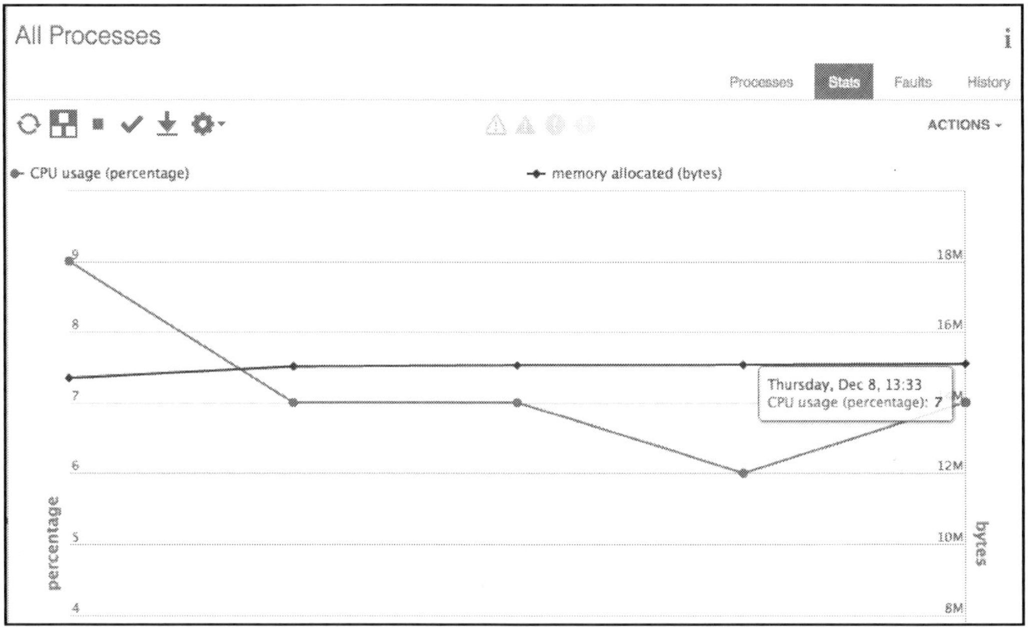

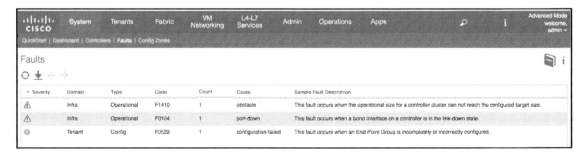

Figure 20

We can also see current and historical faults and events from the **Processes** menu.

The last menu option under **Controllers** is **Controller Policies**, where we can set policies for exporting diagnostic information. We will look at this in the troubleshooting section.

The final two options are **Faults**, in which we can see a couple of examples and **Config Zones**.

Figure 21

[35]

We do not have any zones, but we can create one from the drop-down menu. Configuration zones allow us to subdivide our ACI fabric, meaning that we can make configuration changes to one zone at a time, reducing the chances of an error affecting the entire fabric. Note that if you get access to the Cisco Devnet sandbox environment, the **Config Zones** option is unavailable. Devnet is a great place to learn the developer side of Cisco's products as well as getting access to hands-on labs and virtual and hardware-based sandbox environments. The virtual ones are fairly limited, but available all the time. The physical rack equipment offers the full range of functionality but does get booked up months in advance. You can find more about Devnet by going to the Devnet site: `https://developer.cisco.com/site/devnet/home/index.gsp`.

Tenants menu

The **Tenants** tab shows us all our tenants. We have three preconfigured (**common**, **infra**, and **mgmt**):

Name	Description	Bridge Domains	VRFs	EPGs	Health Score
common		1	2	0	100
infra		1	1	1	100
mgmt		1	2	0	100

Figure 22

If we select a tenant and go through the options, we can see the application profiles assigned to it, the networking configuration, layer 4-layer 7 service parameters, and all of the policies. We will go through these in greater detail in the next chapter when we set up some tenants.

This is where we will create new tenants.

Fabric menu

From the **Fabric** menu, in the **Inventory** submenu, we can see our topology:

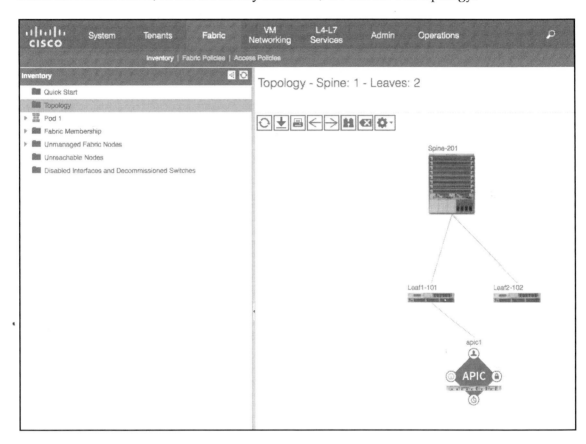

Figure 23

Understanding Components and the ACI Fabric

If we expand the pod out, we can see all of our leaf and spine nodes:

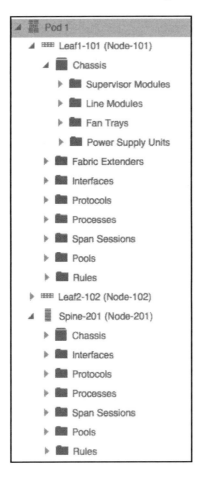

Figure 24

Going through these, we can see our interfaces, routing tables, processes, pools, and rules. One thing to note here is that we have many more routing options with a leaf node than we do with a spine node:

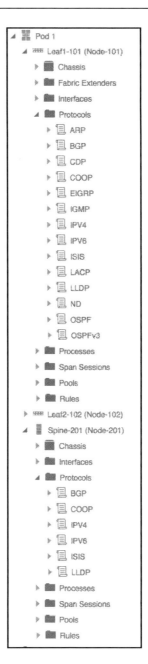

Figure 25

Under the **Fabric Membership** option, we have a list of our leaf and spine nodes, which shows us the serial numbers, ID, name, model, role, and assigned IP address. It also gives us the certificate information, so we know that SSL is healthy and IFM can function.

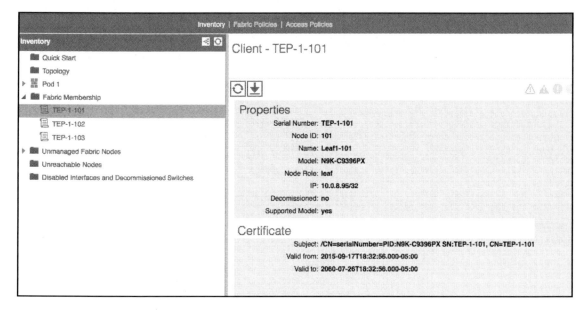

Figure 26

The last three options in this menu are for the nodes we may be having issues with, whether they are currently unmanaged, unreachable, or disabled and decommissioned.

The other options in the **Fabric** submenu are our policies. Here, we can set up callhome policies, monitoring, troubleshooting, spanning tree and VPC policies, whether we want to have CDP turned off or on, and various layer-2 policies. Many of these options have three options; take LLDP for example. We have an option for **LLDP-OFF** (disabled), **LLDP-ON** (enabled), and default (Receive State is enabled, and Transmit State is enabled). Similarly, for CDP we have **CDP-OFF** (disabled), **CDP-ON** (enabled), and default (where the Admin State is **Disabled**).

VM Networking

Under the **VM Networking** menu is where we would start connecting ACI into our third-party vendors. The default options are **Microsoft**, **OpenStack**, and **VMWare**.

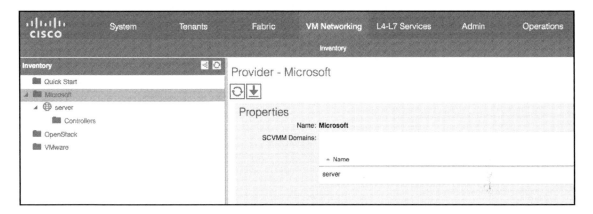

Figure 27

L4-L7 Services

L4-L7 Services allows us to further extend our ACI fabric with additional third-party solutions. This is performed through the addition of packages, which we can import from the **Packages** submenu's **Quick Start** option. This is something we will look at in a later chapter.

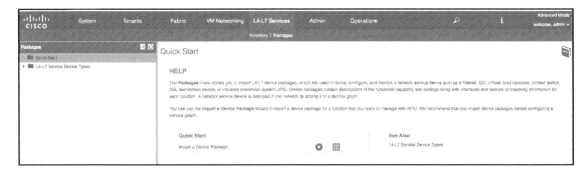

Figure 28

Admin

Under the **Admin** menu is where we configure **AAA (Authentication, Authorization, and Accounting)**. Here, we can set up RBAC and also connect to authentication providers, such as LDAP; for example, Microsoft Active Directory, RADIUS, or TACACS+. We can also set up PKI to use certificate chains.

We can create maintenance schedules, either one-off tasks or regular ones. We can configure our log retention policies, upgrade our firmware, and configure callhome (after setting up the policies in the **Fabric** menu), SNMP, and Syslog. The **Admin** menu is also where we would perform configuration rollbacks and the importing of configuration files and exporting of technical support files.

Figure 29

Operations

The final menu option is **Operations**. This is where will can perform most of our troubleshooting, should the need arise. From here, we find endpoints and look at the traffic path, along with any faults along the path. We can perform a traceroute as well to check the data plane. This is something we will look at in Chapter 9, *Troubleshooting ACI*.

We can also check out usage with the **Capacity Dashboard**, create Optimizer configuration templates, track our endpoints, and even look at a traffic map.

Chapter 1

Figure 30

For now, though, it's time to start configuring!

2
Configuring Policies and Tenants

In this chapter, we will cover the following recipes:

- Creating fabric policies
- Creating access policies
- Creating tenants
- Configuring bridge domains
- Configuring contexts
- Creating application network profiles
- Creating endpoint groups
- Using contracts between tenants
- Creating filters
- Creating contracts within tenants
- Creating management contracts

Introduction

We will start configuring the ACI fabric by creating some policies and a couple of tenants.

The ACI policy model is all about mapping application requirements to policies. We need tenant A to talk to an SQL server; we create a policy for that. We also need tenant A to talk the storage system, so we create a policy for that.

The APIC looks after the policies. When we make a change to an object within the fabric, it is the job of the APIC to apply this change to the policy model, which then makes the change to the affected endpoint. Such an example would be adding a new device to the fabric. Communication with the new device is prohibited until the policy model is updated to include the new device.

There are different policies, but they can be split into fairly distinct groups: those that govern the ACI fabric as a whole and those that are concerned with tenants.

All the policies are recorded in the **MIT**, or **management information tree**.

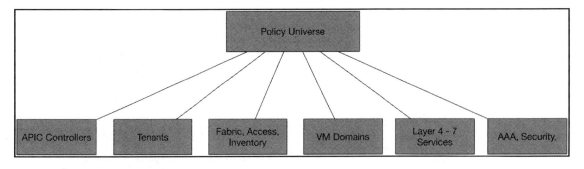

The MIT

In this chapter, we will start by creating a fabric policy to enable **NTP (Network Time Protocol)**, as it is an essential service for the smooth functioning of the fabric (along with DNS, which is covered in `Chapter 4`, *Routing in ACI*). We will look at access policies and enable **CDP (Cisco Discovery Protocol)** across the fabric.

We will then create our first tenant and set it up for networking by creating the networking and application components, and then we will give it something to do by creating a contract that we will provide to a second tenant to consume.

This is a basic idea of what we will be configuring:

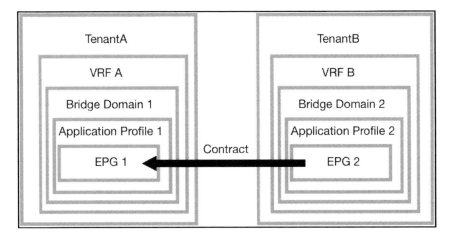

We will also look at creating a management contract for permitting SNMP traffic, which we will need for Chapter 8, *Troubleshooting ACI*.

Creating fabric policies

In this recipe, we will create an NTP policy and assign it to our pod. NTP is a good place to start, as having a common and synced time source is critical for third-party authentication, such as LDAP and logging.

In this recipe, we will use the Quick Start menu to create an NTP policy, in which we will define our NTP servers. We will then create a POD policy and attach our NTP policy to it. Lastly, we'll create a POD profile, which calls the policy and applies it to our pod (our fabric).

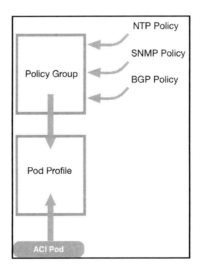

We can assign pods to different profiles, and we can share policies between policy groups. So we may have one NTP policy but different SNMP policies for different pods:

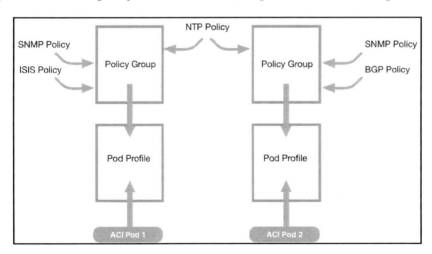

The ACI fabric is very flexible in this respect.

Chapter 2

How to do it...

1. From the Fabric menu, select **Fabric Policies**. From the **Quick Start** menu, select **Create an NTP Policy**:

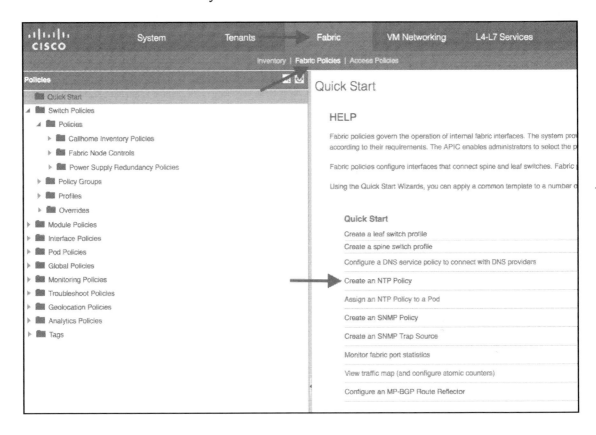

Configuring Policies and Tenants

2. A new window will pop up, and here we'll give our new policy a name and (optional) description and enable it. We can also define any authentication keys, if the servers use them. Clicking on **Next** takes us to the next page, where we specify our NTP servers.

3. Click on the plus sign on the right-hand side, and enter the IP address or **Fully Qualified Domain Name (FQDN)** of the NTP server(s):

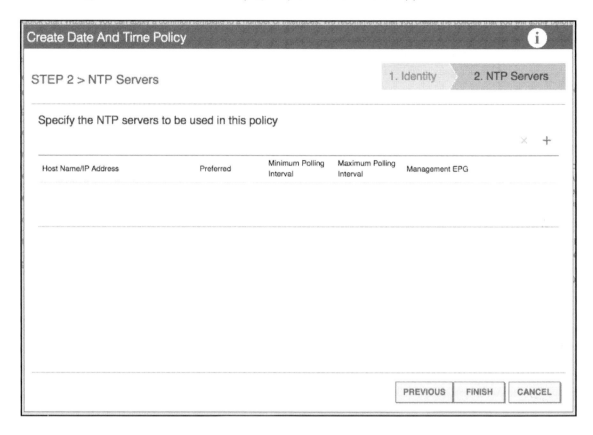

Configuring Policies and Tenants

4. We can also select a management EPG, which is useful if the NTP servers are outside of our network. Then, click on **OK**.

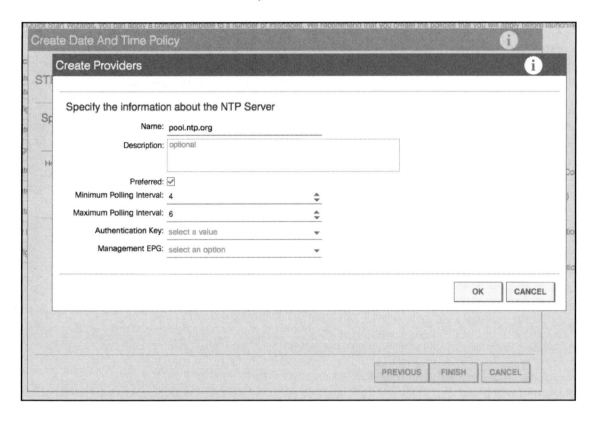

Chapter 2

5. Click on **Finish**.

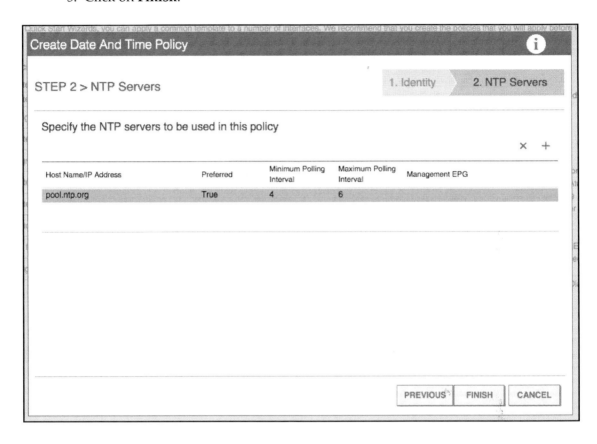

Configuring Policies and Tenants

We can now see our custom policy under **Pod Policies**:

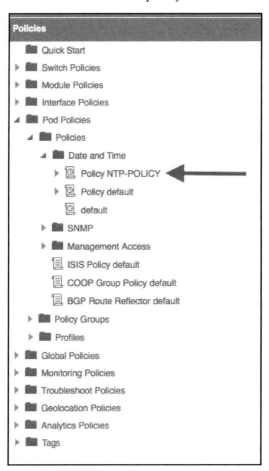

At the moment, though, we are not using it:

Chapter 2

6. Clicking on **Show Usage** at the bottom of the screen shows that no nodes or policies are using the policy.

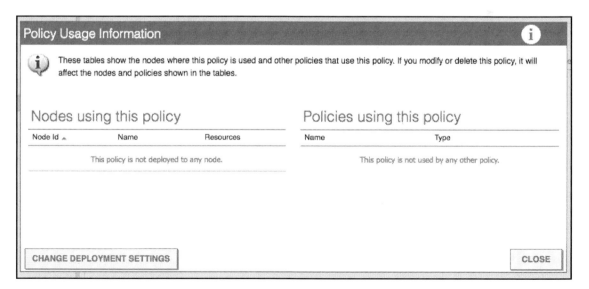

Configuring Policies and Tenants

7. To use the policy, we must assign it to a pod, as we can see from the **Quick Start** menu:

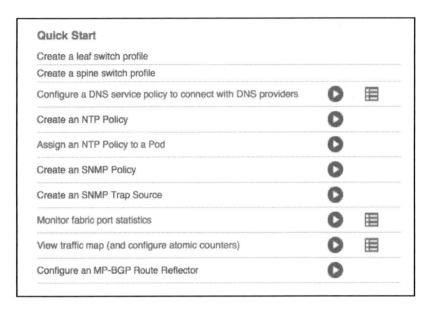

8. Clicking on the arrow in the circle will show us a handy video on how to do this. We need to go into the policy groups under **Pod Policies** and create a new policy:

9. To create the policy, click on the **Actions** menu, and select **Create Pod Policy Group**.

Chapter 2

10. Name the new policy `PoD-Policy`. From here, we can attach our **NTP-POLICY** to the PoD-Policy. To attach the policy, click on the drop-down next to **Date Time Policy**, and select **NTP-POLICY** from the list of options:

[57]

Configuring Policies and Tenants

We can see our new policy.

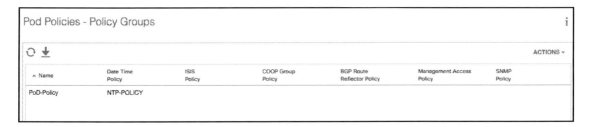

11. We have not finished yet, as we still need to create a POD profile and assign the policy to the profile. The process is similar as before: we go to **Profiles** (under the **Pod Policies** menu), select **Actions**, and then **Create Pod Profile**:

12. We give it a name and associate our policy to it.

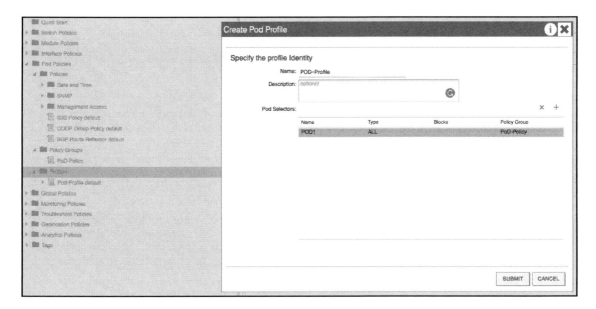

How it works...

Once we create a policy, we must associate it with a POD policy. The POD policy must then be associated with a POD profile.

We can see the results here:

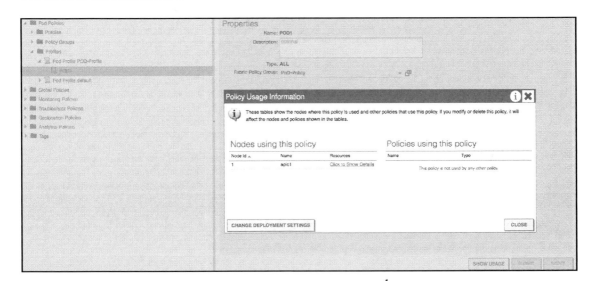

Our APIC is set to use the new profile, which will be pushed down to the spine and leaf nodes.

We can also check the NTP status from the APIC CLI, using the command show ntp (you may want to add NTP servers using the IP address until the DNS recipe from Chapter 4, *Routing in ACI*, is completed).

```
apic1# show ntp
 nodeid        remote          refid      st    t    when   poll    reach    delay
 offset      jitter
-------- - ---------------- -------- ----- -- ------ ------ ------- -------
-------- --------
 1             216.239.35.4    .INIT.     16    u    -       16     0        0.000
 0.000       0.000
apic1#
```

Configuring Policies and Tenants

Creating access policies

Access policies control the operation of switch ports, allowing connectivity to resources such as storage and compute, hypervisors, and layer 4 to layer 7 devices and protocols such as CDP, LLDP, and STP.

In this recipe, we are going to look at access policies and enable a preconfigured policy. We will then look at how to override this policy on a per-port basis, and also to override blocks of ports on a leaf.

How to do it...

1. From the Fabric menu, select **Access Policies**. Go to **Interface Policies** | **Policies** | **CDP Interface**. We can see that there is already a **default** policy:

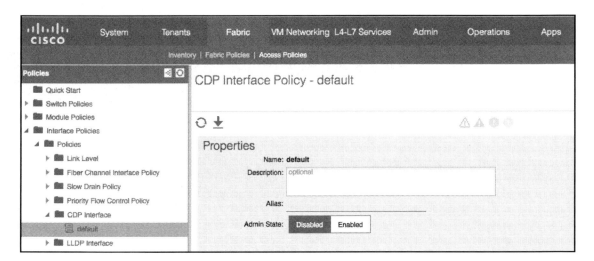

2. The default is for CDP to be disabled. So switch the **Admin State** to **Enabled**, and click on **SUBMIT** in the bottom corner of the window:

Chapter 2

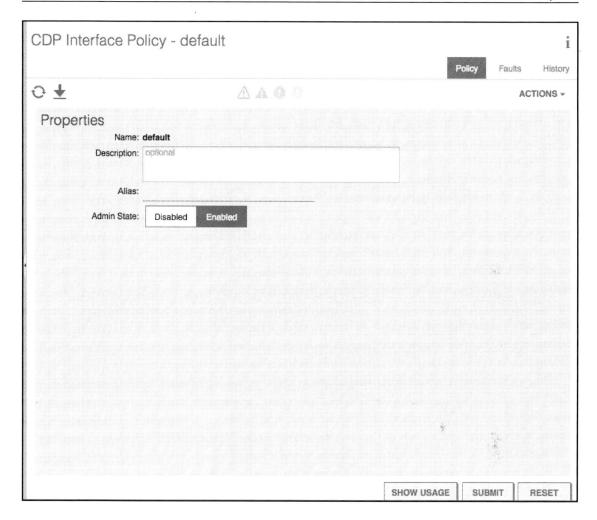

3. This has enabled CDP globally, but what if we need to be a little more selective and disable on a single port?

Configuring Policies and Tenants

4. Right-click on **CDP Interface** and select **Create CDP Interface Policy**.

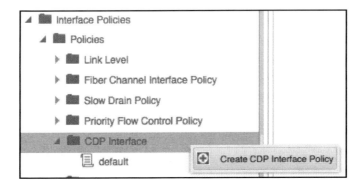

5. Name the new policy CDP-OFF and set the state to **Disabled**.

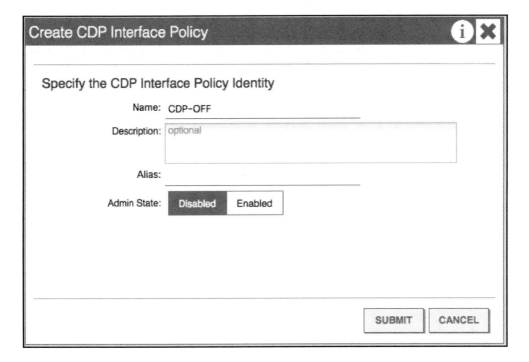

6. Click on **SUBMIT**.
7. We now have two policies, one with CDP enabled, and the other has CDP disabled.

Chapter 2

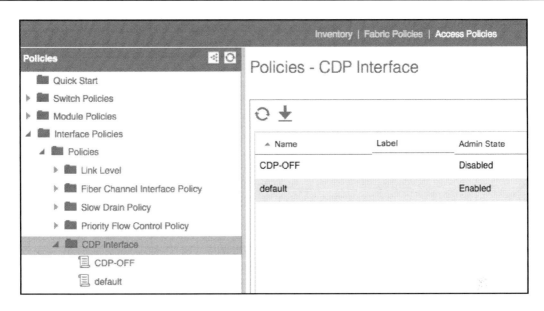

8. We can now create a leaf policy group (well, we should create two, actually). Right-click on **Leaf Policy Groups** and select **Create Leaf Access Port Policy Group**.

Configuring Policies and Tenants

9. Name the new policy `CDP-Off` and choose the **CDP-OFF** policy from the drop-down menu next to **CDP Policy**.

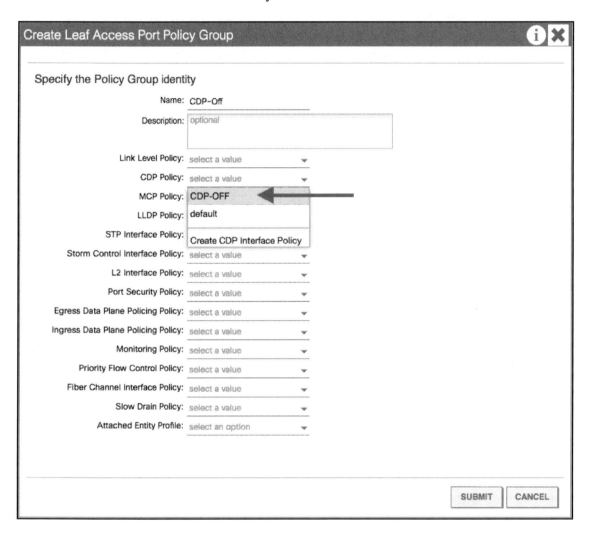

10. Click on **SUBMIT**.
11. Repeat the process to create a second leaf access port policy group, this time selecting **default** from the **CDP Policy** dropdown. The results should look like this:

Chapter 2

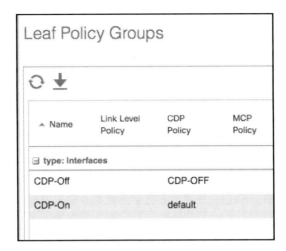

12. Navigate to **Interface Policies** | **Interface Overrides** | **Leaf Interface Overrides**, and select **Create Leaf Interface Override**.

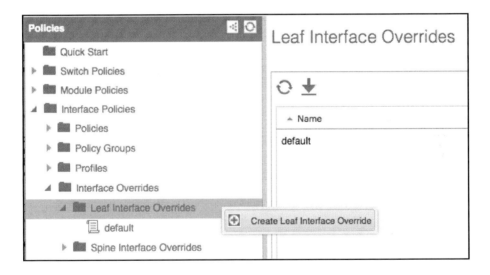

Configuring Policies and Tenants

13. Enter a name for the override and select the port from the drop-down list.

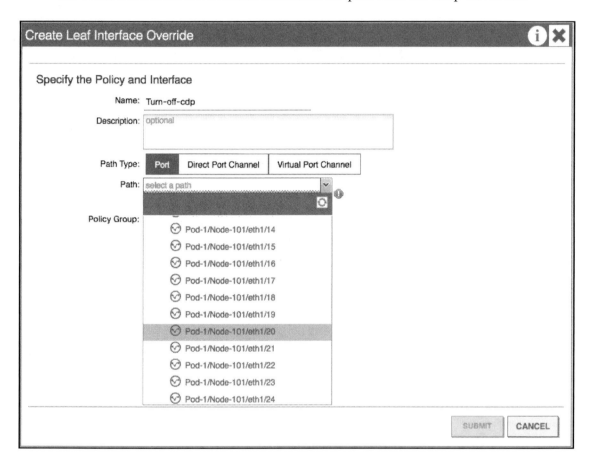

Chapter 2

14. From the **Policy Group** drop-down, select the **CDP-Off** policy created earlier.

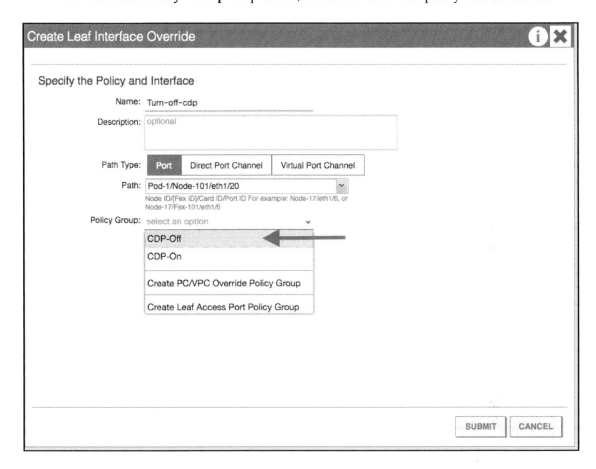

[67]

Configuring Policies and Tenants

15. Click on **SUBMIT**.

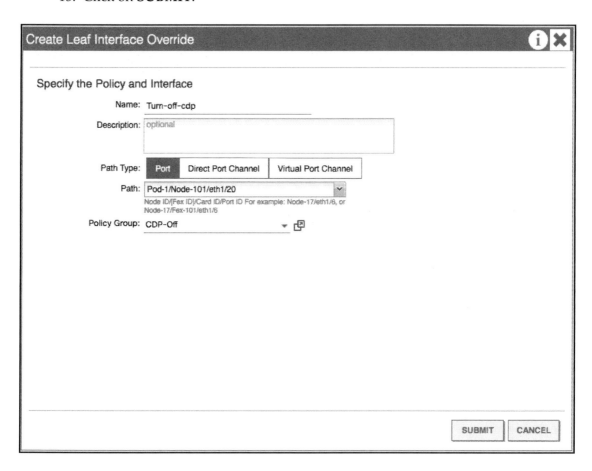

How it works...

There are many preconfigured policies, which will cover the majority of the day-to-day configuration changes you will need to support your infrastructure. Many of these will already be enabled, or disabled, allowing you to tweak them as needed. Not all the defaults will suit every environment. Consider CDP: we may need to turn it off on a single port, as we did before by creating an override.

Chapter 2

By looking at the policy, we can check that the override is working as expected.

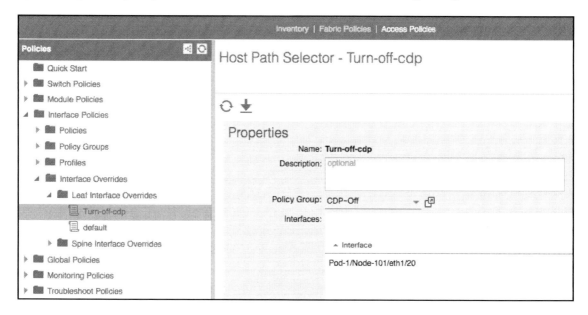

If we click on **Show Usage** down in the bottom right-hand corner, we can see that the policy is being used by **Leaf-1**.

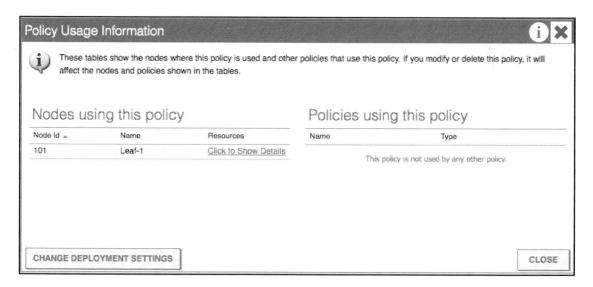

[69]

Clicking on **Click to Show Details** will show us the port that is the object of the override.

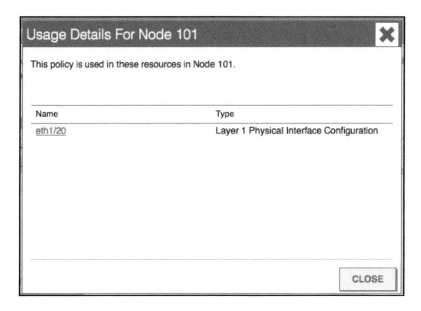

There's more...

The aforementioned solution would not be appropriate, though, if we wanted to turn CDP off for a range of ports.

To turn off CDP for a range of ports, we would need to create a leaf interface profile. To do this, we navigate to **Interface Policies** | **Profiles** | **Leaf Profiles**, right-click on it, and select **Create Leaf Interface Profile**.

Chapter 2

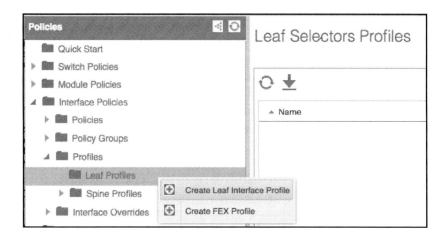

Name the profile and click on the plus sign next to **Interface Selectors**.

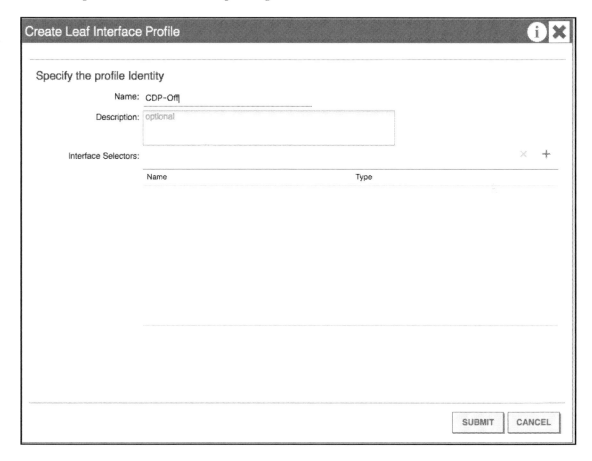

Configuring Policies and Tenants

Enter a name for the port selector, and enter the ports in the **Interface IDs** row. Select **CDP-Off** as the **Interface Policy Group** from the drop-down list.

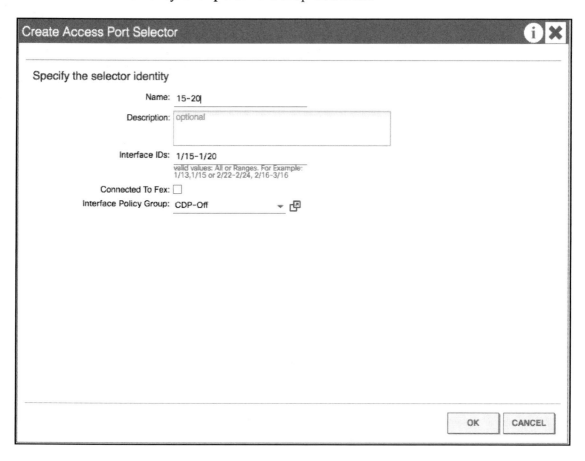

Click on **OK**.

Chapter 2

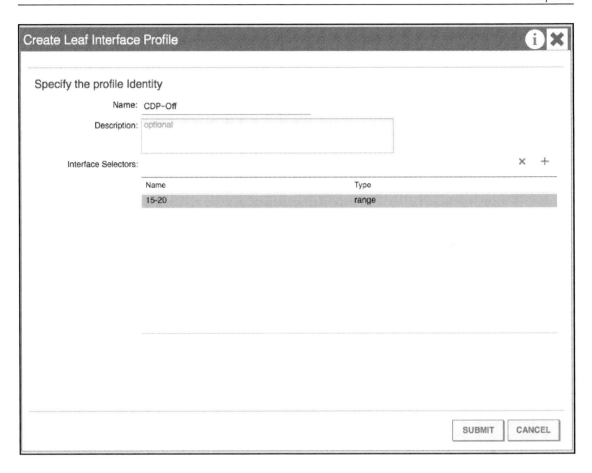

Click on **SUBMIT**.

The next step is to create a switch profile. Navigate to **Switch Policies** | **Profiles**. Right-click on **Leaf Profiles** and select **Create Leaf Profile**.

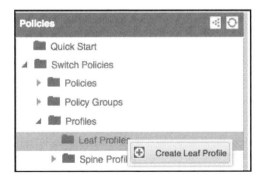

[73]

Configuring Policies and Tenants

Name the profile and then click on the plus sign next to **Leaf Selectors**. Select **Leaf-1** and click on **UPDATE**.

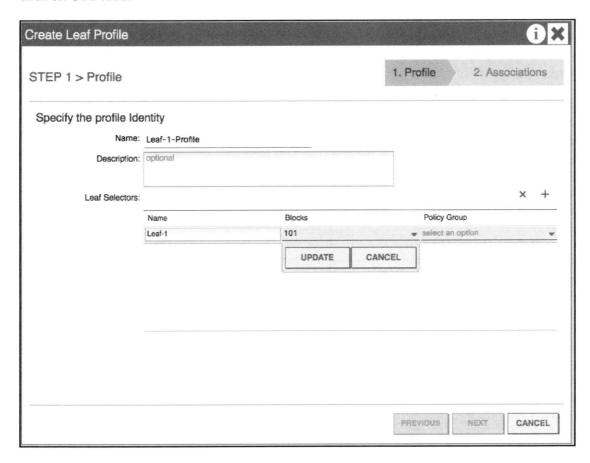

Click on **NEXT**.

Chapter 2

In the next window, select the **CDP-Off** profile.

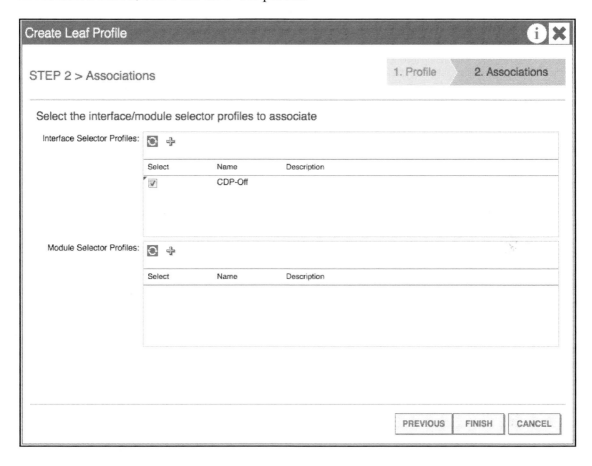

Click on **FINISH**.

Configuring Policies and Tenants

To check the deployment, navigate to **Interface Policies** | **Profiles** | **Leaf Profiles** | **CDP-Off**, and select 15-20. Click on **Show Usage** in the bottom right-hand corner. We can see that the policy is being used by the **Leaf-1** node, and clicking on the link under **Resources** will show that the six interfaces (1/15 to 1/20) are using the **CDP-Off** policy group.

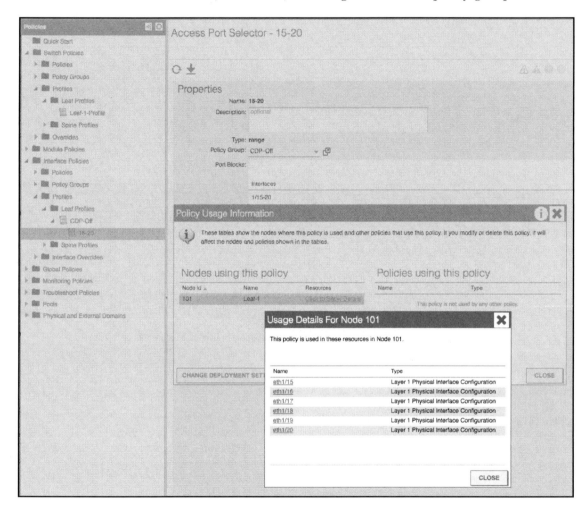

This methodology allows us to have very granular control over the fabric.

Creating tenants

Tenants can be anything we want them to be (within reason): they can be a customer, a business unit within an enterprise, or a grouping of policies. The term 'tenant' is flexible, but each tenant is (by default) an isolated unit within the fabric. It is a logical container, one that can remain self-contained or, through contracts, share resources with other tenants.

The MIT for the tenant is as follows:

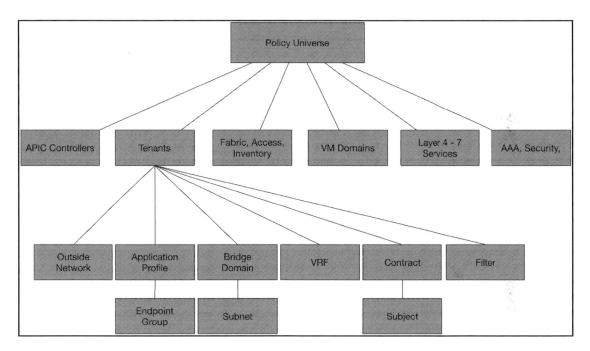

Tenant MIT

As you can see from the diagram, tenants contain some different components, including application profiles, bridge domains, VRFs (also referred to as *contexts*), and contracts. Some of these components, such as bridge domains, have their own components, such as subnets.

We have a couple of tenants preconfigured. These are the "common" tenant (**common**), which holds policies for shared services, such as firewalls and DNS settings; the "infrastructure" tenant (**infra**), which holds policies and VXLAN pools; and the "management" tenant (**mgmt**), which is used for out-of-band access and fabric discovery. The tenants we configure fall under the heading of "user" tenants, and in this recipe, we will create our first tenant.

Configuring Policies and Tenants

How to do it...

1. From the **Tenants** menu, click on the **Actions** menu and select **Create Tenant**.

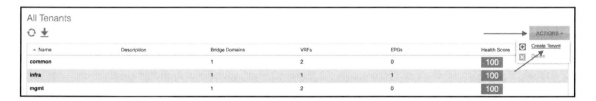

2. In the pop-up window, give the tenant a name, and click on **Submit**.

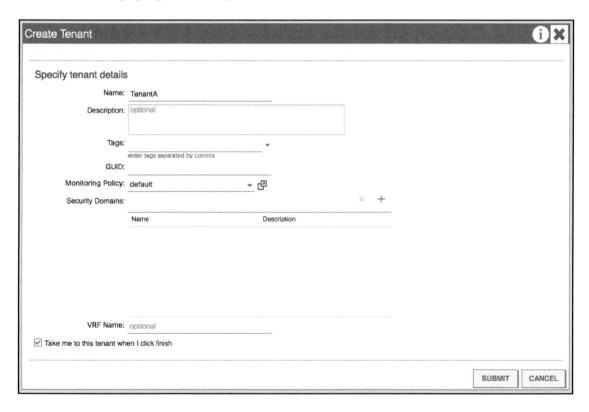

We do not need to enter anything for the other fields. Leaving these empty will not prevent us from creating the tenant.

How it works...

By creating a tenant, we are creating a container. If we look at it from the **Tenants** menu, we can see that we can now drag and drop the components needed into it.

We do not have any components yet, so let's start by configuring a bridge domain.

Configuring bridge domains

Bridge domains (**BDs**) provide layer 2 forwarding within the fabric as well as a layer 2 boundary. A BD must be linked to VRF and must have at least one subnet associated with it. BDs define the unique layer 2 MAC address space and also the flood domain (if flooding is enabled).

Bridge domains can be public, private, or shared. Public bridge domains are where the subnet can be exported to a routed connection, whereas private ones apply only within the tenancy. Shared bridge domains can be exported to multiple VRFs within the same tenant, or across tenants when part of a shared service.

In this recipe, we will create a bridge domain and, along with it, define a VRF and a subnet for communication within the tenancy.

How to do it...

1. We start by going into the tenant we created in the previous recipe and going to **Networking** | **Bridge Domains**.

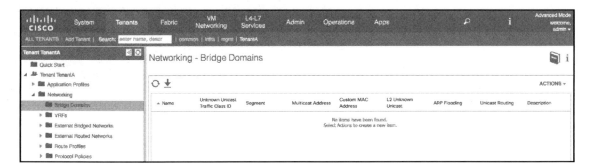

2. Click on **Actions**, and then on **Create Bridge Domain**.

Chapter 2

3. This launches a new window. Here, we name our bridge domain and assign a VRF to it if we have already created one, or create a new VRF.

Configuring Policies and Tenants

If we choose **Create VRF**, it brings up another window:

Because we have not created any timer policies for BGP or OSPF or a monitoring policy, we can leave these fields empty and use the default values.

Chapter 2

4. Once we click on **SUBMIT**, the new VRF is selected:

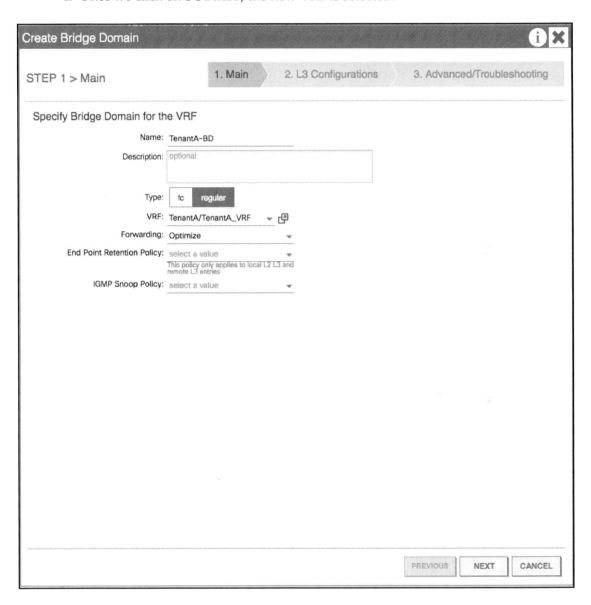

[83]

Configuring Policies and Tenants

5. We can set the forwarding to **Optimize**. Leave the End Point Retention Policy and IGMP Snoop Policy at the defaults, and click on **NEXT** to take us to the **L3 Configurations** window.

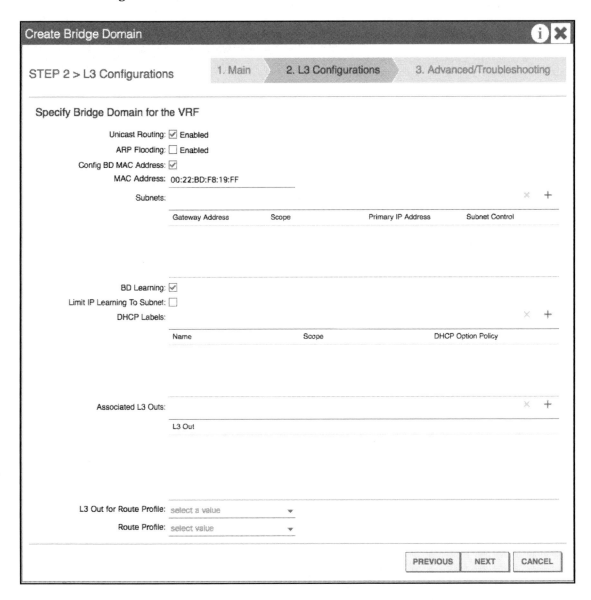

This is where we enable Unicast Routing and ARP flooding (if we want to), specify a MAC address and create a subnet.

> ARP flooding is disabled by default. The fabric will convert any ARP broadcast traffic into unicast traffic and push it to the destination leaf node. If we want to enable traditional ARP flooding behavior, this is where we would enable it.

6. To create a subnet, click on the plus sign, which brings up another window:

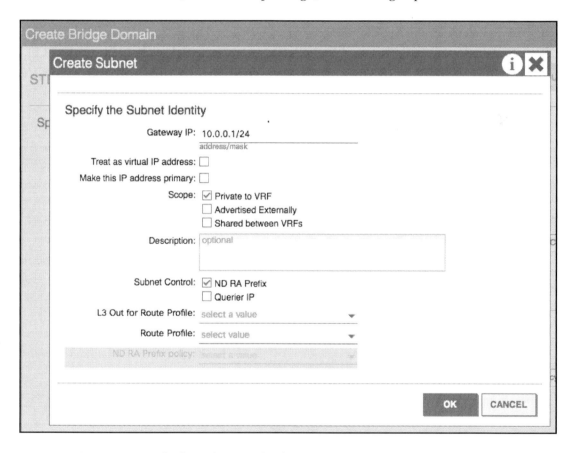

7. Here, we specify the subnet and subnet mask for the network and set the scope to be private, public (**Advertised Externally**), or shared.

Configuring Policies and Tenants

Private to VRF means that the subnet will not be advertised externally (outside of the VRF). **Advertised Externally** means just that, and will be flagged for advertising through a routing protocol to an external device. **Shared between VRFs** is similar to advertising externally, but is kept within the fabric. Because we are only concentrating on tenant A, at this stage, we will use the **Private to VRF** scope.

8. Click on **OK**, which will take us back to the **L3 Configurations** window.
9. Click on **NEXT** to take us to the final window, where we can select a monitoring policy.

10. Click on **FINISH**.

How it works...

We can see the bridge domains we have created from the **Networking - Bridge Domains** menu within the tenant settings.

This page gives us an overview of all of the bridge domains associated with a tenant, including the multicast address.

Chapter 2

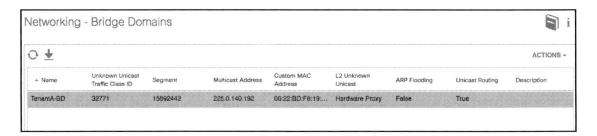

Because bridge domains permit multicast traffic but at the same time isolate it from other bridge domains, each bridge domain will get its own multicast address.

Clicking on a particular bridge domain takes us into all of the settings for it and allows us to change the associated VRF as well as changing the flooding settings and policies.

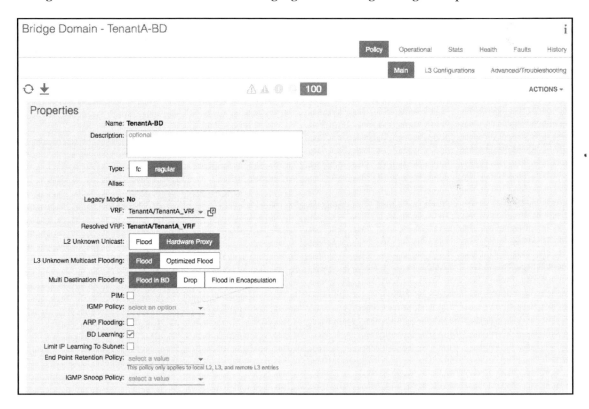

Configuring Policies and Tenants

The subnet we created can be found by going to the **Bridge Domains** menu, under the **Configured Bridge Domain** menu, and then the **Subnets** menu:

Lastly, the VRF we created can be found under the **Networking - VRFs** menu:

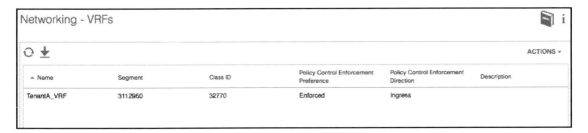

We can create additional VRFs if we want to, which we shall do in the next recipe.

Configuring contexts

So far, we have configured a tenant and created a bridge domain and context for it. A context, also known as a **VRF (Virtual Routing and Forwarding)** is a unique layer 3 forwarding domain. We can have multiple VRFs within a tenant, and VRFs can be associated with more than one bridge domain (but we cannot associate a bridge domain with more than one VRF).

Chapter 2

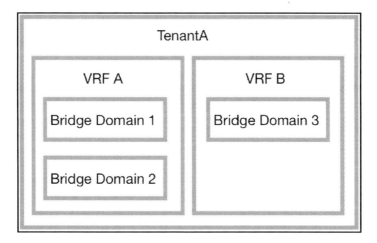

In this recipe, we will create a second VRF under TenantA and a new bridge domain.

How to do it...

1. From the **Networking** menu under the tenant, select **VRFs**.

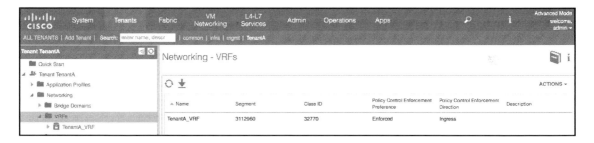

2. From the **Actions** menu, select **Create VRF**.

Configuring Policies and Tenants

3. Give the VRF a name, and select any applicable options. Here, I have chosen to add a DNS label of **VRF2**. We can create a new bridge domain (this is the default option) at this stage as well.

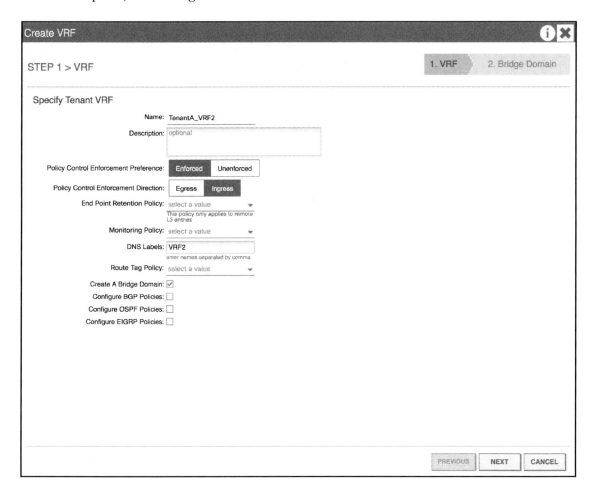

4. Click on **NEXT**, select the **Forwarding** setting (such as Optimize), and change any defaults (which I have not changed here).

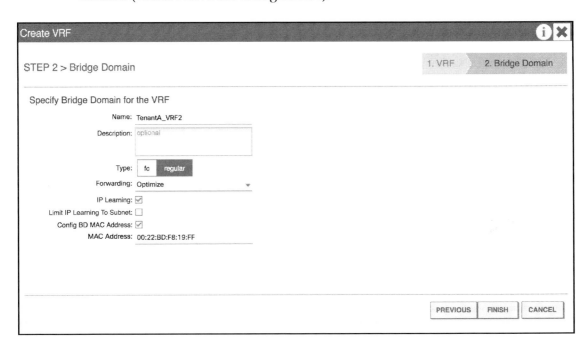

5. When you have done this, click on **FINISH**. The new VRF will be shown underneath the first VRF we created.

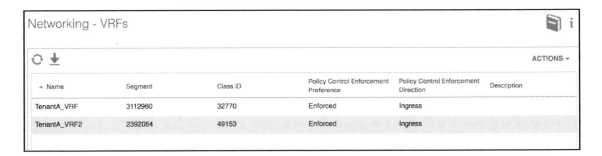

Configuring Policies and Tenants

How it works...

Selecting the newly created VRF from the left-hand side, we can click on **Show Usage** to see which bridge domain it is associated to:

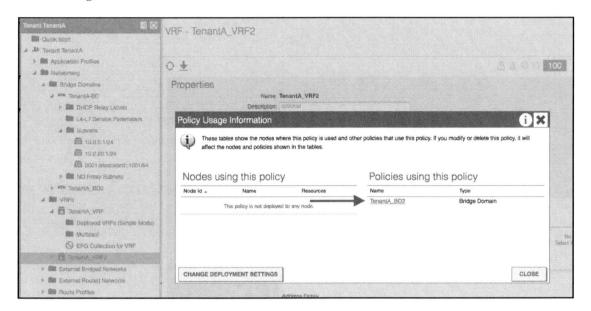

Going into the VRF, we can see the policy details, as we saw previously. We can also look at associated EPGs and external routed networks from the Operational tab.

Using the **Stats** menu, we can see a graph of the traffic (unicast and multicast) that passes through the VRF.

From the **Health** menu, we can look at the health of the VRF and, as we get further with configuring our fabric, a diagram of the relationships between objects. This view will also allow us to troubleshoot the entire path.

We can also see any faults that may have occurred as well as the history for the VRF, such as the audit log.

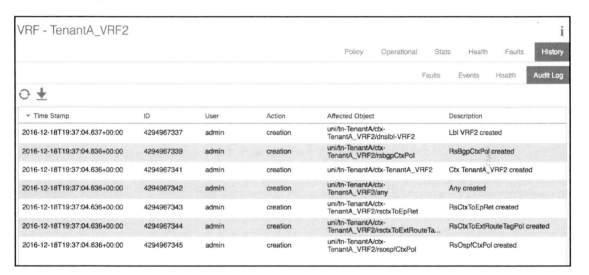

Looking at the audit is useful for two reasons. Firstly, we can see that we will have full tracking of actions through RBAC. Each action is timestamped along with the user who made the change. Secondly, we can start to see the kinds of commands used by the API.

There's more...

If we wanted our new bridge domain (**TenantA_BD2**) to be associated with our first VRF (from the bridge domains recipe), we could do this. We select the bridge domain and, from the VRF dropdown, select **TenantA/TenantA_VRF**.

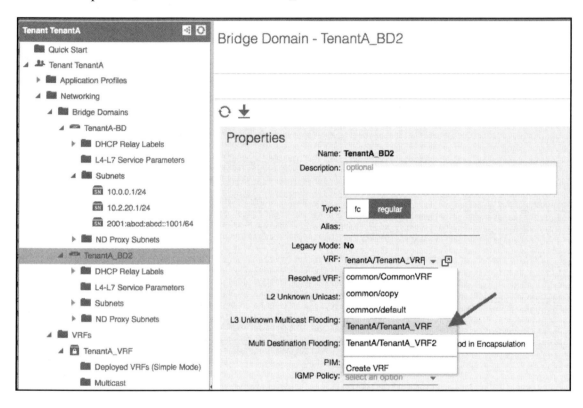

Click on **SUBMIT** and accept the policy change warning popup. The VRF will change along with the resolved VRF.

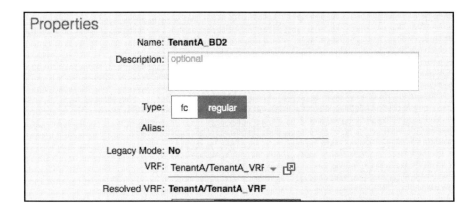

Creating application network profiles

Application profiles (**APs**) are containers for the grouping of **endpoint groups** (**EPGs**). We can have more than one EPG with an AP. For example, an AP could group a web server with the backend database, with storage, and so on. EPGs are assigned to different bridge domains.

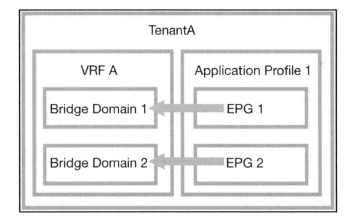

Application profiles define different aspects to the tenancy, governing security, **quality of service** (**QoS**), **service-level agreements** (**SLAs**), and layer 4 to layer 7 services.

Configuring Policies and Tenants

APs are so intrinsically linked to EPGs (and contracts to a lesser extent) that it is harder to create these as separate tasks. For this reason, we will create them in one recipe. As you can see from the following screenshot, we are even guided in the **Quick Start** menu to create the EPGs and contacts when we create the application profile.

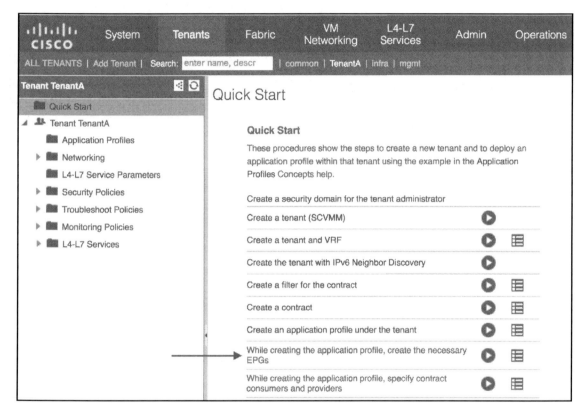

If we click on the grid-style icon next to the play button, the help window for the task will pop up.

How to do it...

1. We can create an AP from the **Quick Start** menu by clicking on the **Create an application profile under the tenant** link. This method is slightly different to selecting **Application Profiles** from the left-hand side menu and then using the actions menu to select **Create Application Profile**. The end result is the same, however.

    The window that appears is as follows:

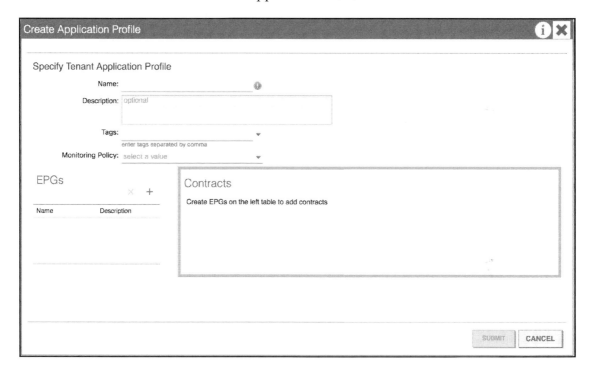

2. We need to enter a name (such as `TenantA_AP1`):

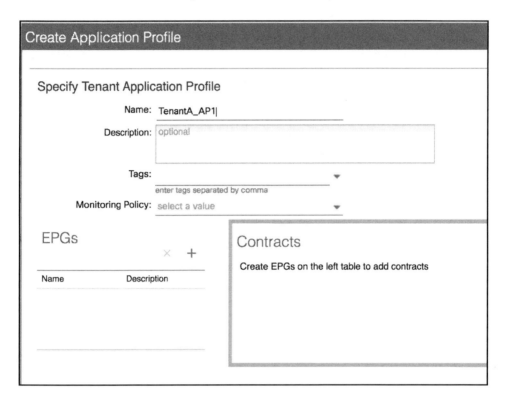

We also need to create an endpoint group, which we will do in the next recipe.

Creating endpoint groups

Endpoint groups are managed objects that (unsurprisingly) contain endpoints. Endpoints are devices that are connected to the network, either directly or indirectly. Endpoints have certain attributes, such as an address and a location; they can be physical or virtual. Endpoint groups are a logical grouping of these, based on common factors. The factors are more business related, such as having common security requirements and whether the endpoints require virtual machine mobility, have the same QoS settings, or consume the same L4-L7 services. Therefore, it makes sense to configure them as a group.

Chapter 2

EPGs can span multiple switches and are associated with one bridge domain. There is not a one-to-one mapping between an EPG and particular subnets, and one cool thing about membership in an EPG is that it can be static for physical equipment or dynamic when we use the APIC in conjunction with virtual machine controllers; again, this will cut down on the number of manual configuration steps.

How to do it...

1. From within the **Create Application Profile** window, click on the plus sign next to **EPGs**.

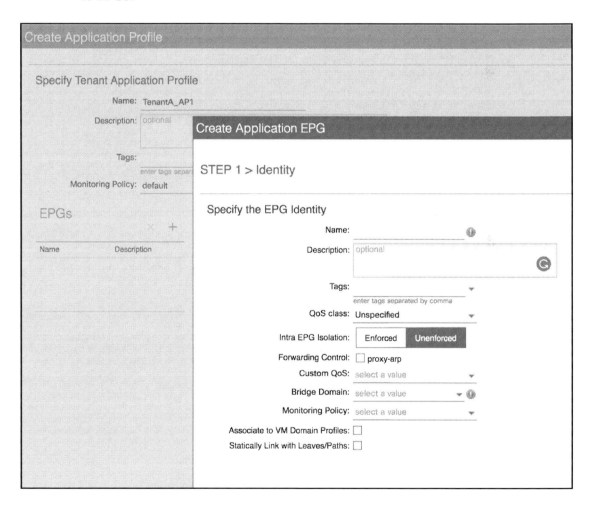

2. Give the EPG a name, and select the bridge domain associated with it:

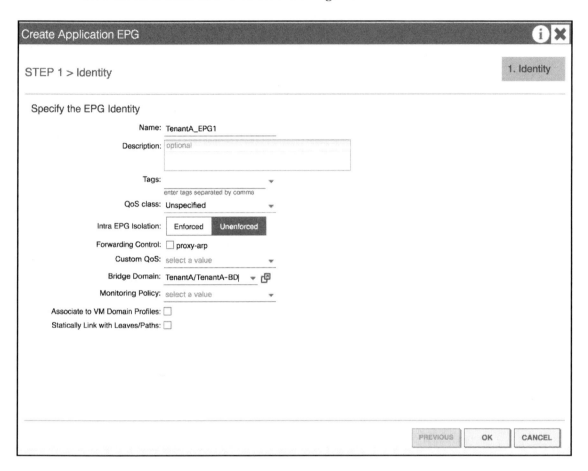

3. We can click on **OK** to be returned to the previous window.

Intra-EPG isolation is designed to prevent endpoints in the same EPG from communicating with each other, useful if you have endpoints belonging to different tenants in the same EPG.

Chapter 2

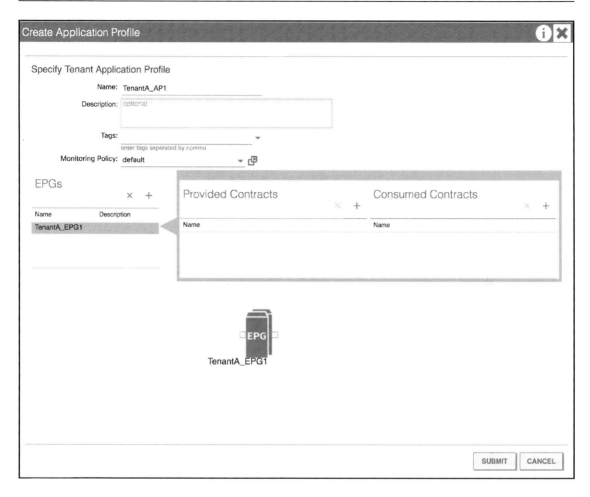

4. We can click on **SUBMIT** here and our AP and EPG will be created, or we can specify some contracts to provide, consume, or both. For the moment, we will just click on **SUBMIT** and create the contract separately in the next recipe.

How it works...

We can start to see the different components of the ACI fabric starting to merge together now, giving us an understanding of how they all tie in together. A virtual machine (endpoint) can be assigned to an endpoint group, which is tied to an application profile. The endpoint group is associated with a bridge domain, which contains the subnet (or subnets), and in turn, the bridge domain is linked to a VRF instance. The VRF controls our routing, and all of these components go to make up the tenant.

The tenant is, at the moment, very isolated. If we were to add another tenant into the mix, the two would not be able to communicate. We can permit inter-tenant communication by using contracts, which is what we will start setting up next.

Using contracts between tenants

Contracts allow EPGs to communicate with each other, according to the rules we set. Contracts can be very granular, including the protocol, port, and direction of the traffic. We do not need a contract for intra-EPG traffic--this is implicitly permitted--but a contract is essential for inter-EPG traffic.

An EPG can be a provider of a contract, a consumer of a contract, or can perform both functions, providing and consuming at the same time. We can also provide or consume multiple contracts simultaneously. Contracts are (to simplify them) access lists. However, they are not bound by the same limitations that access lists are. To read about why contracts are better than access lists, refer to `http://www.cisco.com/c/en/us/td/docs/switches/datacenter/aci/apic/sw/1-x/aci-fundamentals/b_ACI-Fundamentals/b_ACI_Fundamentals_BigBook_chapter_0100.html#concept_0DEE0F8BB4614E3183CD568EA4C259F4`. To try and simplify the definition of provider and consumer, we have two contracts. One opens up HTTP access to a particular destination (it provides), the other permits access from the other EPG to the HTTP server (consuming). We can also be less stringent and have full TCP and UDP access between two EPGs, so would have two contracts and both EPGs would consume one and provide the other, allowing full bidirectional connectivity.

How to do it...

1. We need to create another tenant for this recipe. Repeat the previous recipes from this chapter using the following settings:
    - **Name:** `TenantB`
    - **Bridge Domain Name:** `TenantB-BD`
    - **VRF Name:** `TenantB_VRF`
    - **Subnet:** `10.0.1.1/24`
    - **Application Profile Name:** `TenantB_AP1`
    - **EPG Name:** `TenantB_EPG1`

Chapter 2

2. This has created another tenant, but at the moment, the two will be unable to communicate. We need to edit the subnets we have created and set them to **Shared between VRFs**. Navigate to **Tenants** | **TenantA** | **Networking** | **Bridge Domains** | **TenantA-BD** | **Subnets** | **10.0.0.1/24**, and tick the **Shared Between VRFs** checkbox. Click on **SUBMIT** and apply the changes. Repeat the process for the TenantB 10.0.1/24 subnet.

3. We are going to create a very basic contract. TenantA will be the provider and TenantB will be the consumer. We start by selecting the **Security Policies** option from the left-hand side menu for TenantA:

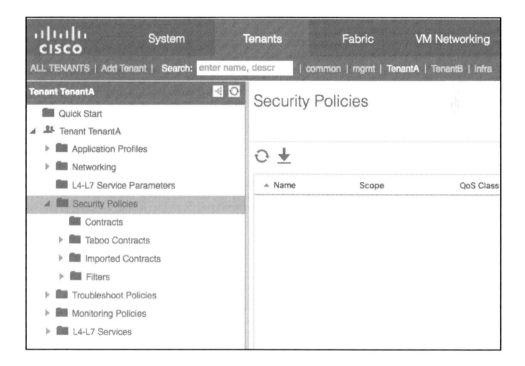

[103]

Configuring Policies and Tenants

4. From here, we select **Create Contract** from the **Actions** dropdown.

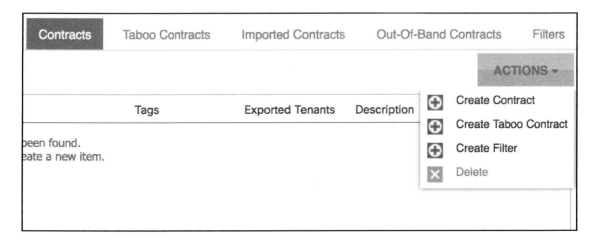

5. We need to give the contract a name and click on the plus sign to create a new subject of the contract:

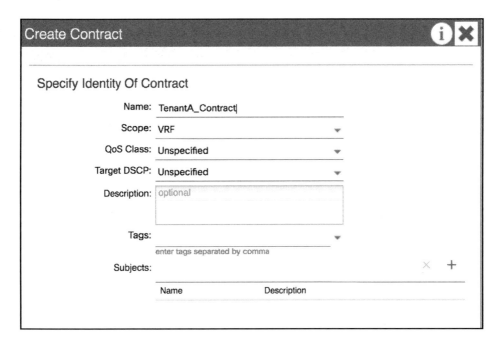

6. In the new window, we need to specify the subject. We assign it a name:

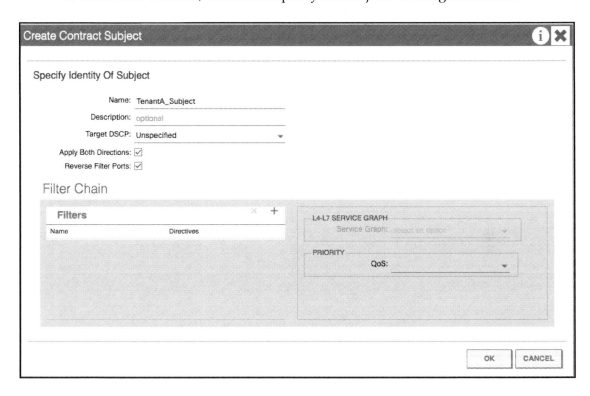

Configuring Policies and Tenants

7. The next step is to create a filter chain. Filter chains are where we classify our traffic (according to which attributes between layer 2 and layer 4 we decide upon). Clicking on the plus sign next to **Filters** gives us a list of filters that exist within the **common** tenant.

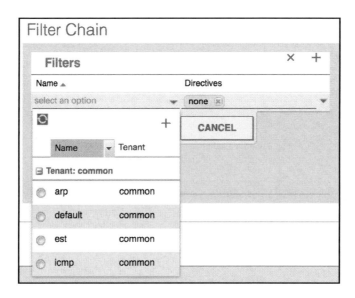

Clicking on the plus sign above the word **Tenant** will allow us to create a custom one.

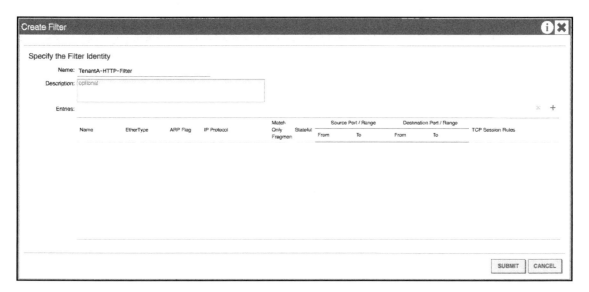

Chapter 2

8. Click on the plus sign next to **Entries** to create an entry for HTTP:

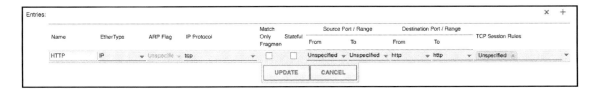

Name the entry and set the **EtherType** to **IP**, the **IP Protocol** to **tcp**, and the destination port range to **http**.

9. Click on **UPDATE**.
10. Click on **SUBMIT**.
11. Back on the **Create Contract Subject** window, click on **UPDATE**.

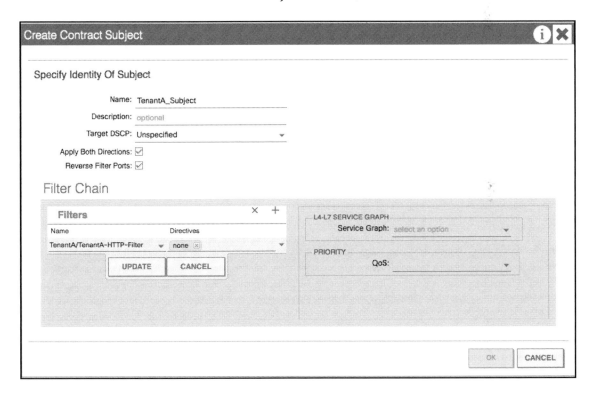

12. Click on **OK**.
13. Click on **SUBMIT**.

Chapter 2

14. Once we click on **SUBMIT**, we can see the contract listed in the security policies.

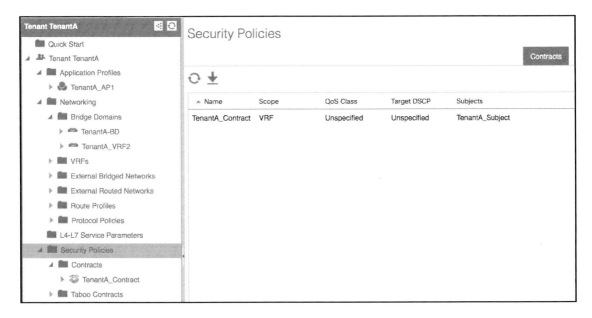

15. The next step is to attach it to the EPG. We do this from the **Contracts** option under the tenant application profile: **TenantA** | **Application profiles** | **TenantA_EPG1** | **Contracts**.

Configuring Policies and Tenants

16. We click on **Actions** and then on **Add Provided Contract** and select the contract we previously created.

We can add contract labels and subject labels.

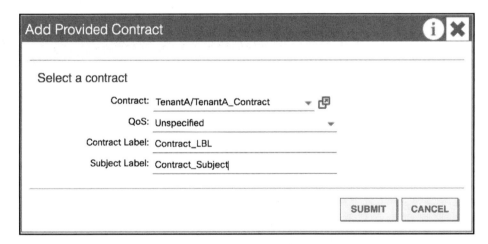

These labels are optional and are used to increase granularity during policy enforcement.

[110]

Chapter 2

17. Once we hit **SUBMIT**, our contract is connected to our EPG.

18. We need to do the same with TenantB, this time setting it as a consumed contract:

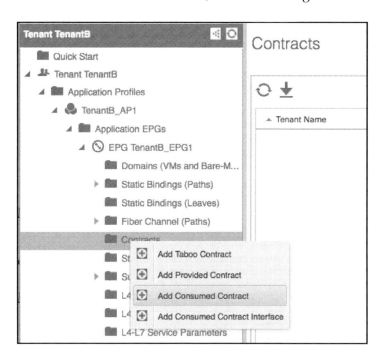

[111]

Configuring Policies and Tenants

If you try and add the previously created contract, you will not find it in the drop-down list.

This is because the scope is set to **VRF**. We need the scope to be set to **Global** so that other tenants can see it.

19. Return to **TenantA**, and navigate to **Security Policies | Contracts | TenantA_Contract**. Click on the **Policy** tab on the right-hand side.

20. Change the scope to **Global**, and click on **SUBMIT** at the bottom right-hand corner. Click on **SUBMIT CHANGES**.
21. We need to export the contract now. From **TenantA | Security Policies**, right-click on **Contracts** and select **Export Contract**.

Chapter 2

22. Set the name for the export, select the contract created earlier, and select **TenantB**.

23. Click on **SUBMIT**.
24. We should now be able to see the exported contract being imported into **TenantB**.

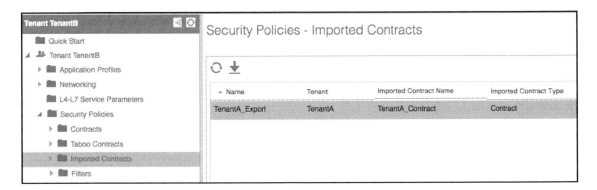

Configuring Policies and Tenants

25. Navigate to **Contracts**, right-click on it, and select **Add Consumed Contract Interface**.

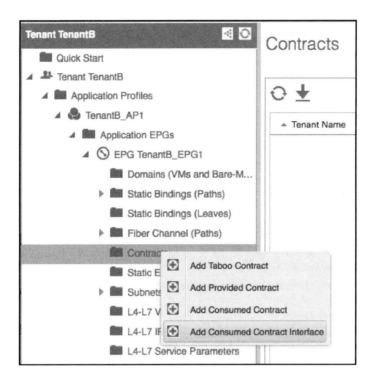

26. Select **TenantB/TenantA_Export**.

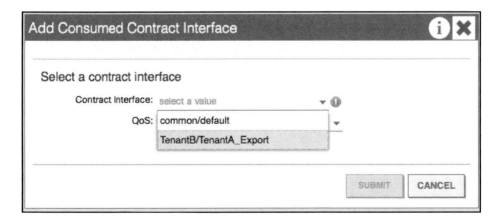

27. Click on **SUBMIT**.
28. We can now see the contract listed.

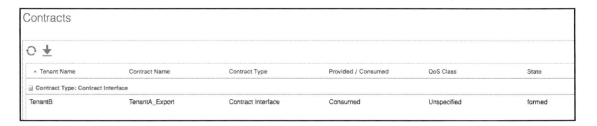

How it works...

We have created a very basic regular contract to provide to another tenant. There are other types of contracts we can create. Taboo contracts are used to deny and log traffic. Like conventional access control lists to deny traffic, these need to come first. An example would be where we are permitting a large number of ports and want to deny one or two particular ports; we would do this with a taboo contract to deny the traffic, created before the regular contract permitting the entire range.

In this recipe, we added a couple of labels. Labels allow us to classify what objects can talk to each other. Label matching is performed first, and if no label matches, then no other contract or filter information is processed. The label-matching attribute can be all, none, at least one, or exactly one.

While filters specify the fields to match on between layer 2 and layer 4, the subject can specify the actual direction of the traffic (unidirectional or bidirectional).

The contract we created was not that exciting but offers a building block onto which we can add more filters.

Creating filters

In this recipe, we will create a filter and apply it to the contract we created previously.

How to do it...

1. From the **TenantA Security Policies** menu, select the **Filters** option. Click on **Actions**, and then click on **Create Filter.**

2. Give the filter a name and (if you want to) description, and then click on the plus sign. The entries in the filter must have a name, but after that, you can be as permissive or restrictive as you need. Here, we have created a filter called **https**, which sets a filter on the layer 3 **EtherType** of **IP**, the layer 4 IP protocol of **tcp**, and the layer 7 protocol of **https** (as the destination port range). This follows the same steps as the previous recipe.

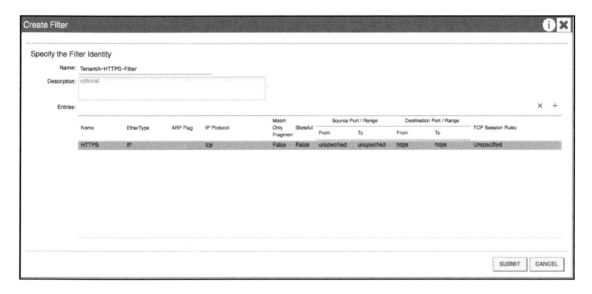

3. We can now click on **SUBMIT**, and we can see the filter listed under the tenant's filters:

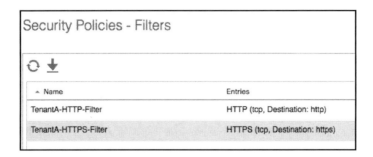

Chapter 2

4. To attach this filter to the contract, we need to select the contract we created earlier. Then, under the **Filters** window, click on the plus sign.

5. In the window that pops up, we can select the new filter from the drop-down menu, we can choose to log the activity, and click on **SUBMIT**:

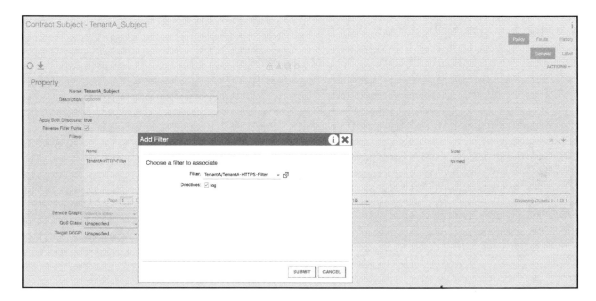

6. Finally, we see our filter sitting alongside the default filter from the previous recipe.

Configuring contracts between different tenants is the harder of the options. By contrast, configuring contracts between EPGs in the same tenant takes much fewer steps, as do management contracts. We will look at these next. This will also help show how contracts work so much more nicely than access lists as you scale the number of APs, EPGs, and tenants.

Configuring Policies and Tenants

Creating contracts within tenants

We will now create another application profile and EPG within TenantA and provide a contract for the other to consume.

How to do it...

1. Create another application profile and EPG within **TenantA**. The end result should look like this:

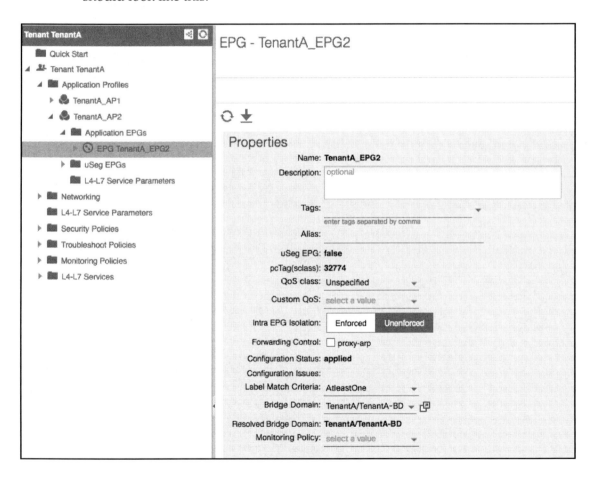

Chapter 2

2. Expand the new EPG, right-click on **Contracts**, and select **Add Consumed Contract**.

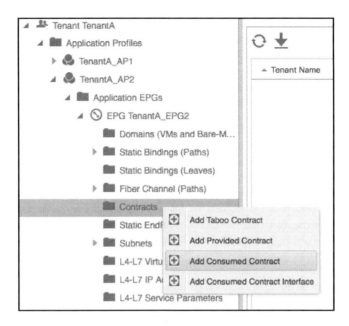

3. From the drop-down list, select the contract.

[119]

Configuring Policies and Tenants

4. Click on **SUBMIT**. We can get a visual representation of this as well.

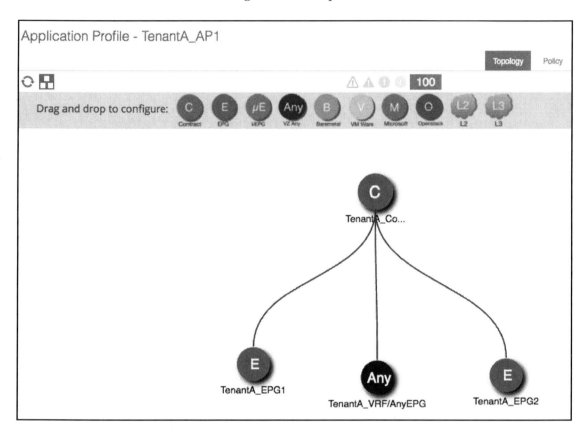

The same method would be used if we had another EPG within the same AP.

Chapter 2

Creating management contracts

The final contract we are going to create is one in the **mgmt** tenant. This one will allow SNMP traffic between the APIC and the SNMP software, which we will be setting up in Chapter 8, *Monitoring ACI*.

How to do it...

1. Create a filter (snmp-contract) in the mgmt tenant (**Tenants** | **mgmt** | **Security Policies** | **Filters**).
2. Create two entries, permitting UDP ports **161** and **162**.

3. Right-click on **Out-Of-Band Contracts** and select **Create Out-Of-Band Contract**.

[121]

Configuring Policies and Tenants

4. Name the contract (OOB-SNMP), and click on the plus sign next to Subjects. Select the **snmp-contract** created previously.

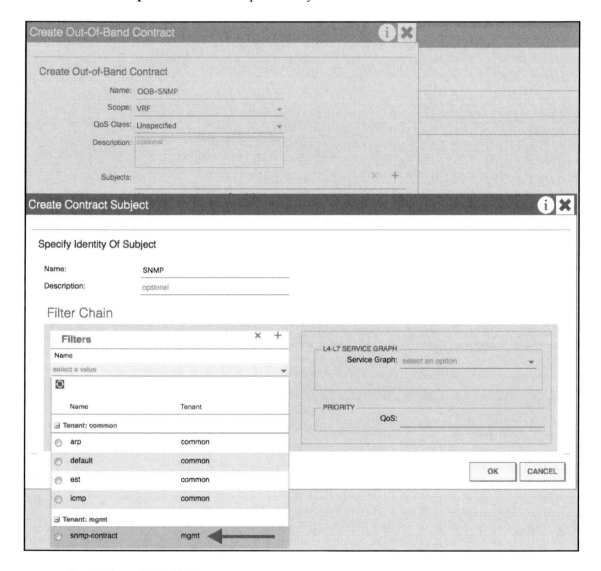

5. Click on **UPDATE**.
6. Click on **OK**.
7. Click on **SUBMIT**.

How it works...

This is an out-of-band contract, which we will be needing later on in the book. Earlier versions of the ACI software did not require this contract, but newer ones do. The contract permits traffic to the UDP ports used by SNMP and for SNMP trap notifications.

3
Hypervisor Integration (and Other Third Parties)

In this chapter, we will cover the following recipes:

- Installing device packages
- Creating VMM domains and integrating VMWare
- Associating vCenter domains with a tenant
- Deploying the AVS
- Discovering VMWare endpoints
- Adding virtual machines to a tenant
- Tracking ACI endpoints
- Integrating with A10
- Deploying the ASAv
- Integrating with OpenStack
- Integrating with F5
- Integrating with Citrix NetScaler

Introduction

ACI is highly extensible. Through device packages, we can add several different devices to our environment, which is referred to (in ACI terms) as **service insertion**.

The packages themselves are small ZIP files. Some require certain permissions from the manufacturer before you can download them (such as Citrix), whereas others just require registering your e-mail address (A10, for example).

Hypervisor Integration (and Other Third Parties)

Inside the ZIP file, we have a few different files. Taking the A10 APIC package as the example here, we have five Python files, one XML file, and one GIF image in a folder called Images. The ZIP file's size is a mere 65 KB. The XML file is, for most, going to be the easiest to understand. This file is called device_specification.xml. It starts with defining the vendor (vnsMDev) along with a package name (which is one of the Python scripts) and the version details (vmsDevScript):

```
<vnsDevScript name="A10" packageName="device_script.py" ctrlrVersion="1.1"
minorversion="1.0" versionExpr="4.[0-9]+.[-A-Za-z0-9]*"/>
```

Next, we define the device profiles (vnsDevProf), whether they are virtual or physical devices, and the number of Ethernet interfaces that they have (note that I have truncated the output):

```
<vnsDevProf name="vThunder" type="VIRTUAL" context="single-Context"
pcPrefix="trunk ">
    <vnsDevInt name="ethernet 1" />
    <vnsDevInt name="ethernet 2" />
    <!-truncated ->
    <vnsDevInt name="ethernet 7" />
    <vnsDevInt name="ethernet 8" />
</vnsDevProf>
<vnsDevProf name="vThunder-ADP" type="VIRTUAL" context="multi-Context"
pcPrefix="trunk ">
    <vnsDevInt name="ethernet 1" />
    <vnsDevInt name="ethernet 2" />
    <!-truncated ->
    <vnsDevInt name="ethernet 7" />
    <vnsDevInt name="ethernet 8" />
</vnsDevProf>
<vnsDevProf name="Thunder" type="PHYSICAL" context="single-Context"
pcPrefix="trunk ">
    <vnsDevInt name="ethernet 1" />
    <vnsDevInt name="ethernet 2" />
    <!-truncated ->
    <vnsDevInt name="ethernet 19" />
    <vnsDevInt name="ethernet 20" />
</vnsDevProf>
<vnsDevProf name="Thunder-ADP" type="PHYSICAL" context="multi-Context"
pcPrefix="trunk ">
    <vnsDevInt name="ethernet 1" />
    <vnsDevInt name="ethernet 2" />
    <!-truncated ->
    <vnsDevInt name="ethernet 19" />
    <vnsDevInt name="ethernet 20" />
</vnsDevProf>
```

After the interface declarations, we define some interface labels for "external" and "internal" (vnsMIfLbl) and some credentials (vnsMCred and vnsMCredSecret). The first big section we get to is next, which is the cluster configuration (vnsClusterConfig). This section covers core functionality, such as time, DNS, hostname, interface numbering, IPv4 and IPv6 functionality, and NTP. We then move to vnsMDevCfg, which is for network interface settings, including Virtual Router Redundancy Protocol (VRRP).

The vnsMFunc tag takes up the bulk of the XML file. These are device-specific entries, so the contents of this tag will vary considerably among the different vendors. However, they must all follow the same schema.

The final tags are vnsComposite (comparisons between two values, such as on or off, tcp or udp, and Yes or No) and vnsComparisons (match a-z and A-Z, or match 0-9, or "is it an IP address or subnet mask?").

```
<vnsComposite name="TrueFalse" comp="or">
   <vnsComparison name="True" cmp="eq" value="true"/>
   <vnsComparison name="False" cmp="eq" value="false"/>
</vnsComposite>
<vnsComposite name="EnableDisable" comp="or">
   <vnsComparison name="enable" cmp="match" value="enable"/>
   <vnsComparison name="disable" cmp="match" value="disable"/>
</vnsComposite>
<vnsComposite name="onOff" comp="or">
   <vnsComparison name="on" cmp="match" value="on"/>
   <vnsComparison name="off" cmp="match" value="off"/>
</vnsComposite>
<!-- Basic comparison Objects -->
<vnsComparison name="isAlpha" cmp="match" value="[a-zA-Z]+"/>
<vnsComparison name="isNumber" cmp="match" value="[0-9]+"/>
<vnsComparison name="isIPAddress"
              cmp="match"

value="([01]?dd?|2[0-4]d|25[0-5]).([01]?dd?|2[0-4]d|25[0-5]).([01]?dd?|2[0-4]d|25[0-5]).([01]?dd?|2[0-4]d|25[0-5])"/>
<vnsComparison name="isIPMask"
              cmp="match"

value="([01]?dd?|2[0-4]d|25[0-5]).([01]?dd?|2[0-4]d|25[0-5]).([01]?dd?|2[0-4]d|25[0-5]).([01]?dd?|2[0-4]d|25[0-5])"/>
```

We also have tags that set the fault codes (vnsMDfcts) and function profiles (vnsAbsFuncProfContr). The function profiles are, again, device specific and, for the A10, specify whether the device is a web server or a web server with high availability.

Hypervisor Integration (and Other Third Parties)

While we, as engineers, do not need to be concerned with what the contents of these XML files are, they do serve as a good reminder of the declarative nature of ACI. The XML files are all based on a common schema, and if the vendor can fit what they need around this schema, then the appliance should run very happily within the ACI framework.

 For a more in-depth look at device packages, refer to the following link: http://www.cisco.com/c/en/us/td/docs/switches/datacenter/aci/apic/sw/1-x/L4-L7_Device_Package_Development/guide/b_L4L7_Package.html

Let's find out how to add a device package.

Installing device packages

Installing a device package from the GUI is very simple.

How to do it...

1. From the **L4-L7 Services** menu, click on **Packages:**

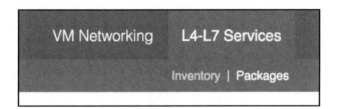

2. The **Quick Start** menu gives us one option: **Import a Device Package**.

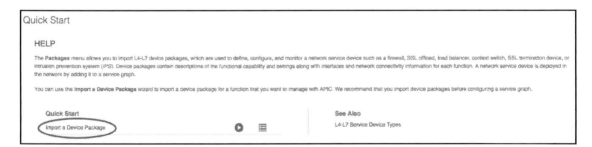

3. Click on this link to bring up the file open dialog box:

4. Click on **BROWSE...** and select the zipped package file you want to import. Do not extract the files.

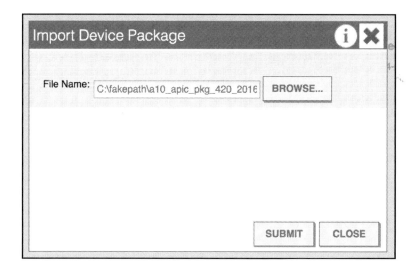

5. Click on **SUBMIT**. You will see another message briefly appear as the file is uploaded to the APIC.

Hypervisor Integration (and Other Third Parties)

How it works...

If we look at **L4-L7 Service Device Types**, we can see the newly added device package.

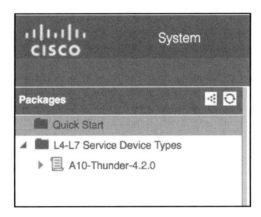

If we expand out the package, we can see a number of options; these should be familiar if you have looked through the package's XML file.

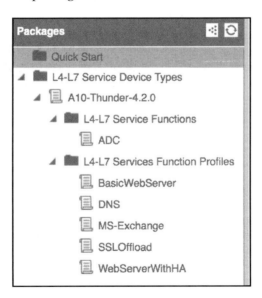

We won't be going through these settings now, as we will look at A10 devices later in this chapter.

There's more...

Here is a link to a list of device packages (some require specific permissions to download, such as ASA):

http://www.cisco.com/c/en/us/solutions/collateral/data-center-virtualization/application-centric-infrastructure/solution-overview-c22-734587.html

Next, we will move on to integrating VMWare with ACI.

Creating VMM domains and integrating VMWare

ACI uses Virtual Machine Manager (VMM) domain profiles to facilitate communication between virtual machine controllers and the ACI fabric. There are a handful of components that make up a domain, and these are:

- Virtual Machine Manager domain profile
- EPG association
- Attachable entity profile association
- VLAN pool association

The Virtual Machine Manager domain profile groups VM controllers together. Within this are two components: the **credential** for connecting to the VM controller, and the **controller,** which specifies how to connect to the VM controller.

The EPG association allows the APIC to push endpoint groups into the VM controller as port groups and also permits the EPG to span across several VMM domains.

The attachable entity profile association associates a VMM domain to the physical network. Here, we use an **attachable entity profile** (**AEP**), which is a network interface template, to set policies on leaf switch ports.

Finally, the VLAN pool association specifies the VLAN ID, or range of IDs, for encapsulation.

How to do it...

 This recipe assumes that you already have a vCenter server set up.

1. From **Fabric** | **Access Policies** | **Pools** | **VLAN**, select **Create VLAN Pool** from the **Actions** menu.
2. Give the pool a name and click on the plus sign to set the block range:

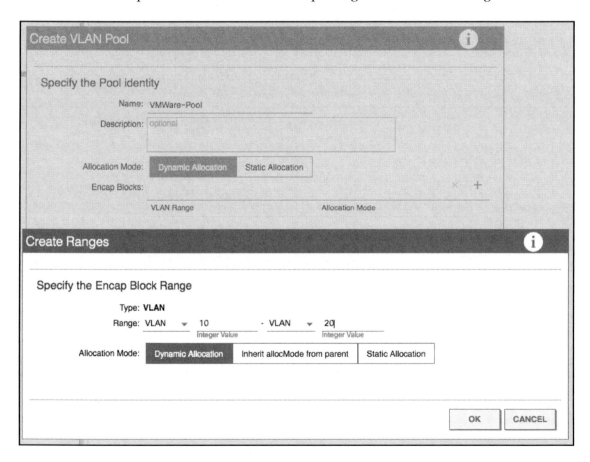

3. Click on **OK**. The new range should be listed under **Encap Blocks**. Click on **Submit**. The new VLAN pool will be listed:

Chapter 3

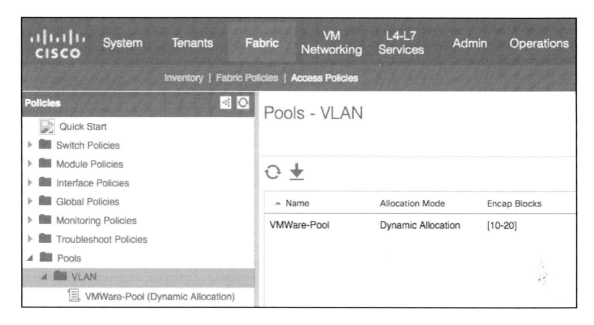

4. From the VM Networking menu, right-click on **VMware** and select **Create vCenter Domain**.

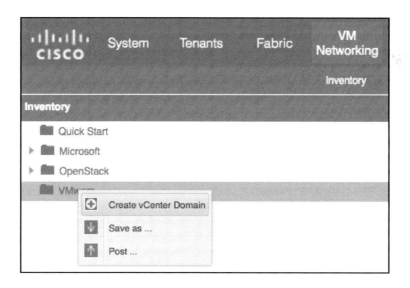

Hypervisor Integration (and Other Third Parties)

5. Fill in the details for the **Virtual Switch Name**, and from the dropdown, select the VLAN pool created earlier.

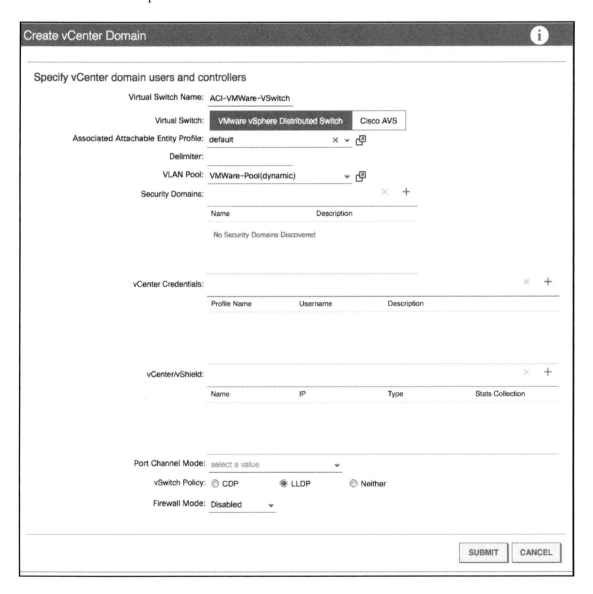

Chapter 3

6. Fill in the **vCenter Credentials** with an appropriate username and password by clicking on the plus sign.
7. Create the relevant credentials. Here, we will name the controller, set the IP address (or hostname), the **distributed virtual switch** (**DVS**) version, the data center (as defined in vCenter), and the associated credential (created in step 6).

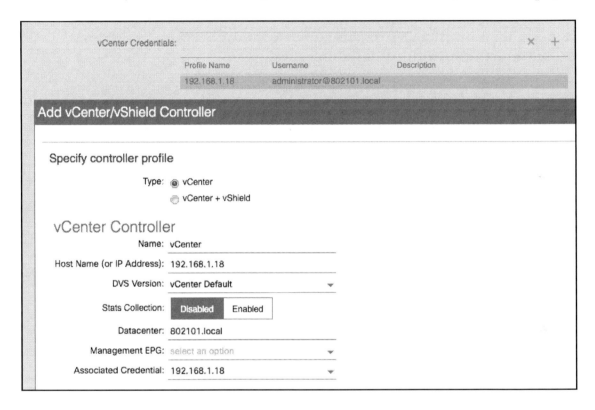

8. We also need to create the **Management EPG**. Clicking on the dropdown arrow next to this option brings up the option to **Create EPG Under Tenant mgmt**. Clicking on this option brings up another window:

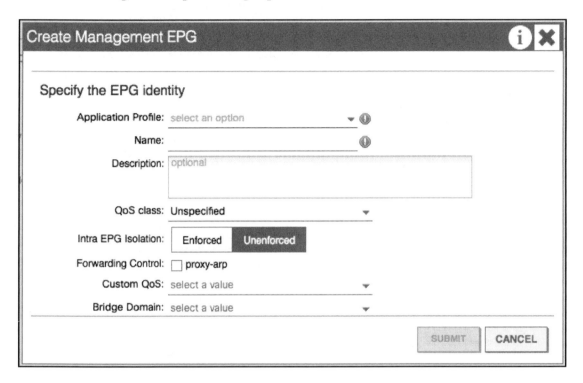

9. We create an **Application Profile** by clicking on the dropdown in the previous screenshot and selecting **Create Application Profile Under Tenant mgmt**:

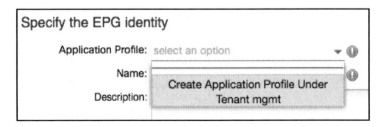

10. We name the application profile and select the monitoring policy (if we have one) and add any tags or descriptions:

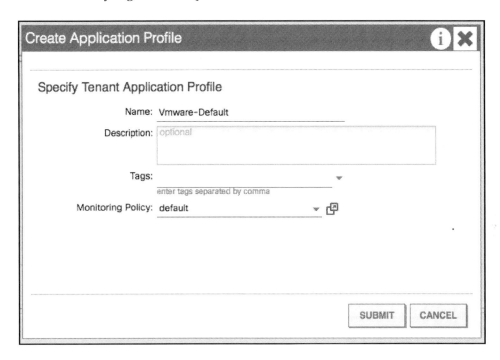

11. Click on **SUBMIT**.

12. Returning to the previous screen, we can name the EPG and accept the default values for the other options.

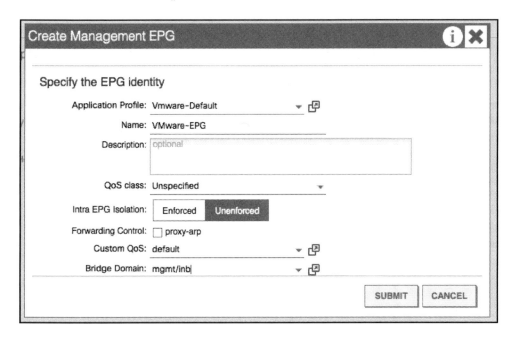

Chapter 3

13. Click on **SUBMIT**.
14. On the final screen, click on **OK**.

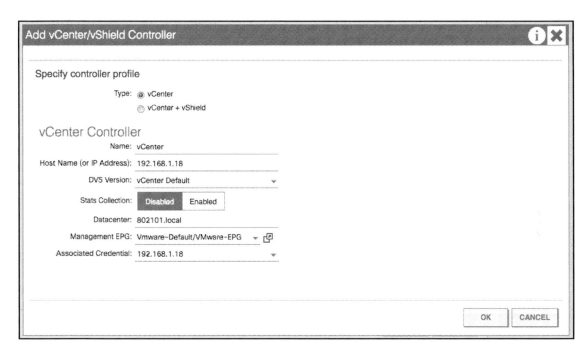

15. Click on **SUBMIT**.

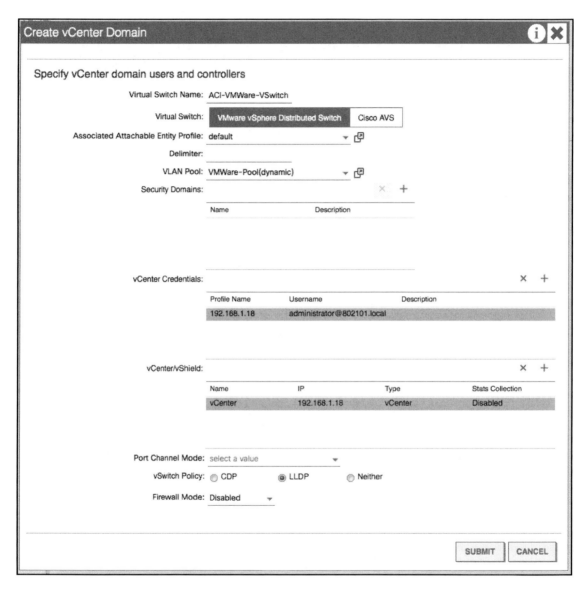

I have set the vSwitch policy to use LLDP, which will be significant later.

Chapter 3

 Note that although we have not specified any **Security Domains** or **Port Channel Mode**, the new configuration is accepted.

16. If we start drilling through the left-hand side menu, we should be able to see any virtual machines running on the ESXi hosts connected to the **vCenter** server:

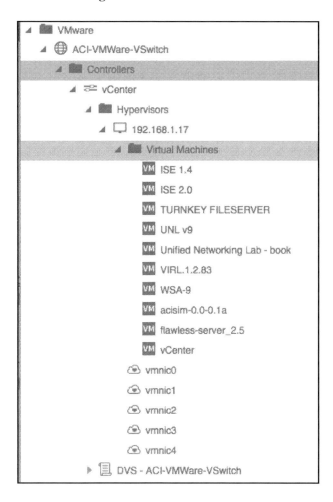

17. We can verify that the DVS is created by looking through the vCenter console:

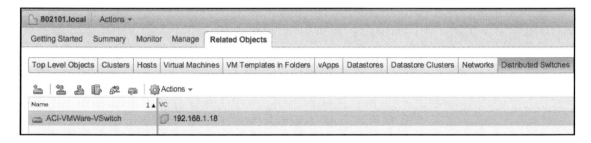

18. If we look at the properties of the vSwitch, we can see that LLDP is enabled (as per the configuration made earlier).

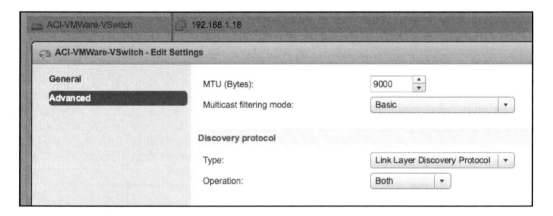

There's more...

There is an ACI plugin for vCenter:

`http://www.cisco.com/c/en/us/td/docs/switches/datacenter/aci/apic/sw/1-x/virtualization/b_ACI_Virtualization_Guide_2_0_1x/b_ACI_Virtualization_Guide_2_0_1x_chapter_01010.pdf`

The plugin allows you to manage the ACI fabric from within the vSphere web client. You can create, modify, and delete tenants, application profiles, EPGs, contracts, VRFs, and bridge domains instead of switching between the different applications. You can install the plugin by visiting `https://<APIC IP>/vcplugin`.

The next step is to associate the vCenter domain with our tenant.

Associating vCenter domains with a tenant

We can associate a vCenter domain with a tenant through the drag and drop interface.

How to do it...

1. Navigate to the tenant's application profile.

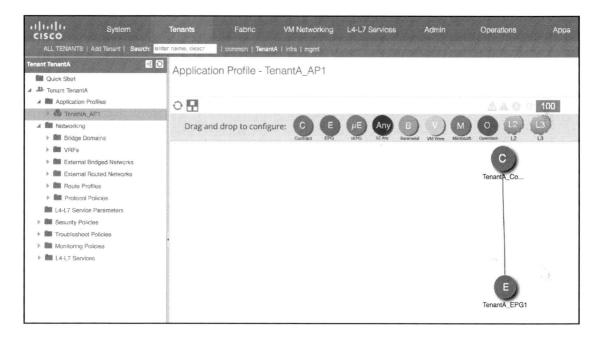

2. Drag a **VM Ware** object onto the tenant EPG. You should see a dotted line appear.

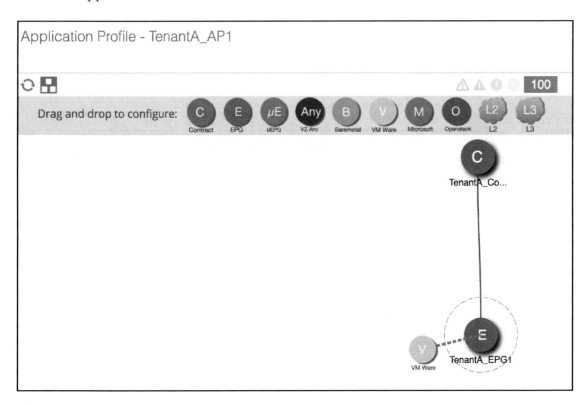

3. Once you release the mouse button, a new window will appear.

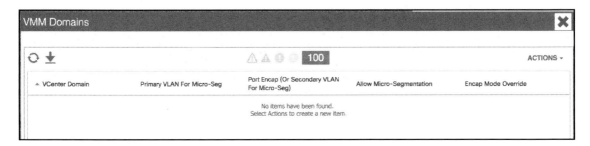

4. Click on the **Actions** menu and select **Add VMM Domain Association**.
5. In the new window, select the vCenter domain added in the previous recipe.

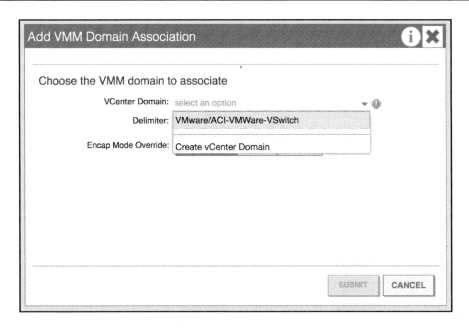

6. Choose the appropriate VLAN mode and encapsulation mode.

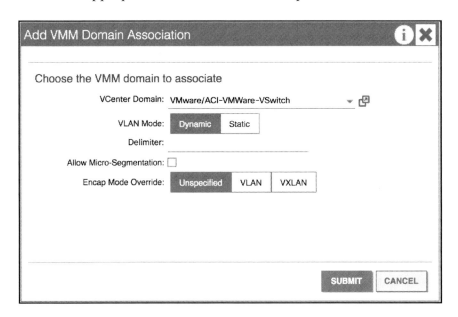

Click on **SUBMIT**.

Hypervisor Integration (and Other Third Parties)

7. The VMM domain will now be associated and appear on the tenant's application profile.

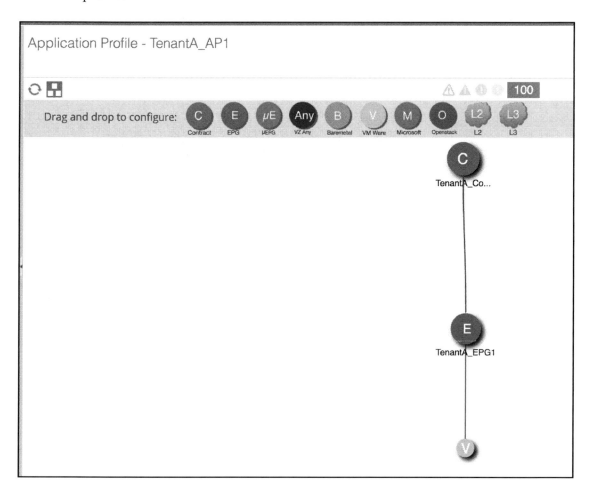

How it works...

We have now created a DVS and, through this, have connected vCenter to the tenant.

There is another way to connect vCenter though: the Cisco way.

Deploying the AVS

The Cisco **Application Virtual Switch** (**AVS**) is an alternative to the **vSphere Distributed Switch** (**VDS**) we set up earlier.

The AVS is based around the Nexus 1000v switch but customized for ACI.

The benefits of the AVS are that it allows you to create a Virtual Tunnel End Point (VTEP) on the VMWare hosts. This enhances scalability (over the VDS) as we are not bound by a one-hop limit. One of the differences between using the DVS and the AVS is that the DVS uses LLDP for VM discovery whereas the AVS uses OpFlex.

We need to install an additional plugin to vCenter to be able to run the AVS. You can download it from https://software.cisco.com/download/release.html?mdfid=282646785&softwareid=286280428&release=1.1 You will require a CCO account and the specific entitlement.

How to do it…

Earlier in this chapter, we created a vCenter domain. As part of this, we created a VDS. The other option would be to use the Cisco AVS (refer to the figure in step 5 in the *Creating VMM domains and integrating VMWare* recipe).

1. Click on **VM Networking**.
2. Right-click on **VMware**.
3. Select **Create vCenter Domain**.
4. Give it a name.

Hypervisor Integration (and Other Third Parties)

5. Select **Cisco AVS as the Virtual Switch**.

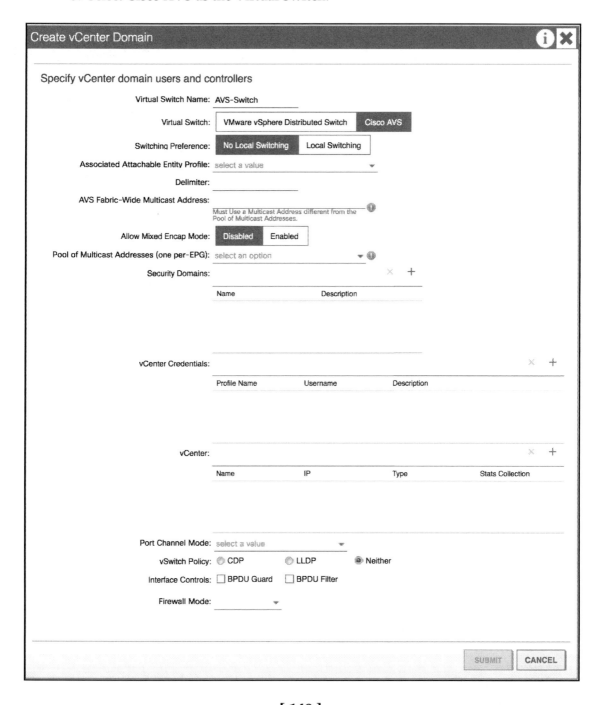

6. Set the **Switching Preference**.
7. Set the **AVS Fabric-Wide Multicast Address**.
8. Set the multicast address pool (creating one if required).
9. Set the **vCenter Credentials** and **vCenter** details (which is the same as the other recipe).
10. Set the **Port Channel Mode**, **vSwitch Policy**, **Interface Controls**, and **Firewall Mode**.

How it works...

Many of the options can be left as the default values. The essential ones will have a red circle with an exclamation mark in it.

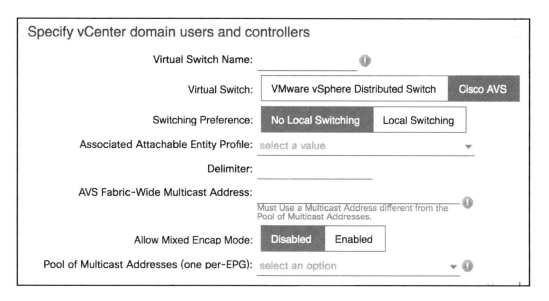

In these settings, **No Local Switching** has been selected (the default setting). With this setting, all traffic between VMs in the same EPG must flow through the leaf node, and VXLAN is the only encapsulation method available. This is also known as "FEX Enable Mode." This is not the recommended method.

The preferred method is **Local Switching** mode. Traffic between VMs in the same EPG is routed by the hypervisor instead of having to flow through the leaf node. Traffic between VMs in different EPGs will still need to flow through the leaf node, but there can still be considerable performance gains with local switching mode. Local switching mode can also use VLAN and VXLAN for encapsulation, and is referred to as "FEX Disable Mode."

There's more...

- For the AVS to work, it needs to be installed. Follow this guide to install the plugin and the AVS:

    http://www.cisco.com/c/en/us/td/docs/switches/datacenter/nexus1000/avs/vsum-getting-started/1-0/b_Cisco_Virtual_Switch_Update_Manager_Getting_Started_Guide_Release_1_0_For_Cisco_AVS/b_Cisco_Virtual_Switch_Update_Manager_Getting_Started_Guide_Release_1_0_For_Cisco_AVS_chapter_01.pdf

- There is also a useful PDF of the differences between the DVS and the AVS:

    http://www.cisco.com/assets/global/DK/seminarer/pdfs/Cisco_Tech_Update-ACI_Hypervisor_integration-22_og_24_september_2015.pdf

Discovering VMWare endpoints

Naturally, there will be additional VMs created within the VMWare environment. As such, we will need the new machines to be reflected in ACI.

We can do this manually.

How to do it...

1. From the **VM Networking** tab, open up the **VMWare** menu, and click on the switch that was created earlier.
2. Right-click on the **vCenter** name in the **Properties** window.

Chapter 3

3. Select **Trigger Inventory Sync**.

4. Click on **YES** to the message that pops up.

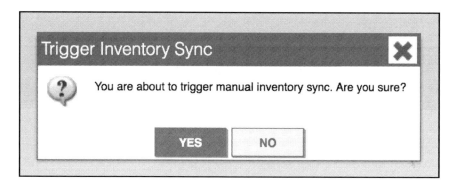

How it works...

When we trigger the inventory sync, ACI polls the connected vCenter servers and pulls in a list of all the virtual machines.

Here are the statistics before the sync:

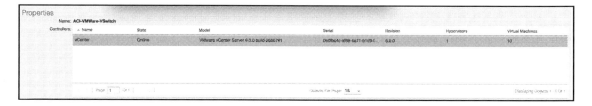

Notice that ACI sees 10 virtual machines.

After the update, we can see 11 virtual machines.

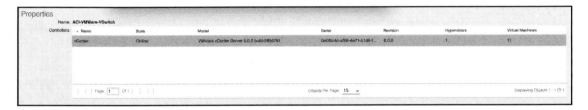

We do not need to perform manual updates all the time, however, as the APIC will do this automatically as well.

Adding virtual machines to a tenant

Now that we have associated our vCenter to the APIC, we need to start associating some virtual hosts to the tenant.

To do this, I set up a new ESXi host in VirtualBox (with the VM set to use two CPUs, two 30 GB hard disks, and 4 GB of memory). If you are short on available hardware and are running the ACI simulator within one ESXi host, this avoids any issues that could be caused by adding the host controlling the ACI simulator to a tenant running within the simulator.

I am not sure whether there would be a problem, but I did not want to encounter any "divide by zero" issues!

How to do it...

1. Add the ESXi host to vCenter and license it.
2. Go to the **Networking** settings, and add the new host to the DVS by right-clicking on the switch and selecting **Add and Manage Hosts**.

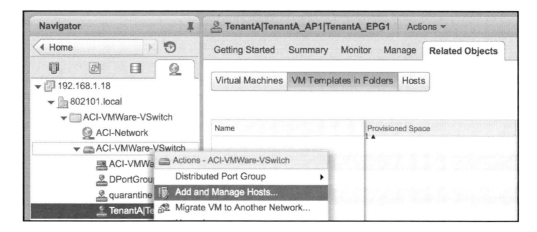

3. Follow the wizard to add the ESXi server. Once this has completed, you should see the host listed.

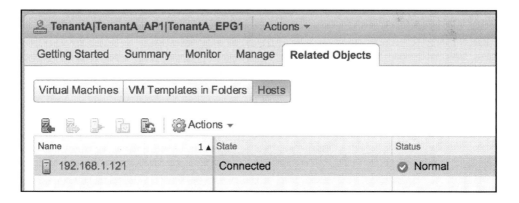

4. Import an OVA file (I am using a Tiny Linux OVA file due to its small footprint), by selecting the import option under **Virtual Machines**. I have called the VM **Tiny-ACI**.
5. You should see the virtual machine from the ACI GUI.

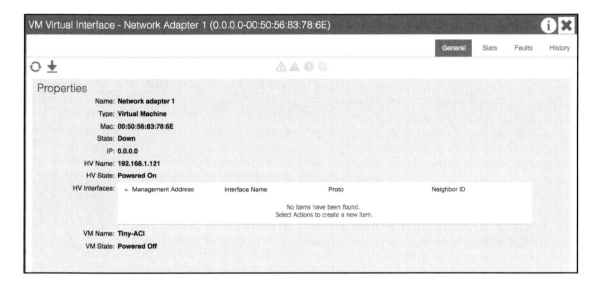

How it works...

By adding an ESXi host to the tenant, we can run virtual machines within the tenant. But once we start adding virtual machines to hosts, how do we keep track of them? Let's find out!

Tracking ACI endpoints

Once the number of tenants increases, it is likely that the number of virtual machines will also increase. How, then, do you keep track of all the VMs and to which tenant they belong?

Thankfully, the ACI Toolkit can help you with this (and a host of other scenarios).

How to do it...

1. Download the ACI Toolkit virtual machine from http://bit.ly/1IzliZY.
2. Deploy the OVA file to create the VMWare guest virtual machine.
3. Update the packages by logging in to the virtual machine using the username and password of `acitoolkit`, then run the command `sudo ~/install`.
4. Connect the APIC to the ACI Toolkit's MySQL database by running the following command:

   ```
   python aci-endpoint-tracker.py
   -u https://192.168.1.205 -l admin -p apicpassword -i
   127.0.0.1 -a root -s mysqlpassword
   ```

5. Log in to MySQL using this command:

   ```
   mysql -u root -p
   ```

   You will be prompted for the password.

6. Switch to the ACI Toolkit database:

   ```
   use acitoolkit;
   ```

7. We can then query the endpoint table by using the following commands:

   ```
   select * from endpoints;
   select * from endpoints where tenant='Tenant_A"
   ```

How it works...

The ACI Endpoint Tracker connects the APIC to a MySQL database, which you can easily query.

For updates to be inserted into the database, the Endpoint Tracker must be running.

There's more...

This recipe is just to whet your appetite. Refer to the developers' documentation for the wealth of functions that the toolkit offers:

- https://acitoolkit.readthedocs.io/en/latest/tutorialpackages.html
- https://acitoolkit.readthedocs.io/en/latest/endpointtracker.html

Integrating with A10

The A10 Thunder is the easiest way to get started with L4-L7 services. This is because you can download a trial of the A10 Thunder and also download the device package from A10. The other services listed are a little more difficult to get started with unless you have a large wallet.

In this recipe, we will be adding a new application profile and EPG so that we can deploy the A10 between the existing TenantA_AP1 and the new web application profile.

How to do it...

1. Create a second application profile, called `TenantA-Web-AP`, using the **TenantA_VRF2** bridge domain created in `Chapter 2`, *Configuring Policies and Tenants*.

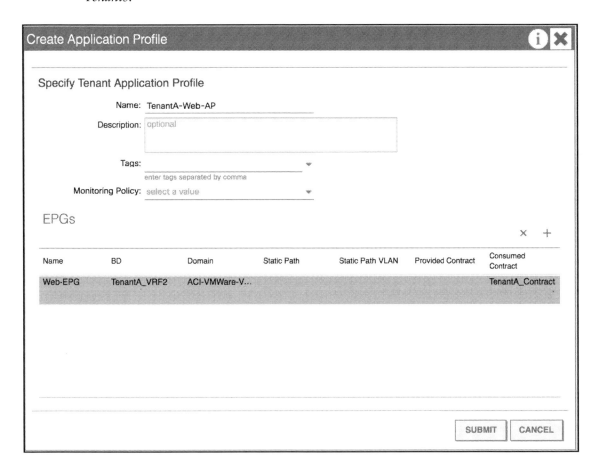

The **Application Profiles** window should look like this:

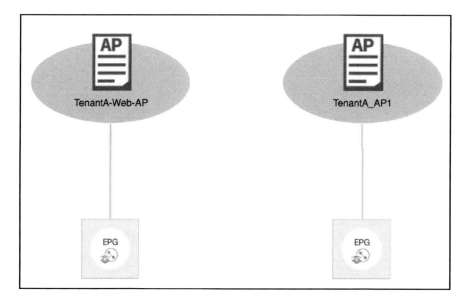

2. Create a subnet for **TenantA_VRF2**:

Chapter 3

3. vCenter should see the new EPG settings:

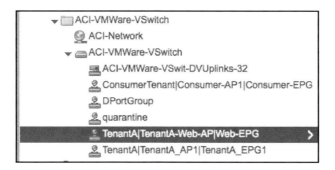

4. We have already covered installing the vThunder device package at the start of this chapter, but you can register to download it from `https://www.a10networks.com/cisco-aci-integration`.

5. Download the trial from `https://www.a10networks.com/products/virtual-ddos-mitigation-load-balancer-application-delivery`.

[159]

6. Deploy the OVA template into vCenter. When you get to section 2d in the deployment wizard (Setup Networks), make sure that the first Ethernet adapter is set to use the management network (often shown as **VM Network**) and that ethernet1 is set to the TenantA's AP1 EPG and ethernet2 is set to use the web EPG. Once the VM has been deployed, the settings should look like this:

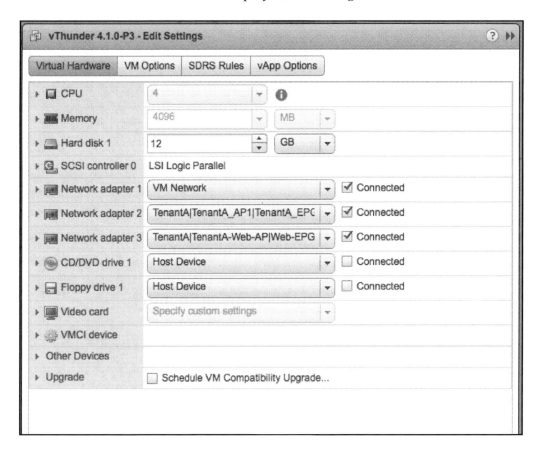

7. The VM will need licensing. There will be a licensing link on the download page; we need to get the current UID to generate the license. We can SSH to the VM (using the password of `a10` when prompted):

```
Stuarts-iMac:~ stu$ ssh admin@192.168.1.223
Password: (type "a10" here)
ACOS system is ready now.
[type ? for help]
vThunder(NOLICENSE)>
vThunder(NOLICENSE)>en
```

```
Password: (press enter here)
vThunder(NOLICENSE)#show license uid
```

8. Copy this license into the licensing page and wait for them to e-mail you the license file.
9. Once you have the file, start up a TFTP server and copy the `trial_license.txt` file to the TFTP server directory.
10. From the vThunder CLI, install the license:

```
vThunder(NOLICENSE)#import license trial_license.txt
tftp://192.168.1.88/trial_license.txt
(make sure that you replace any IP addresses with
ones for your environment)
```

11. We now need to assign the device to the tenants. From TenantA, click on **L4-L7 Services**, and select **Create a L4-L7 device**:

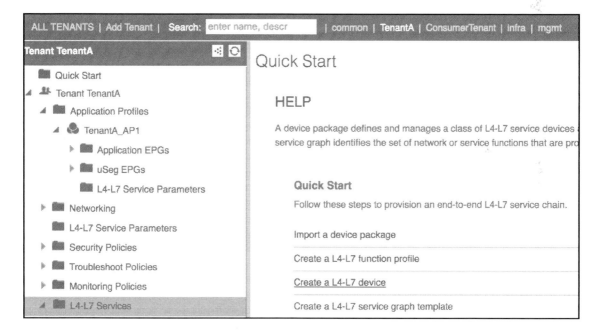

Hypervisor Integration (and Other Third Parties)

12. As mentioned earlier, the essential fields will have red exclamation circles next to them.

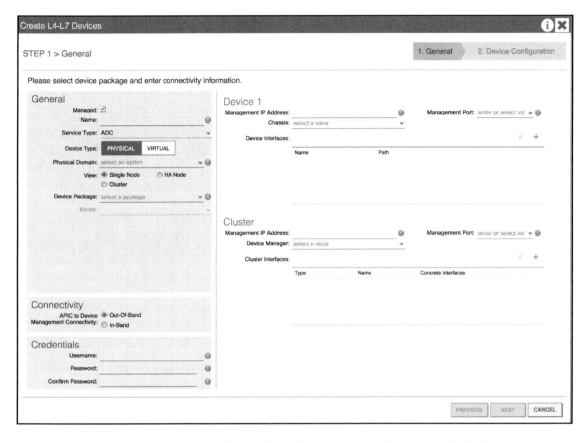

In the **General** field, fill in the **Name**, **Device Type**, VMM Domain, and **Device Package**:

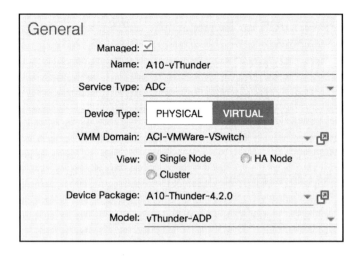

Leave the **Connectivity** setting to **Out-Of-Band**.

For the **Credentials**, use the username of admin and a password of a10:

13. For the **Device 1** field, set the IP address and port. Do not change the HTTPS port; otherwise, you will see errors in the APIC about an "unsupported port." Select the VM from the drop-down list and set the interfaces. Note that we need to set Ethernet 1 to the VM's second network adapter (which has been mapped to AP1) and set Ethernet 2 to the VM's third network adapter (assigned to the web AP).

14. In the **Cluster** settings, the management IP address and port will be copied from the device one settings. Click on the plus sign to create a new cluster interface, setting the type as **provider**; give it a name (`From-TenantA`) and a concrete interface to Ethernet 1. Do the same again, setting the type as **consumer**; give it a name (**To-Consumer**) and the interface to Ethernet 2.

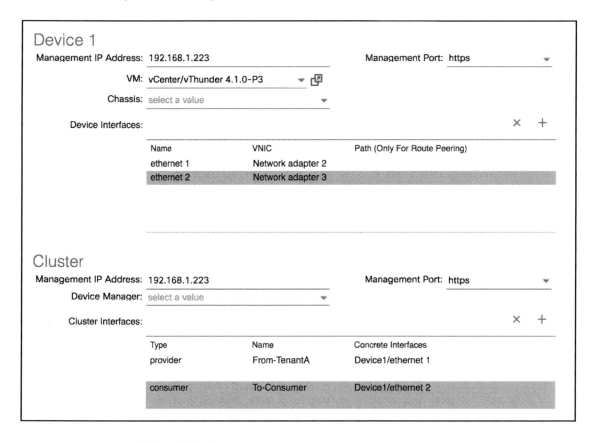

Click on **NEXT**.

15. Click on **FINISH**.
16. The next step is to create a service graph template. From the **L4-L7 Services** menu (under the tenant), select **L4-L7 Service Graph Templates**. Click on the **Actions** menu, and select **Create L4-L7 Service Graph Template**.

Chapter 3

17. Set the graph name (`Tenant-A-Provider`) and drag the **TenantA/A10-vThunder** object between the consumer EPG and the provider EPG. Select the profile in the window that pops up (**Basic Web Server**).

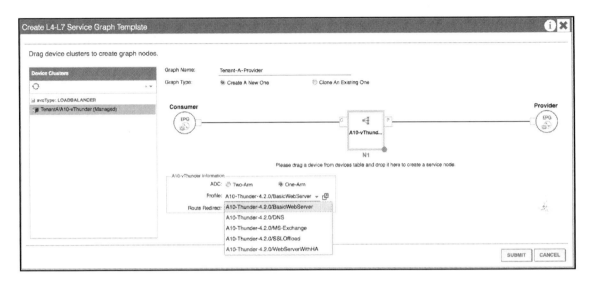

18. Click on **SUBMIT**.
19. Right-click on the graph name, and select **Apply L4-L7 Service Graph Template**.

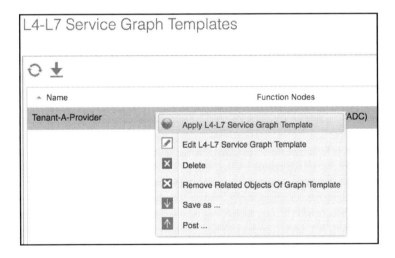

[165]

Hypervisor Integration (and Other Third Parties)

20. Set the consumer and provider EPGs. The provider EPG will be TenantA, and the consumer will be the web AP. Set the contract to be the **TenantA_Subject** contract we created in `Chapter 2`, *Configuring Policies and Tenants*.

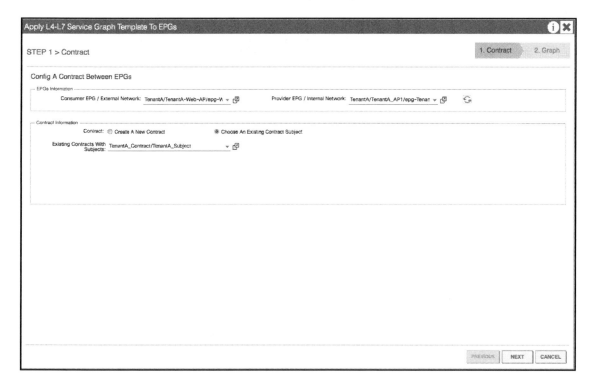

21. Click on **NEXT**.

[166]

Chapter 3

22. Set the cluster interface.

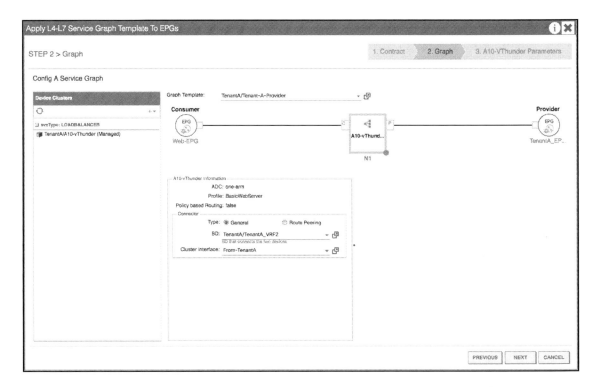

23. Click on **NEXT**.

24. We need to set some values for vThunder here. You can edit the fields by double-clicking on them, typing in the relevant details, and clicking on **APPLY**. If any required fields are not completed, you will receive a message when you click on **FINISH**.

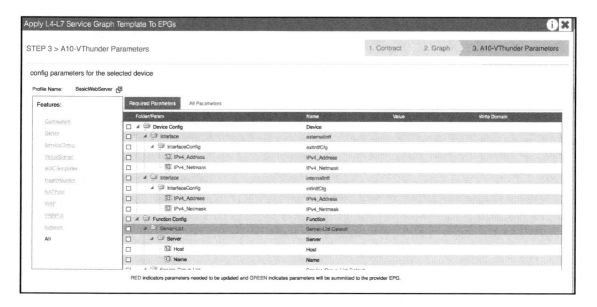

25. Click on **FINISH**.

How it works...

In this recipe, we created a second EPG within TenantA. We created a new subnet and inserted an A10 Thunder virtual appliance between the two EPGs, one of which is the provider, the other the consumer.

There's more...

Refer to the following PDF for the full walkthrough:

```
https://www.a10networks.com/sites/default/files/A10-DG-16143-EN.pdf
```

Deploying the ASAv

Deploying the ASAv consists of two parts. Firstly, we need to upload the ASAv device package, and then, we need to deploy the OVA file to create the ASAv guest on the ESXi hosts. This is the same method as the A10 deployment in the previous recipe.

How to do it...

We start by installing the device package, following the same steps as the *Installing device packages* recipe earlier.

The ASAv device package and OVA file do require specific entitlements from Cisco before you can download them.

1. From **L4-L7 Services**, select packages and click on **Import Device Package**.
2. Browse to the package location and upload it. The package name will be something like `asa-device-pkg-1.2.4.8`.
3. The new device should be visible from the **L4-L7 Service Device Types** window in the GUI.
4. From vCenter, choose the option to deploy the OVA template (**File | Deploy OVF Template**).
5. Select the appropriate download option. If you are using a standalone ESXi server, use the file named asav-esxi.ofv; if you are using vCenter, use the file named `asav-vi.ovf`.
6. Follow the installation wizard, accepting the terms and conditions, and set the hostname, management IP address, and firewall mode.

OOB (out-of-band) management must be enabled!

7. Click on **FINISH** to deploy the ASAv.
8. Power on the ASAv virtual machine.
9. Connect to the console of the virtual machine and configure a username and password:

```
username admin password admin123 encrypted privilege 15
```

10. Enable HTTP access:

    ```
    http server enable
    http 0.0.0.0 0.0.0.0 management
    ```

11. From the ACI GUI, select the tenant that will be using the firewall.
12. Go to **L4-L7 Services**.
13. Right-click on **L4-L7 Devices**.
14. Click on **Create L4-L7 devices**. This will open the device import wizard. Use the following settings:

    - **General**:
        - **Managed**: (Selected)
        - **Service Type**: Firewall
        - **Device Type**: Virtual
        - **Mode**: Single
        - **Function**: GoTo
        - Select the appropriate VMM domain, device package, and model
    - **Connectivity**:
        - **Out-Of-Band**
    - **Credentials**:
        - **Username**: `admin` (or username set in step 9)
        - **Password**: `admin123` (or password set in step 9)
    - **Device 1**:
        - **Management IP address**: The IP address assigned to the ASAv during setup
        - **Management Port**: https
        - **Device Interfaces**: Assign the appropriate interfaces to the desired path
    - **Cluster**:
        - Set the consumer and provider contract information and interfaces

15. We need to create a **Service Graph Template** like we did with the A10 device in the previous recipe, but with a couple of differences. Start by right-clicking on **Function Profiles**, which is in the **L4-L7 Services** menu option within the tenant.

16. Select the option to **Create L4-L7 Services Function Profiles Group**". Give the group a name.
17. The new group should appear underneath. Right-click on the newly created group, and select **Create L4-L7 Services Function Group**.
18. As we will be setting the firewall up in router mode (GoTo mode in ACI-speak) we need to select **WebPolicyForRoutedMode** in the profile dropdown.
19. Set the IP addresses for the internal and external interfaces, along with the security level.
20. Because of the profile we chose, HTTP and HTTPS will be allowed through the firewall, but here we can also add any new rules we want to implement.
21. Click on **SUBMIT** when you have set the appropriate options.
22. Create the service graph template, give it a name, and drop the firewall cluster object between the two EPGs. Set the firewall to be Routed, and set the function profile to the one we created a moment ago.
23. Apply the template.
24. The steps here are, again, very similar to the A10 setup: we set the consumer and provider EPGs, create a new contract, and set a filter if we want to. It is advisable not to set the filter here; instead, we select **No Filter (Allow All Traffic)**, which means that all traffic filtering performed is decided upon by the contents of the access list set earlier (step 20).
25. Click on **NEXT**.
26. Select the appropriate BDs (bridge domains) and cluster interfaces.
27. Click on **NEXT**.
28. Set the config parameters.
29. Click on **FINISH**.

We will be setting up the ASAv in `Chapter 10`, *An end-to-end example using the NX-OS CLI*.

How it works...

Configuring the ASA is very similar to the A10, with a few additional steps. In fact, once you have added one device package and set up the corresponding device, each additional device, no matter the vendor, is all very similar--the hardest part is getting access to the package file and the virtual machine! The steps are very different from adding a hypervisor, though, so let's run through that another time, by adding OpenStack to our environment.

Hypervisor Integration (and Other Third Parties)

There's more...

For a complete guide to configuring the ASAv on the APIC, refer to the link below.

http://www.cisco.com/c/en/us/support/docs/cloud-systems-management/application-policy-infrastructure-controller-apic/200428-ASAv-in-GoTo-L3-Mode-with-the-Use-of-A.html

Integrating with OpenStack

The easiest way to get started with OpenStack is, by far, the Mirantis OpenStack bundle. It is easy to set up and comes with everything you need to get started with OpenStack if this is the first time you're putting your toe in this particular pool. You will still require the correct Cisco subscription to get the package file.

How to do it...

1. Install the Mirantis OpenStack virtual machines by following the guide at https://www.mirantis.com/how-to-install-openstack/. This takes about 20 minutes or so to complete and once completed will give you one FUEL controller and three OpenStack nodes to play with.

2. Download the FUEL plugin from http://plugins.mirantis.com/repository/a/c/aci_opflex/. Copy the plugin to the OpenStack controller:

   ```
   scp aci_opflex-9.0-9.0.12-1.noarch.rpm root@10.20.0.2:/tmp
   root@10.20.0.2's password: r00tme
   aci_opflex-9.0-9.0.12-1.noarch.
   rpm 100%   615KB 615.1KB/s    00:00    Stuarts-iMac-
   2:Downloads stu$
   ```

3. Log in and install the plugin:

   ```
   ssh root@10.20.0.2
   root@10.20.0.2's password: r00tme
   [root@fuel ~]#
   [root@fuel /]# fuel plugins --install
   /tmp/aci_opflex-9.0-9.0.12-1.noarch.rpm
   ```

4. Upload the `.rpm` file downloaded from Cisco:

   ```
   scp aci_opflex-9.0-9.0.12-1.noarch.rpm
   10.20.0.2:/var/www/nailgun/plugins/aci_opflex-
   7.0/repositories/ubuntu/
   ```

5. Update the `Packages` file in this directory:

   ```
   dpkg-scanpackages -m . /dev/null | gzip -9c > Packages.gz
   ```

   You may need to install dpkg-dev for the command to work.

6. From the FUEL GUI, create a new OpenStack environment.
7. Name the new environment and select the relevant OpenStack release. Click on **NEXT**.
8. Select either **KVM** or **Qemu** as the hypervisor. Click on **NEXT**.
9. On the **Networking Setup** page, select Neutron with VLAN or VLXLAN segmentation (depending on your requirements). Click on **NEXT**.
10. Assign a minimum of one controller node and one compute node.
11. Click on the **Settings** icon for the nodes and enable the **ACI OpFlex** plugin. Complete all the fields, making sure that the driver mode is set to ML2.
12. Click on **NEXT** through the remaining fields until you finish the environment creation.

How it works...

The new environment should appear as a new tenant within the APIC GUI. The plugin links the Neutron component of OpenStack to ACI; nodes added to OpenStack will appear as nodes within the APIC.

There's more...

If you would like to read more on getting started with OpenStack, visit this link:
https://www.mirantis.com/how-to-install-openstack/

For a great video on integrating ACI and OpenStack, watch this video:
https://www.youtube.com/watch?v=pWMXTb237Vk

Integrating with F5

F5 stopped support for the standard ACI package back in December 2016. This is not to say, though, that they have shunned ACI--quite the opposite. They continue to embrace ACI, but getting the two technologies to coexist works slightly differently.

In this recipe, we will create a basic virtual server on the F5 BIG-IP and set this up on our APIC.

Getting ready

Before we can configure the APIC, we need to make sure that the F5 components are running and configured.

For this, we need iWorkflow (version 2.0.0 or higher) and a BIG-IP appliance. I am using **iWorkflow-2.1.0.0.0.10285-scsi.ova** and **BIGIP-13.0.0.0.0.1645.ALL-scsi.ova**. These are available for download from the F5 website (`https://downloads.f5.com`), and you can download free trials.

These need to be imported into vCenter and the VMs started. Once started, run through the configuration wizards to set up the basic IP addressing, NTP, and DNS configuration. The BIG-IP device should be added into iWorkflow.

How to do it...

1. From the **F5 BIG-IP GUI**, navigate to **iApps** | **Templates**. Select the inbuilt **f5.http** template, and scroll to the bottom of the screen. Click on **Copy** and give the template a name.

   Make sure you name it correctly as it must be in the format `name_v1.1.1` or `name.v1.1.1`, so **ACIHTTP_v1.1.2** will work fine, whereas **ACIHTTP-v1.1.2** will not work as this does not follow the iWorkflow naming convention.

2. Click on **FINISH**. The resulting template will look like this:

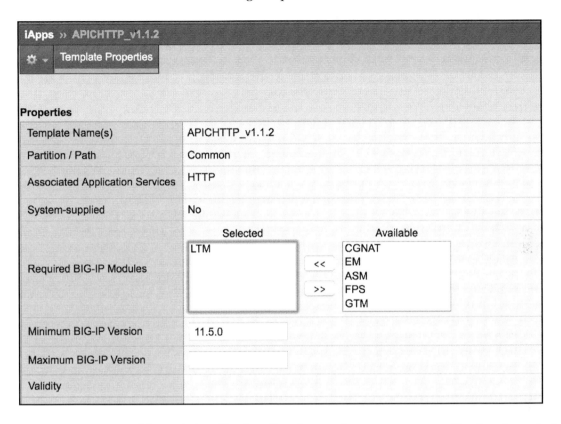

3. Navigate to **iApps** | **Application Services** and create a new application. I created one called **HTTP** and used the template created in step 1. There are some required fields, such as the virtual server IP address, port, and DNS address.

4. Click on **FINISH**. The resulting service should look a little like this:

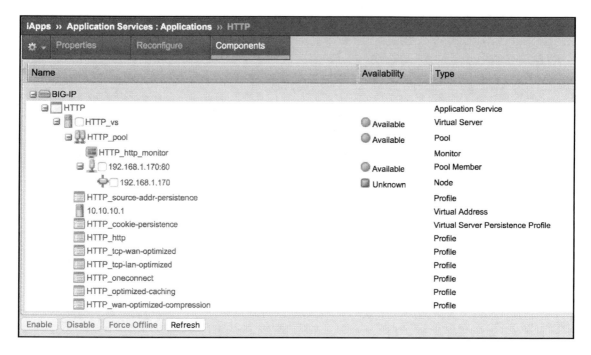

5. Return to **iApps | Templates**. Select the template created in step 1 and click on **Export**. Download the template file.
6. In iWorkflow, navigate to **Clouds and Services | iApps Templates**.

7. Create a new template, selecting the template downloaded in step 5. Use the JSON file from BIG-IP device, selecting it from the drop-down menu.

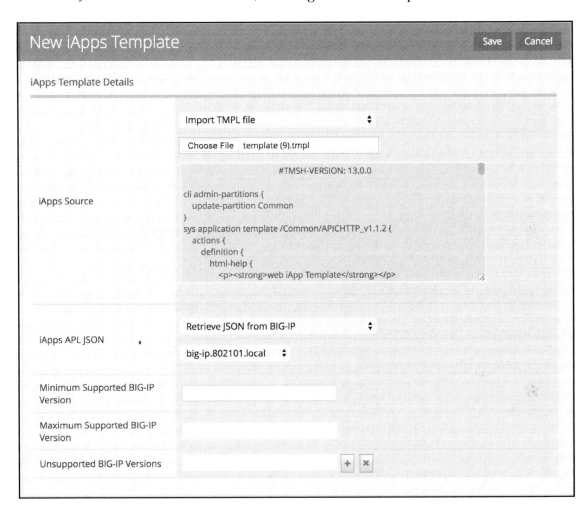

8. Click on **SAVE**.

Hypervisor Integration (and Other Third Parties)

9. Navigate to **Clouds** and create a new cloud, setting the connector type to **Cisco APIC**.

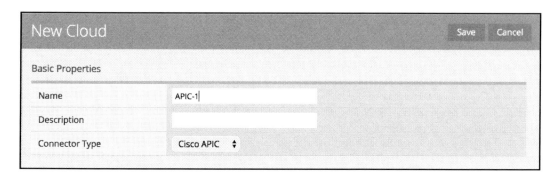

10. Create a service template, setting the **Cloud** to the one created in the previous step and the template to that created in step 7. Depending on the template, you may need to enter some more information, such as the **Name**, **Virtual Address**, and **Virtual Port**:

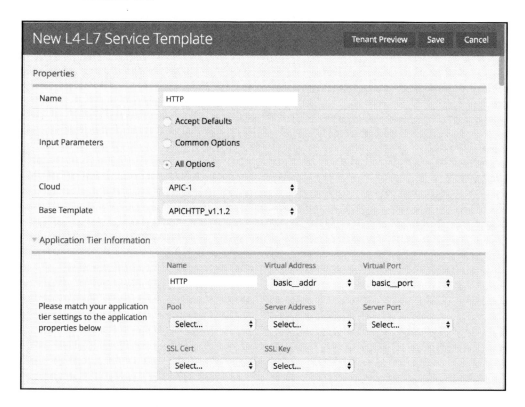

[178]

11. Click on SAVE.
12. Go back to **Clouds**, and select the APIC cloud created in step 9.

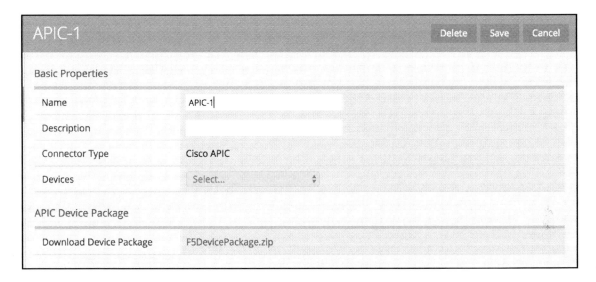

13. Click on **F5DevicePackage.zip** to download it.
14. Import the device package into the APIC (**L4L7 Services** | **Packages** | **Import a Device Package**).

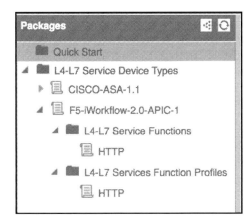

15. Navigate to the tenant and import the device (go **L4-L7 Services | L4-L7 Devices**, right-click on it, and select **Create L4-L7 Device**).
16. Fill in the details.

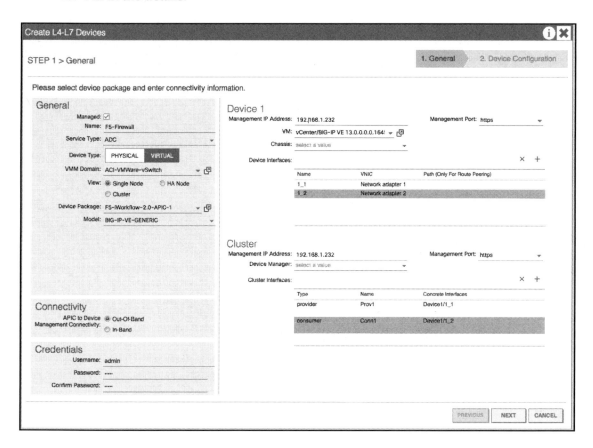

17. Click on **NEXT**.
18. Click on **FINISH**.
19. From the **L4-L7 Service Graph Templates** menu, create a new service graph template.

Chapter 3

20. Name the graph and then drag the F5 object between the Consumer and Provider EPGs.
21. Select the HTTP function profile.

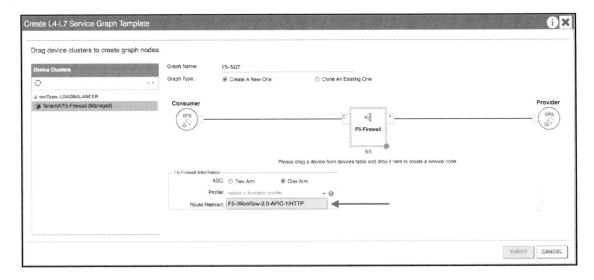

22. Click on **SUBMIT**.

[181]

Hypervisor Integration (and Other Third Parties)

After that, you would create the contract between the provider and consumer, setting the service template to be the one created in the previous steps.

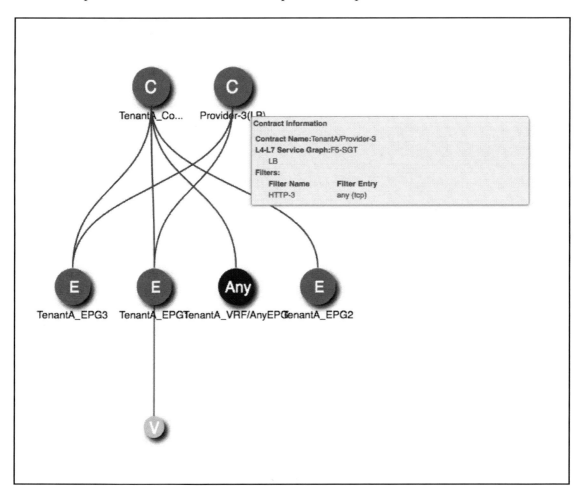

In the previous screenshot, we can see a contract between **TenantA_EPG3 (provider)** and **TenantA_EPG1 (consumer)**.

There's more...

If this recipe has whetted your appetite, you can read the full setup document:

https://support.f5.com/kb/en-us/products/iworkflow/manuals/product/iworkflow-cisco-apic-administration-2-0-0/6.html

There are a couple of good videos on YouTube showing how to integrate F5 with ACI:

- https://www.youtube.com/watch?v=VTE7Ei4Nj6c
- https://www.youtube.com/watch?v=gBAQeMUwgJE

Integrating with Citrix NetScaler

ACI works with Citrix NetScaler MPX, SDX, VPX, and the 1000V series. Integrating the two is very straightforward, and if you have run through either the A10 or ASA recipes, then integrating NetScaler will not be any different.

Getting ready

You will need to download the package from Citrix using the following link. This is restricted content, so you may need to speak to your account manager.

https://www.citrix.com/downloads/netscaler-adc/components/netscaler-device-package-for-cisco-aci.html

How to do it...

The documents from Citrix highlight how easy it is to integrate NetScaler and ACI. Their document lists seven steps:

1. Install the NetScaler devices.
2. Configure the management interfaces and credentials.
3. Install the NetScaler device package onto the APIC.
4. Create a device cluster within the APIC to manage the device.
5. Define the logical interfaces and define a VLAN pool.
6. Define the service graph.
7. Associate the service graph and the device cluster with a logical device and add it to the application profile contract.

We have covered all these steps in the previous recipes.

There's more...

For the official Citrix documentation, refer to these links:

- https://www.citrix.com/content/dam/citrix/en_us/documents/products-solutions/implementing-cisco-application-centric-infrastructure-with-citrix-netscaler-application-delivery-controllers.pdf
- https://www.citrix.com/blogs/2015/06/04/citrix-netscaler-and-cisco-aci-how-it-all-works/

4
Routing in ACI

In this chapter, we will look at:

- Creating a DHCP relay
- Utilizing DNS
- Routing with BGP
- Configuring a layer-3 outside interface for tenant networks
- Associating a bridge domain with an external network
- Using route reflectors
- Routing with OSPF
- Routing with EIGRP
- Using IPv6 within ACI
- Setting up multicast for ACI tenants
- Configuring multicast on the bridge domain and interfaces
- ACI transit routing and route peering

Introduction

ACI works extremely well by itself; however, as the great John Donne once said, "no man is an island." Here, we will look at how to extend ACI through routing. Before we delve into the world of routing, we will look at helping our nodes get IP addresses by creating a DHCP relay and help them resolve names through DNS. Once we have covered this, we will look at configuring **Border Gateway Protocol (BGP)**, **Open Shortest Path First (OSPF)**, and **Enhanced Interior Gateway Routing Protocol (EIGRP)**. We will then look at how easy IPv6 and multicast support is within ACI, before finishing the chapter looking at transit routing.

Creating a DHCP relay

By default, ACI-wide flooding is disabled. Because flooding is disabled, connecting to a DHCP server is only possible if it is in the same EPG as the client (as flooding within a bridge domain is enabled).

The options, therefore, are to have one DHCP server per-EPG, which would be wasteful on "compute" resources and on administrative time, or to use a DHCP relay and have one, central, server.

In this recipe, we will be setting up a DHCP relay.

How to do it...

We will be using the Common tenant for this (first), as it is best practice to place resources within this tenant if they are to be shared across multiple tenants. Using the Common tenant is not the only way, though; we can also use the Fabric Access policies to achieve the same goal for the Infrastructure tenant.

Why would you use one tenant over the other?
Using the Common tenant means that the DHCP relays can be used by *any* tenant. If we use the Infrastructure tenant, the DHCP relay policies are *selectively* exposed to the other tenants. Configuring a global DHCP relay under the Fabric Access means that any tenant can use the DHCP relays and we have a higher level of control.

Chapter 4

Creating a DHCP relay using the Common tenant

1. From **Tenants** | **Common** | **Networking** | **Protocol Policies** | **DHCP**, right-click on **Relay Policies** and select **Create DHCP Relay Policy**.

2. Name the policy, and click on the plus sign next to **Providers**.

3. Select the **EPG Type** (which should be **Application EPG**).
4. Select the **Application EPG** where the DHCP server is located (for this, we are going to use one that would be situated within TenantA).

Chapter 4

 Notice that the Common tenant has access to all of the tenants, their application profiles, and their EPGs.

5. Enter the **DHCP Server Address**.

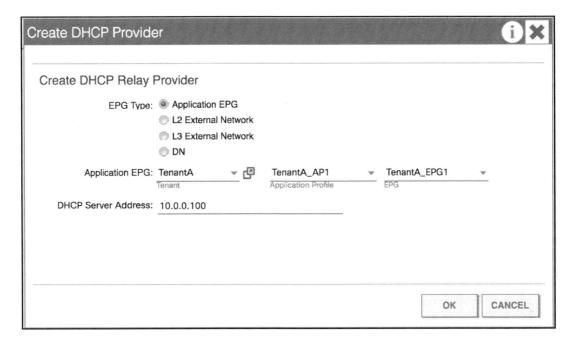

6. Click on **OK**.

7. Click on **SUBMIT**.

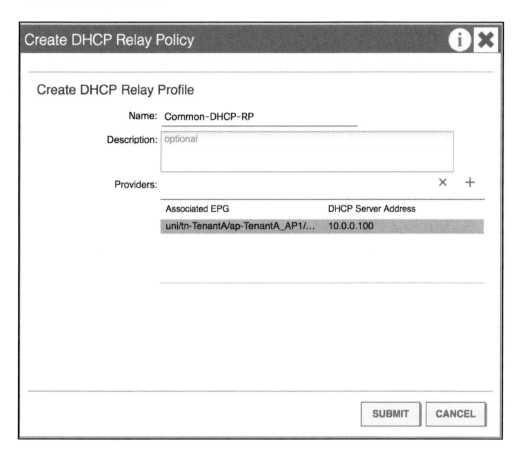

Next, we need to create the labels.

8. From **TenantA**, go to **Networking** | **Bridge Domains** | **TenantA-BD**. Right-click on**DHCP Relay Label**s and select **Create DHCP Relay label**.

Chapter 4

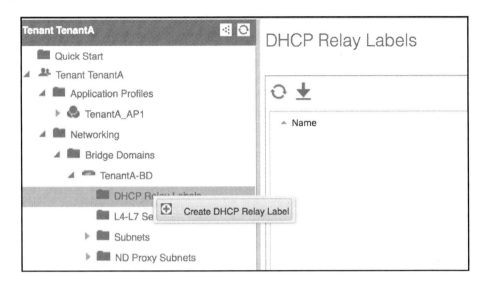

9. Set the scope to **tenant**.
10. Select the Tenant DHCP relay policy we created earlier.

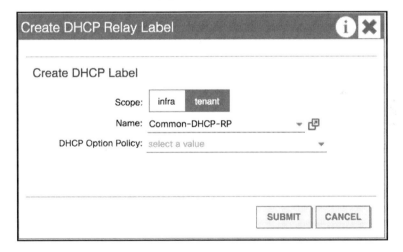

11. Click on **SUBMIT**.

The second method we will look at is creating an access policy for a global DHCP relay.

Creating a global DHCP relay

1. From **Fabric** | **Access Policies** | **Global Policies** DHCP Relay Policies, right-click and select **Create DHCP Relay Policy**.

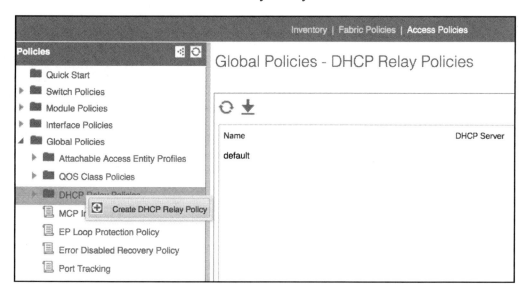

2. Name the policy and click on the plus sign next to **Providers**.

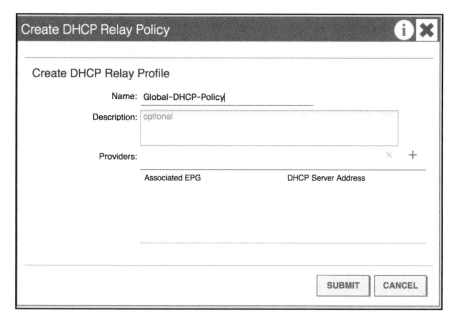

3. Select the **EPG Type** (**Application EPG**).
4. Choose the **Application EPG** where the DHCP server is.
5. Enter the **DHCP Server Address**.

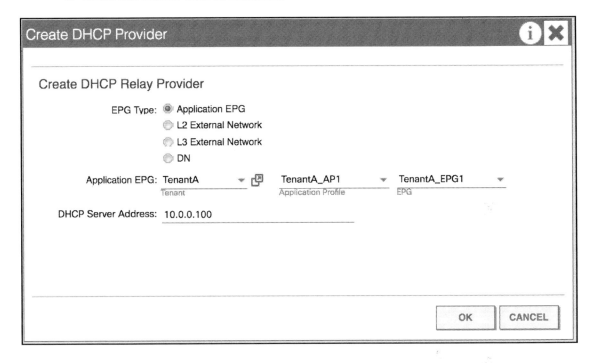

6. Click on **OK**.

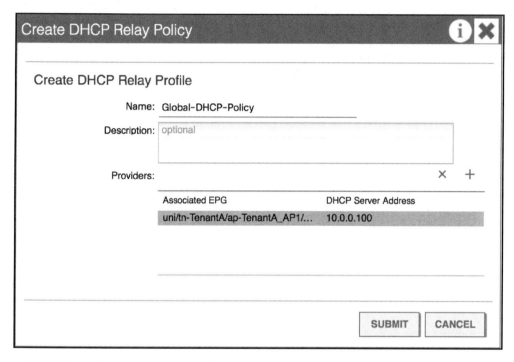

7. Click on **SUBMIT**. We need to create another set of labels here, as we did in the first method.

 I have created a second tenant for this, called TenantB. Jump ahead to Chapter 7, *Network Programmability with ACI*, if you want to create it yourself using the REST client, or drop back to Chapter 2, *Configuring Policies and Tenants*, if you want to set it up by hand (just replace "TenantA" with "TenantB" and use the subnet 20.0.0.1/24).

8. From **TenantB**, go to **Networking** | **Bridge Domains** | **TenantB-BD**.
9. Right-click on **DHCP Relay Labels** and select **Create DHCP Relay Label**.

Chapter 4

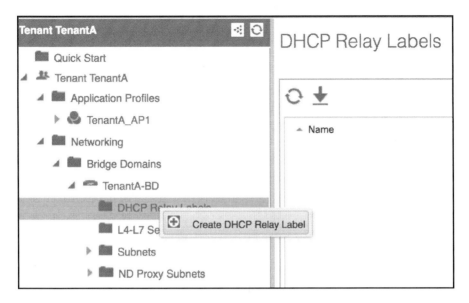

10. Set the scope as **infra**.
11. Select the global DHCP relay policy created earlier.

12. Click on **SUBMIT**.

[195]

How it works...

For this to work between EPGs, we would need to have routing in place as well as a contract to permit the DHCP traffic. Refer to *Chapter 2* for how to create contracts.

There's more...

In a multitenancy environment, tenants will require separate DHCP servers; otherwise, they could receive incorrect IP addresses, gateway addresses, DNS server addresses, and much more.

Utilizing DNS

A DNS policy will be required to connect to external servers by their name, rather than their IP address. Such services could be AAA, RADIUS, or vCenter.

The DNS service policy is a shared policy, in that any tenant and VRF that uses this service must be configured with the particular DNS profile label.

How to do it...

1. From **Fabric**, select **Fabric Policies** | **Global Policies** | **DNS profiles**. Right-click on **DNS Profiles** and select **Create DNS Profile**.

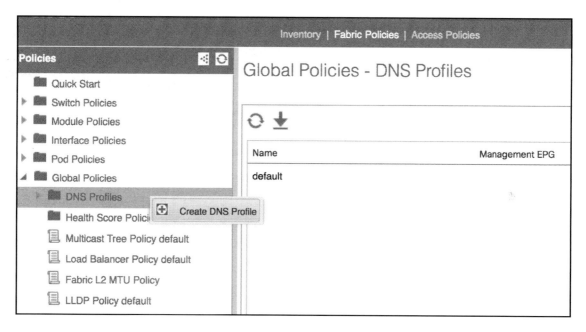

2. Name the profile and select the **default (Out-of-Band)** option next to **Management EPG**.

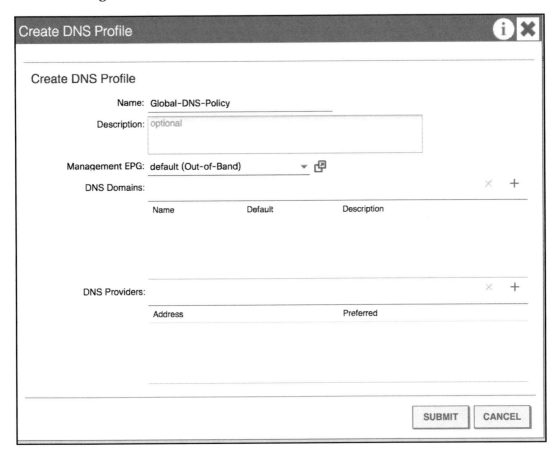

3. Click on the plus sign next to **DNS Providers** and add the IP addresses of the DNS servers. Select the **Preferred** tick box if you want to.

Chapter 4

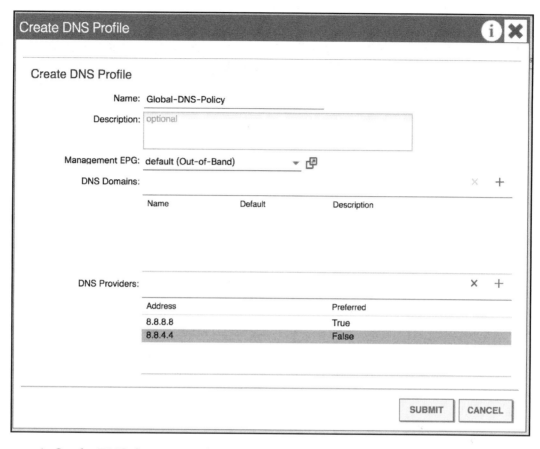

4. Set the DNS domains in the same manner.
5. Click on **SUBMIT**. We need to set the labels, again.
6. From **Tenants**, select the **mgmt**. tenant.
7. Go to **Networking**, then to **VRFs**, and select **oob**.
8. Scroll down the page in the working pane until you see the **DNS labels** box.

9. Enter the **DNS label (Global-DNS-Policy)**.

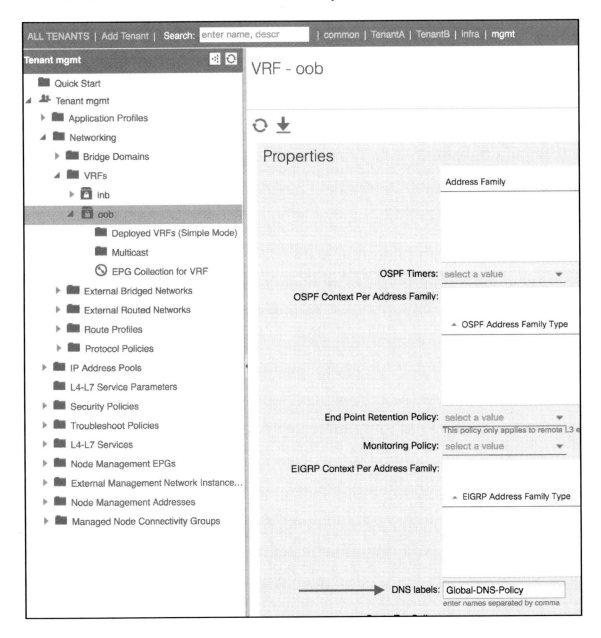

10. Click on **SUBMIT**.

Perform steps 6 to 10 with TenantA to provide the tenant with access to the same global DNS profile.

How it works...

Because the APIC uses a Linux-based operating system, this recipe adds entries to the /etc/resolv.conf file. We can check the contents of this by running the command cat /etc/resolv.conf.

```
apic1# cat /etc/resolv.conf
# Generated by IFC
nameserver 8.8.8.8

nameserver 8.8.4.4

apic1#
```

There's more...

In this recipe, there is the assumption that TenantA will require the same DNS resolution as the APIC management. In an environment where there are multiple tenants, who may have overlapping address spaces (as is often the case with RFC1918 private addresses), then they will need to deploy their own DNS servers to overcome this issue. To facilitate upstream DNS resolution (that is, names outside of their own network), they would need to employ some sort of external routing within their own VRFs. We will look at external routing next.

Routing with BGP

ACI supports three routing protocols: BGP, OSPF, and EIGRP. We will start by looking at BGP.

Routing in ACI

As we go forward, we will see that the steps taken to implement OSPF and EIGRP are very similar. The steps, from a 10,000-foot view, are to create an "external routed network," configure an interface, and associate this interface to a bridge domain. To get a visualization of the type of deployment we would be looking at, refer to this figure:

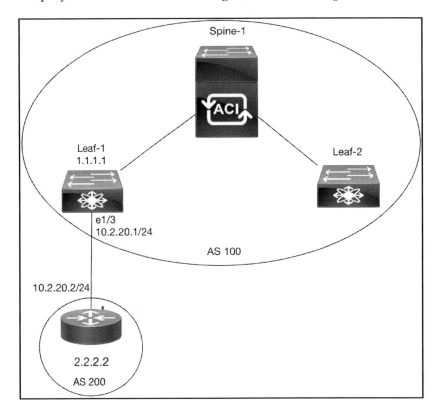

How to do it...

1. Navigate to **TenantA | Networking | External Routed Networks**.
2. Right-click on this and select **Create Routed Outside**.

Chapter 4

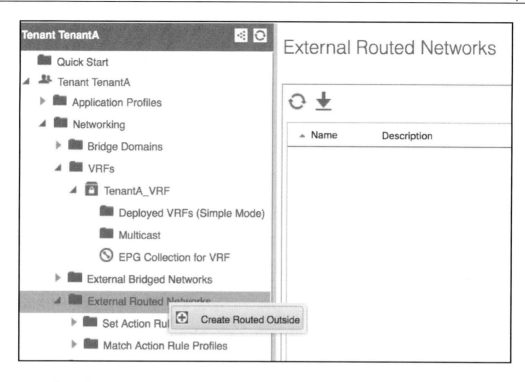

3. Give the new Routed Outside a name.
4. Select the **BGP** checkbox.
5. Select the desired VRF.

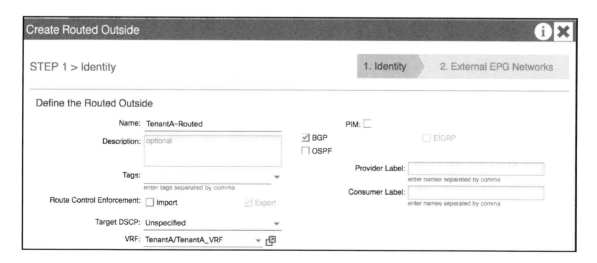

6. Click on **NEXT**.
7. Click on **FINISH**.

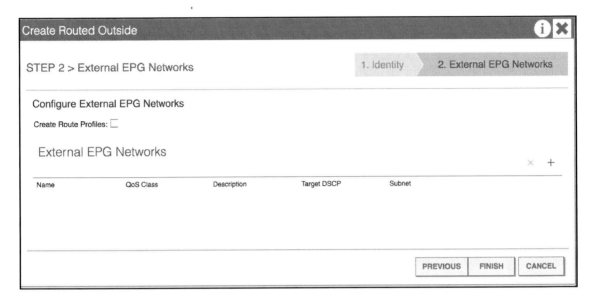

8. The new profile will appear in the work pane. Selecting it will show us the options we have configured so far.

Chapter 4

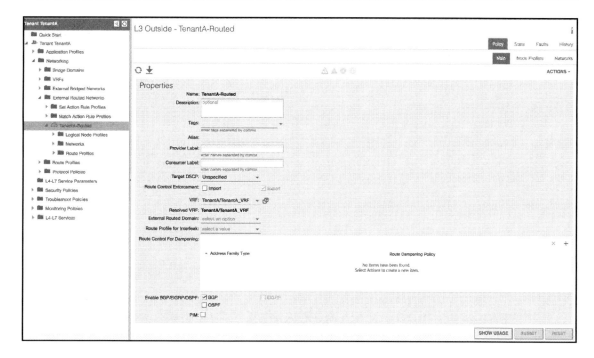

9. Select **Node Profiles** on the right-hand side and click on the plus sign.

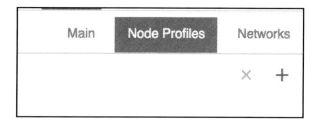

10. Name the profile, and click on the plus sign next to **Nodes**.

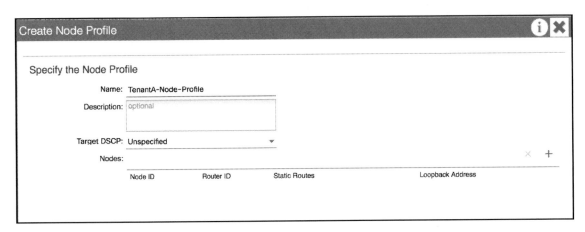

11. Select a node from the drop-down menu.

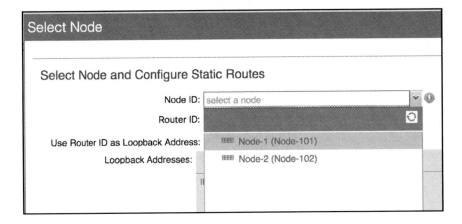

12. Enter a **Router ID**.

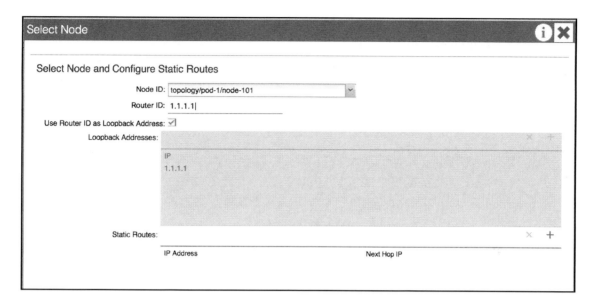

 Whenever you create a router ID on a leaf switch; it creates an internal loopback interface with that IP address.

13. Click the plus sign next to **BGP Peer Connectivity Profiles**.

14. Enter the peer address, the remote AS number, and the local AS number.

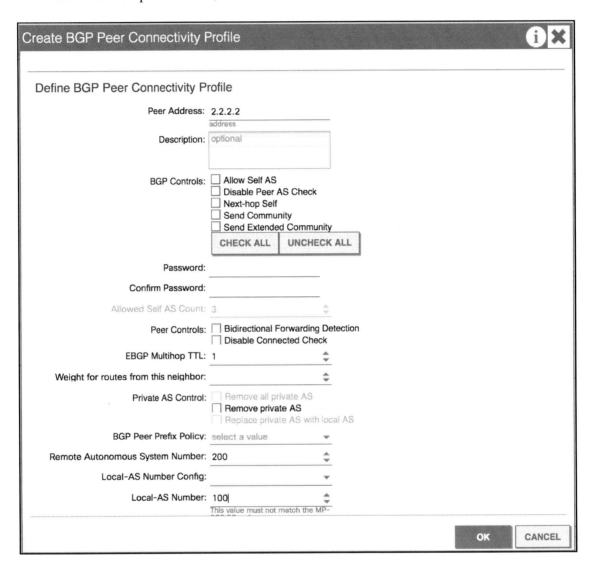

15. Click on **OK**.
16. Click on **SUBMIT**. We can now create an external network.
17. Click on **Networks** from the top right-hand side, and click on the plus sign.

Chapter 4

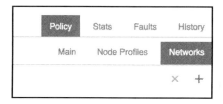

18. Name the network, and click on the plus sign next to **Subnet**.
19. Set the IP address and subnet.

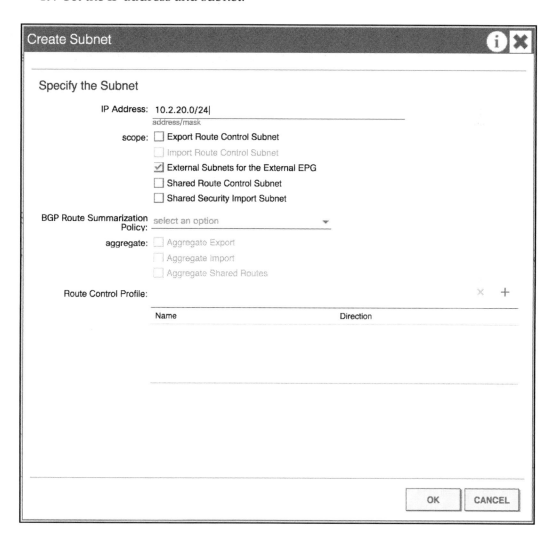

[209]

20. Click on **OK**.
21. Click on **SUBMIT**.

 You can learn more about BGP from my book *BGP For Cisco Networks, CreateSpace Independent Publishing Platform* (https://www.amazon.com/BGP-Cisco-Networks-Protocol-Switching/dp/1496169212).

We now need to create an interface to connect through.

Configuring a layer-3 outside interface for tenant networks

We can create three types of interfaces for routing; they are:

- Routed interfaces
- SVIs
- Routed sub-interfaces

We will create one of each!

How to do it…

First, we will create routed interfaces, which are physical interfaces that have an IP address.

Creating routed interfaces

1. Navigate to **TenantA** | **Networking** | **External Routed Networks** | **TenantA-Routed**.
2. Expand **Logical Node Profiles**.

Chapter 4

3. Expand **TenantA-Node-Profile**.
4. Right-click on **Logical Interface Profiles**.
5. Select **Create Interface Profile**.

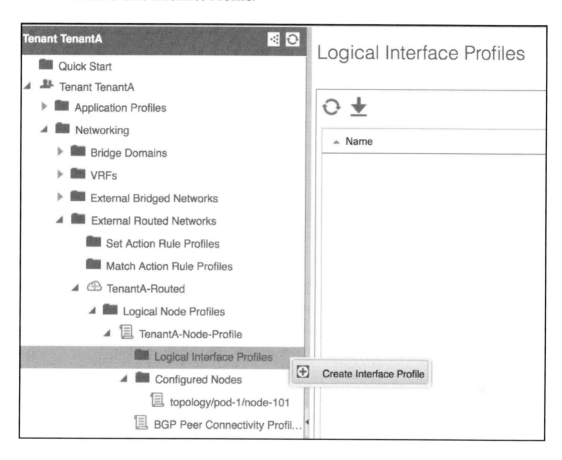

Routing in ACI

6. Name the interface profile and select the interface type (Routed Interface).

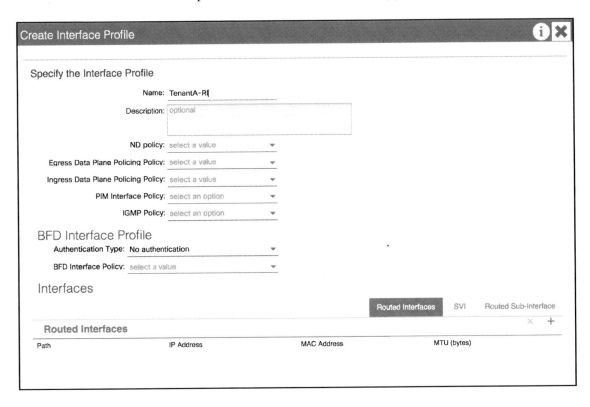

7. Click the plus sign to open **Select Routed Interface**.
8. Select the desired leaf node and interface from the drop-down. This interface would connect to another device, such as a switch or router, with which it would form the BGP peering.

Chapter 4

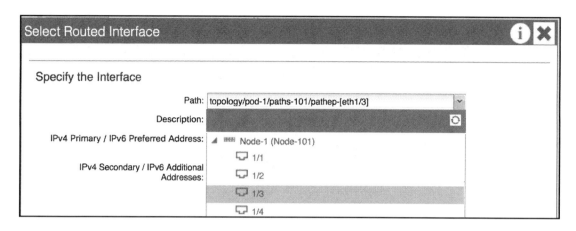

9. Set the **IP address** (I have chosen 10.2.20.1/24).
10. Set the peer-specific **BGP Peer Connectivity Profiles**.
11. Click on **SUBMIT**.

Configuring an external SVI

SVIs, or switch virtual interfaces, are virtual interfaces like the ones we would use in VLAN routing.

1. Follow steps 1-6 from the previous recipe, selecting SVI as the interface type.
2. Choose the interface from the drop-down menu.

Routing in ACI

3. Set the IP address and subnet mask (10.20.20.101/24 here).
4. Click on **OK**.

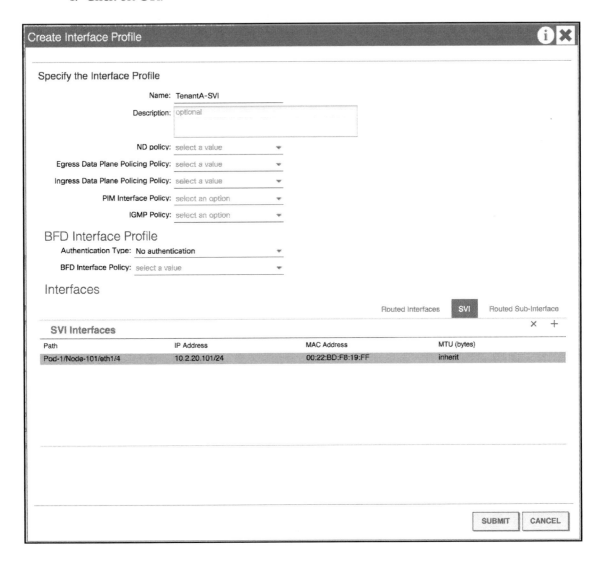

5. Click on **SUBMIT**.

Configuring routed sub-interfaces

A sub-interface is a virtual interface created *within* a physical interface. It uses dot1q encapsulation.

Follow the steps for the SVI recipe, but select **Routed Sub-Interface** as the interface type.

The result should look like this:

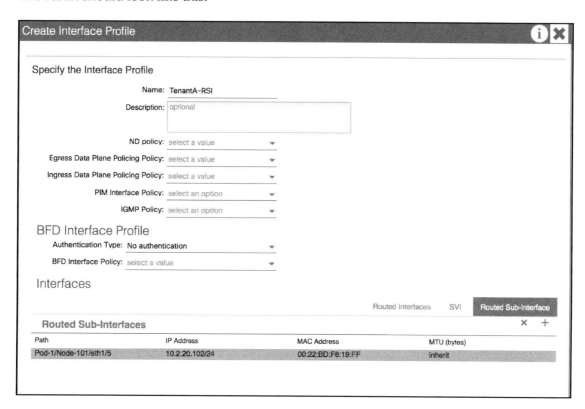

Associating a bridge domain with an external network

Now that we have a routed interface, we must associate it with the bridge domain.

How to do it...

1. Navigate to **TenantA** | **Networking** | **Bridge Domains** | **TenantA-BD**.

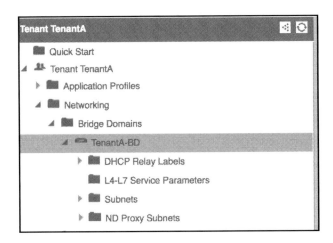

2. Click on **L3 Configurations** on the right-hand side.
3. If required, you can add additional subnets here as well. In the following screenshot, I have added the `10.2.20.0/24` subnet.
4. Select **TenantA-Routed** for **L3 Out** under **Associated L3 Outs**.

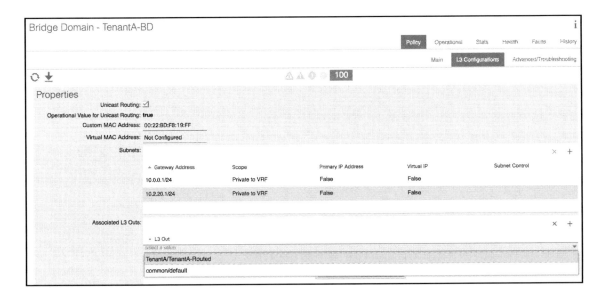

5. Select the same **L3 Out** for the **L3 Out for Route Profile**.

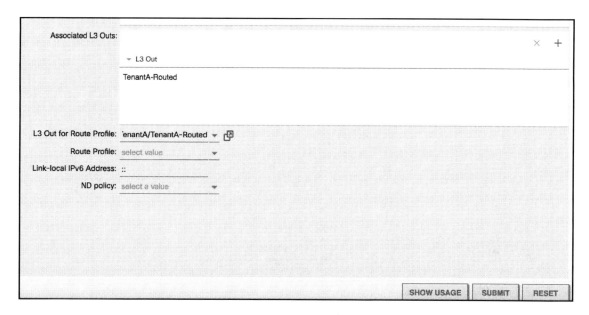

6. Click on **SUBMIT**. One issue here is that we will not be advertising any routes. If you have a successful peering to another BGP speaker, you will see that you will receive routes advertised to you, but the other speaker will not receive any prefixes from the tenant. Therefore, we must make a small change.

Routing in ACI

7. Navigate to **TenantA** | **Networking** | **Bridge Domains** | **TenantA-BD** | **Subnets**, and click on the `10.2.20.1/24` subnet.

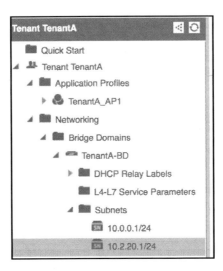

8. Tick the **Advertised Externally** box.

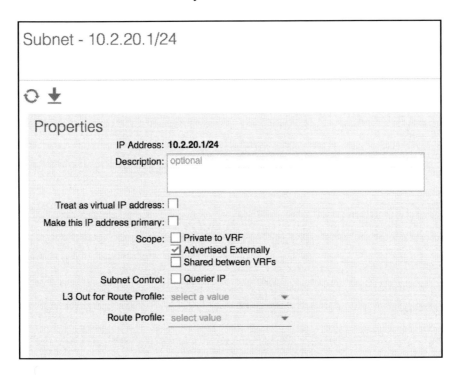

9. Click on **SUBMIT**.
10. Return to the TenantA-BD bridge domain, and look at the L3 Configurations tab. You will now see that the scope for the `10.2.20.1/24` subnet has now changed to **Advertised Externally**.

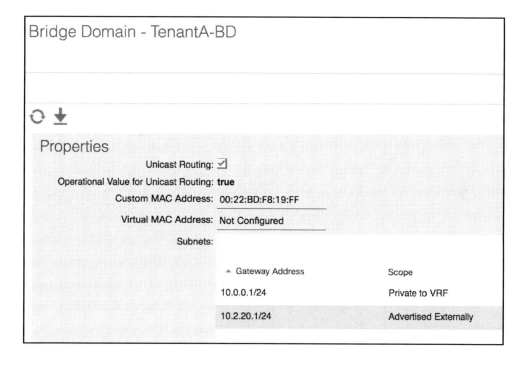

Using route reflectors

We will now enable (on a very limited scale) route reflection in BGP. To do this, we will be reusing the pod policy we created earlier (**PoD-Policy**), back in *Chapter 2*.

This is the same method you would use if you wanted to implement multiprotocol BGP. Strictly speaking, however, route reflection is not the same as multiprotocol BGP (MP-BGP). Route reflection reflects routes from one route reflector client to another, through a "server," bypassing the need for a full mesh between BGP speakers. MP-BGP is used to carry both IPv4 and IPv6 traffic (as well as MPLS VPN traffic), using "address families." The two can be implemented together; you can have route reflection within MP-BGP, but to say that configuring BGP route reflectors also implements MP-BGP is not quite correct. We are looking at this from an ACI standpoint, though, so let's refer to this as an "alternative fact" and move on to configuring MP-BGP.

Routing in ACI

Within ACI, MP-BGP serves to distribute the routes received from external sources, within the ACI fabric (from spine to spine). It is not used to connect to external sources.

By default, MP-BGP is disabled. We should enable it.

How to do it...

1. Navigate to **Fabric | Fabric Policies | Pod Policies | Policies | BGP Route Reflector default**.

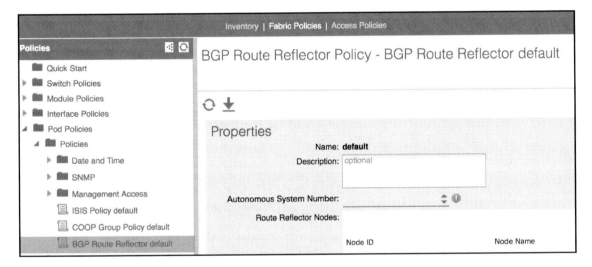

2. Set the AS number and add the spine nodes using their node IDs, which you can find from the **Fabric | Inventory page** (Fabric Membership).

Chapter 4

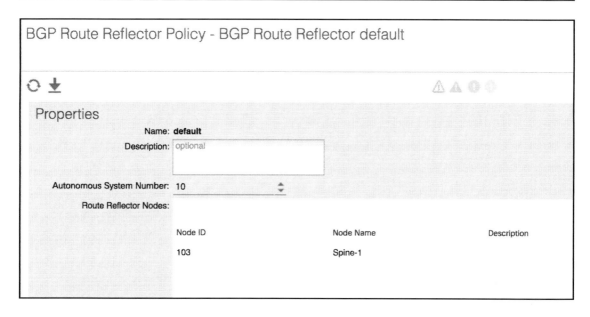

3. Click on **SUBMIT**.
4. Navigate to **Fabric** | **Fabric Policies** | **Pod Policies** | **Policy Groups**.
5. Select the **PoD-Policy** created in the second chapter.

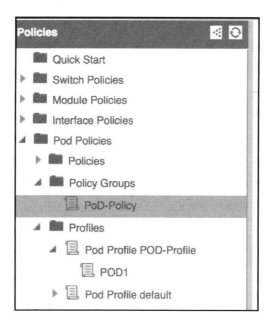

6. Select **default** from the dropdown next to **BGP Route Reflector Policy**.

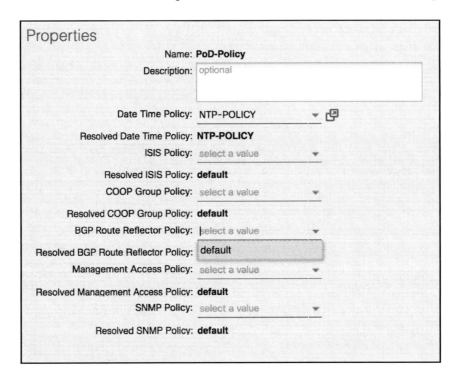

7. Click on **SUBMIT**.
8. You will get a warning (because you are editing an existing, in-use policy group).

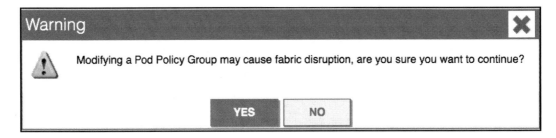

9. Depending on whether you are running a production environment or not, you may want to make this change out of hours. Or just click on **YES**.

How it works...

If you have added more than one node (as you should do), then the BGP relationships should form between the spines and the leaf nodes should become route reflector clients of the spines. To check the state, navigate to **Fabric** | **Inventory** | **Fabric** | **Pod 1** | **Spine-1** | **Protocols** | **BGP** | **BGP** for **VRF-overlay-1** | **Sessions**. The state should show **Established**.

Routing with OSPF

In this recipe, we will cover routing with OSPF, including configuring an OSPF interface policy and profile.

How to do it...

1. Start by creating an external routed network. Navigate to **Tenants** | **TenantA** | **Networking** | **External Routed Networks**. Right-click on this and select **Create Routed Outside**.
2. Name it, choose **OSPF**, and set the **OSPF Area ID**. Cisco ACI supports NSSA, regular areas, and stub areas.

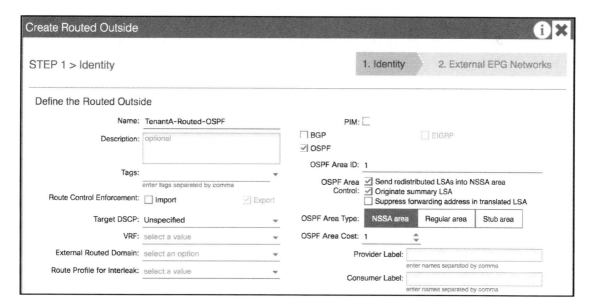

3. Click on the plus sign next to **Nodes And Interfaces Protocol Policies**.
4. Name the policy.

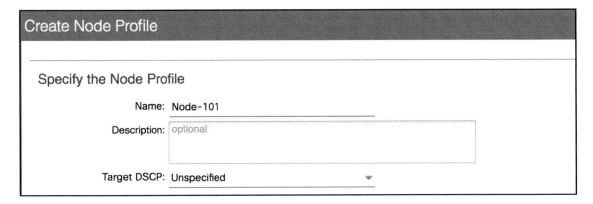

5. Click on the plus sign next to **Nodes**.
6. Select the node and set a router ID.
7. Set any static routes that may be required.

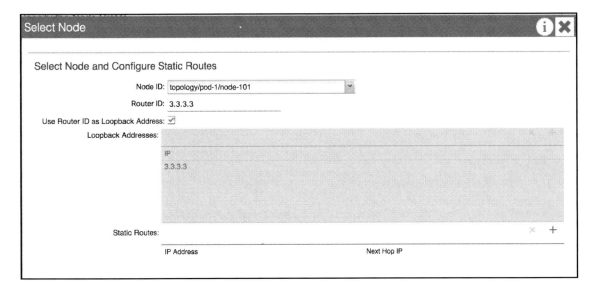

8. Click on **OK**.
9. Click on the plus sign next to **OSPF Interface Profiles**.
10. Name the profile and set any authentication settings and BFD (BiForwarding Detection) configurations.

Chapter 4

11. Configure the interface type (again, choosing from Routed, SVI or Routed Sub-Interface).
12. Click on the plus sign to create the interface.

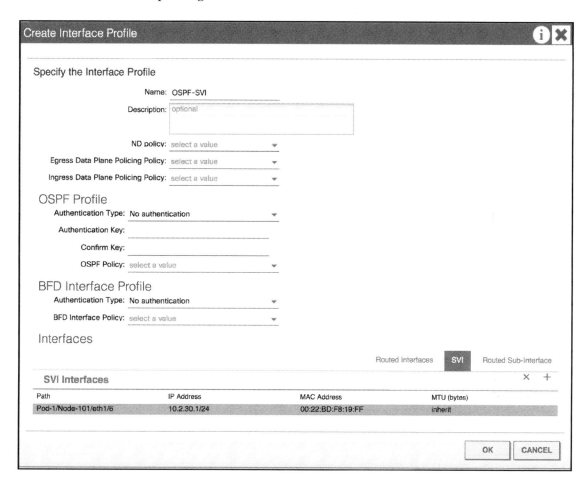

Routing in ACI

13. Click on **OK**.

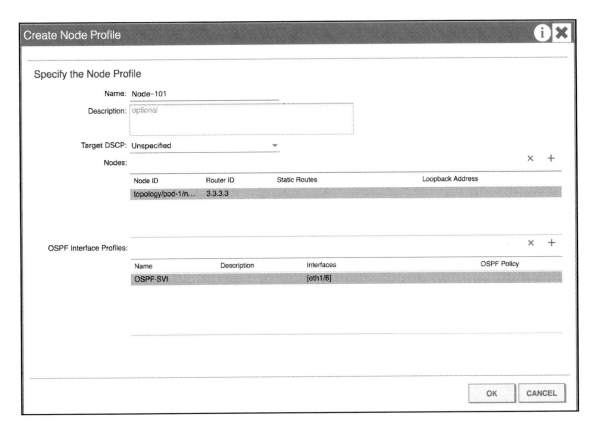

14. Click on **OK** again.

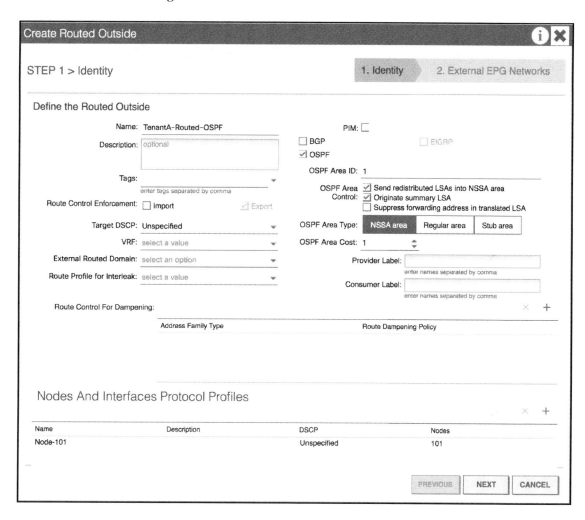

15. Click on **NEXT**.
16. On the **Configure External EPG Networks** page, enter a name.

17. Click on the plus sign to create the subnet.
18. Click on **OK**.

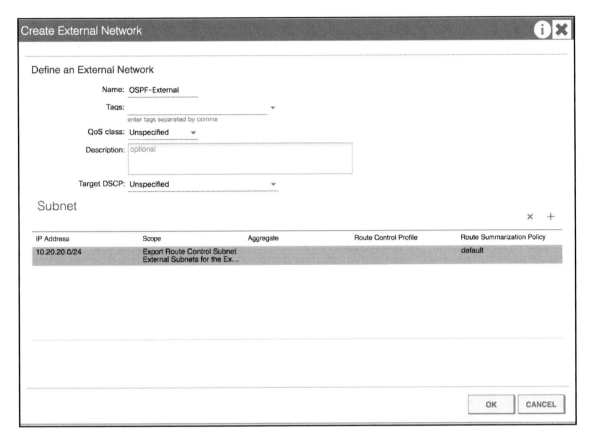

19. Click again on **OK**.

Chapter 4

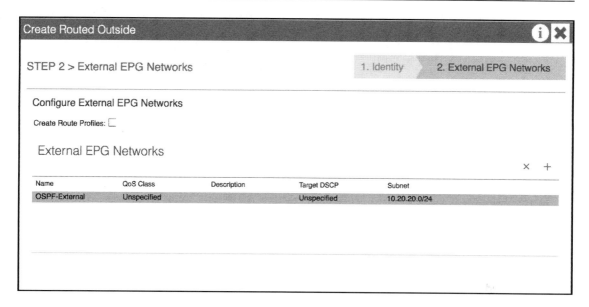

20. Click on **FINISH**.

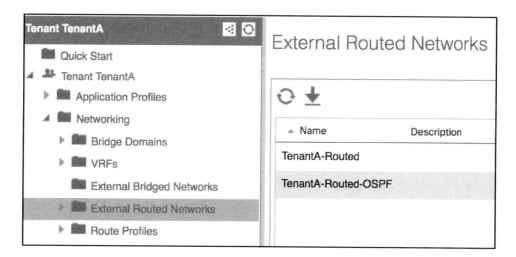

21. Return to **TenantA-BD** and select the **L3 Configurations** tab.
22. Click on the plus sign next to **Associated L3 Outs**.

23. Select **TenantA/TenantA-Routed-OSPF L3 Out**.

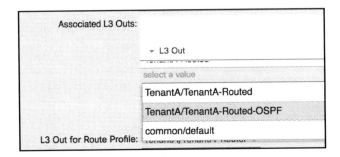

24. Click on **UPDATE**.
25. Change the **L3 Out** for **Routed Profile** to be **TenantA/TenantA-Routed-OSPF**.
26. Click on **SUBMIT**.

Routing with EIGRP

Configuring EIGRP within ACI is no different than configuring BGP or OSPF.

How to do it...

1. Create the external routed network (**TenantA | Networking | External Routed Networks | Create Routed Outside**).
2. Name the new identity.
3. Select the **EIGRP** checkbox.
4. Set the AS number.
5. Click on the plus sign next to **Nodes And Interfaces Protocol Policies**.
6. Name the **Node Profile**.
7. Click on the plus sign to add the node.
8. Select the **Node ID**.
9. Set the router ID.
10. Set any static routes needed.
11. Click on **OK**.
12. Click on the plus sign next to **EIGRP Interface Profiles**.

Chapter 4

13. Name the new profile.
14. Now we need to create an EIGRP policy or use the default one. This field will show the red circle next to it, showing that it is a required field.
15. Create the interface.
16. Set the **IP address**.
17. Click on **OK**.

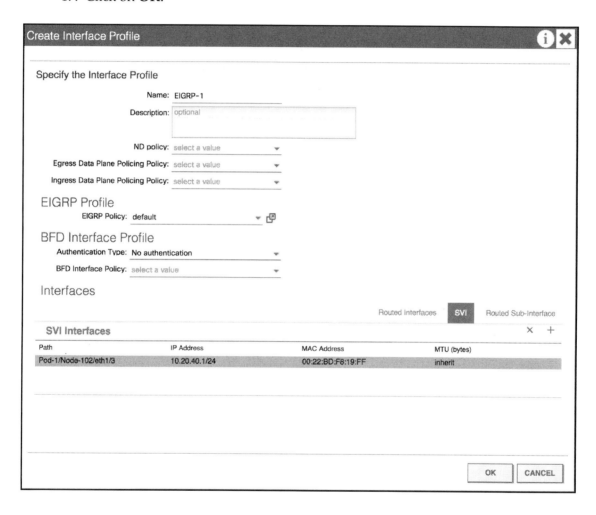

18. Click **OK** once more.

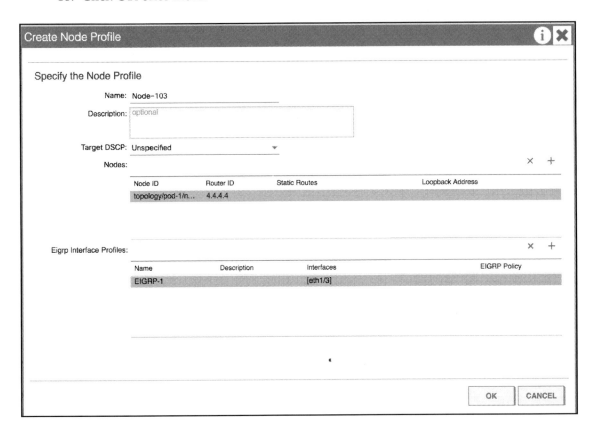

19. Click **OK** yet again.
20. Click on **NEXT**.
21. Configure the external EPG networks.

Chapter 4

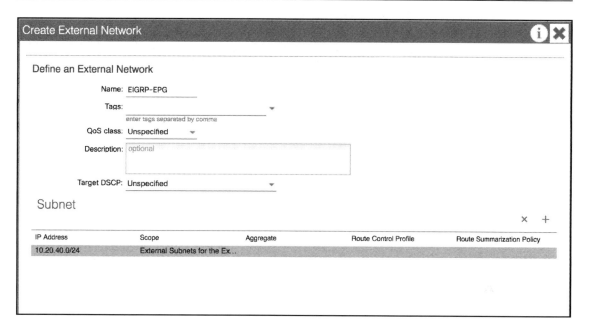

22. Click on **OK**.
23. Click on **FINISH**.
24. Add it to the bridge domain (as per steps 21-26 from the previous OSPF recipe).

Using IPv6 within ACI

Implementing IPv6 is very simple compared to traditional IOS routers. It is so simple that Cisco has not even made any distinction between IPv4 addresses and IPv6 addresses in the GUI.

How to do it...

We will add another subnet to TenantA. This time, it will be an IPv6 subnet.

1. Navigate to **TenantA** | **Networking** | **Bridge Domains** | **TenantA-BD** | **Subnets**.
2. Click on **Actions** and select **Create Subnet**.

3. Enter the IPv6 address and subnet mask.

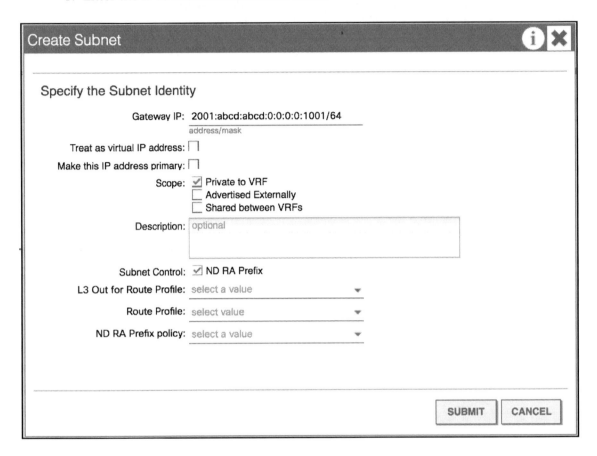

4. Click on **SUBMIT**.

How it works...

The new IPv6 subnet is added in the same way that we added IPv4 subnets.

Chapter 4

As you will have noticed from the other recipes in this chapter, routing with IPv6 is treated no differently to IPv4 routing--there is no graphical distinction between the two.

If we switch to the command line, using the NX-OS CLI, we can see that the subnets are all configured in one area (just SSH to the APIC controller):

```
apic1# sh run tenant TenantA
# Command: show running-config tenant TenantA
 tenant TenantA
   vrf context TenantA_VRF
     exit
   bridge-domain TenantA-BD
     vrf member TenantA_VRF
     exit
   application TenantA_AP1
     epg TenantA_EPG1
       bridge-domain member TenantA-BD
       exit
     exit
   interface bridge-domain TenantA-BD
     ip address 10.0.0.1/24 secondary
     ip address 10.2.20.1/24 secondary scope public
     ipv6 address 2001:abcd:abcd::1001/64
     exit
  exit
apic1#
```

Easy, right? Possibly not as easy as multicast, though!

[235]

Setting up multicast for ACI tenants

Let's set up multicast on the fabric for TenantA.

Ready?

How to do it...

1. Navigate to **TenantA** | **Networking** | **Bridge Domains** | **VRFs** | **TenantA_VRF** | **Multicast**.
2. Click on the button that says **YES, ENABLE MULTICAST**.

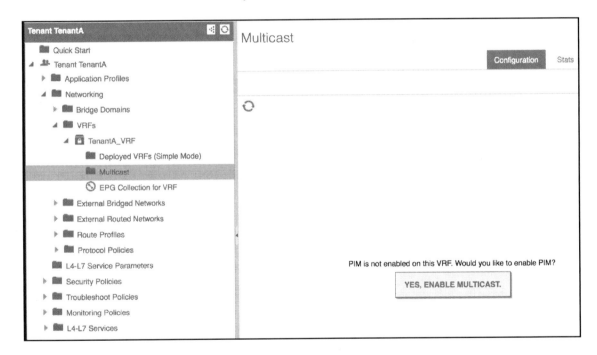

How it works...

From the NX-OS CLI, we can see that **Protocol Independent Multicast(PIM)** is enabled for the VRF:

```
apic1# sh run tenant TenantA
# Command: show running-config tenant TenantA
```

```
tenant TenantA
  vrf context TenantA_VRF
    ip pim
    exit
  bridge-domain TenantA-BD
    vrf member TenantA_VRF
    exit
  application TenantA_AP1
    epg TenantA_EPG1
      bridge-domain member TenantA-BD
      exit
    exit
  interface bridge-domain TenantA-BD
    ip address 10.0.0.1/24 secondary
    ip address 10.2.20.1/24 secondary scope public
    ipv6 address 2001:abcd:abcd::1001/64
    exit
  exit
apic1#
```

So maybe I was a little overenthusiastic about the simplicity that ACI brings to traditionally complex tasks, but this is not without reason. ACI is very easy to learn.

We have not quite finished with multicast, however. Multicast must be enabled at three levels: the VRF (which we have covered) and also at the bridge domain and L3 out levels, which, if you have clicked on the button, you will now see:

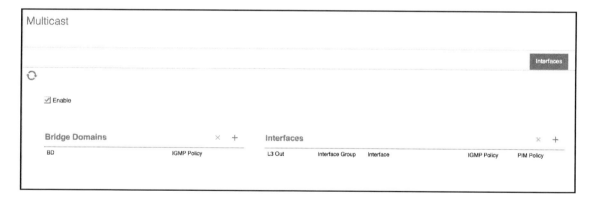

Routing in ACI

Configuring multicast on the bridge domain and interfaces

The second step in configuring multicast is to set it up on the bridge domain and at the interface level.

How it works...

We will start by adding the bridge domain:

1. Click on the plus sign next to **Bridge Domains**.
2. From the drop-down menu, select the **TenantA/TenantA-BD** bridge domain.
3. Click on **SELECT**.

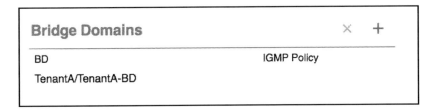

Next, we will add an L3 Out.

4. Click on the plus sign next to **Interfaces**.
5. Select an **L3 Out** from the dropdown.

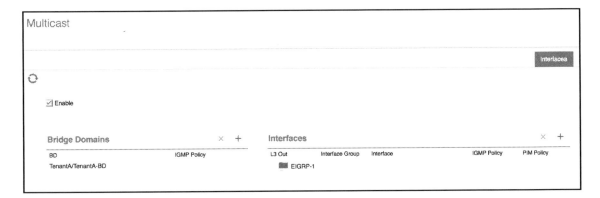

How it works...

We now have a multicast-enabled interface, with which we will be able to join a multicast group.

There's more...

The configuration (from the CLI) now looks like this:

```
apic1# sh run tenant TenantA
# Command: show running-config tenant TenantA
  tenant TenantA
    vrf context TenantA_VRF
      ip pim
      exit
    l3out EIGRP-1
      vrf member TenantA_VRF
      ip pim
      exit
    bridge-domain TenantA-BD
      vrf member TenantA_VRF
      exit
    application TenantA_AP1
      epg TenantA_EPG1
        bridge-domain member TenantA-BD
        exit
      exit
    external-l3 epg __int_EIGRP-1_topo l3out EIGRP-1
      vrf member TenantA_VRF
      exit
    interface bridge-domain TenantA-BD
      ip address 10.0.0.1/24 secondary
      ip address 10.2.20.1/24 secondary scope public
      ip multicast
      ipv6 address 2001:abcd:abcd::1001/64
    exit
  exit
apic1#
```

As you can see, we now have the VRF, the L3 Out, and the bridge domain all enabled for multicast.

That was not too difficult, right?

Let's kick it up a notch and talk about transit routing and route peering.

Routing in ACI

ACI transit routing and route peering

ACI transit routing allows the ACI fabric to pass routing information from one routing "domain" to another. An example of this would be a server connected to one leaf sending and receiving data from a network segment connected to another leaf. The way this works is very similar to MPLS, in that the ACI fabric does not appear as a hop within the routes.

Route peering is where the ACI fabric is used for BGP or OSPF transit between pods.

Many of the steps in configuring this have already been covered in this and previous chapters (detailed in this recipe's *How it works...*), so instead of reinventing the wheel, let's cover some of the theory and less-discussed specifics.

We have a router connected to **Leaf-1**. It is in the subnet **10.10.10.0/24**.

We also have a database server connected to another leaf (**Leaf-2**), in the subnet **20.20.20.0/24**. The router needs to be able to reach this server by ICMP. The router and the database server are in OSPF area 100, advertising their subnets.

An ASA is connected to **Leaf-2** by two interfaces.
This is how everything looks:

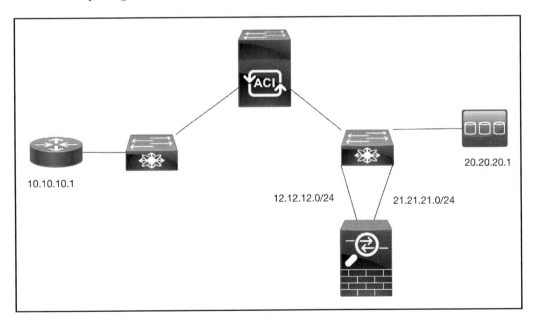

So, how do we get from the router at **10.10.10.1** to the web server at **20.20.20.1**?

How to do it...

1. Create a tenant (DB-Tenant).
2. We will need to add the ASAv package, following the *Deploying the ASAv* recipe in *Chapter 3*.
3. We need to create three L3 Outs.

Name	VRF	Subnets
L3OutInternet	CommonVRF	10.10.10.0/24 (import) 20.20.20.0/24 (import)
L3OutExternal	CommonVRF	12.12.12.0/24 (import) 20.20.20.0/24 (import) 10.10.10.0/24 (export)
L3OutInternal	DB-Tenant	21.21.21.0/24 (import) 10.10.10.0/24 (import) 20.20.20.0/24 (export)

4. The ASA's 12.12.12.0/24 and 21.21.21.0/24 networks will act as the "transit."
5. Route redistribution needs to be enabled so that through MP-BGP, the routes between the router and the database server are exchanged between the L3OutInternet and L3OutExternal interfaces.

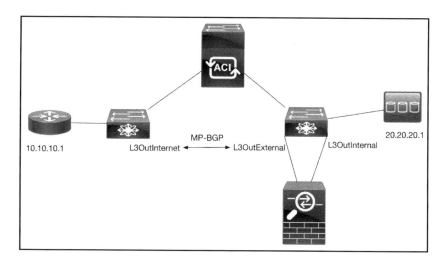

6. A contract will be required for the traffic to pass between the router and the database server.

How it works...

Much of the theory in this recipe has been covered in previous recipes. The ASA was covered in Chapter 3, *Hypervisor Integration (and other 3rd Parties)*, we covered tenant creation as well as bridge domain and VRFs in Chapter 2, *Configuring Policies and Tenants*, and we looked at creating L3 Out interfaces in this chapter. So why reinvent the wheel with this recipe?

While many of the mechanics of transit routing and route peering happen behind the scenes, there are a few aspects we need to pay attention to. The main one is making sure that we are exporting and importing the correct subnets in the correct direction and with the correct scope.

Look at L3OutExternal, for example. We are importing the 12.12.12.0/24 and 20.20.20.0/24 subnets and exporting the 10.10.10.0/24 subnet. Route direction is important. If we do not export the 10.10.10.0/24 subnet, the database server will never see it; the reverse is true for the 20.20.20.0/24 subnet. If we do not import the 12.12.12.0/24 subnet, then we will not be able to act as a transit. We also need to set the scope to act as a transit:

Chapter 4

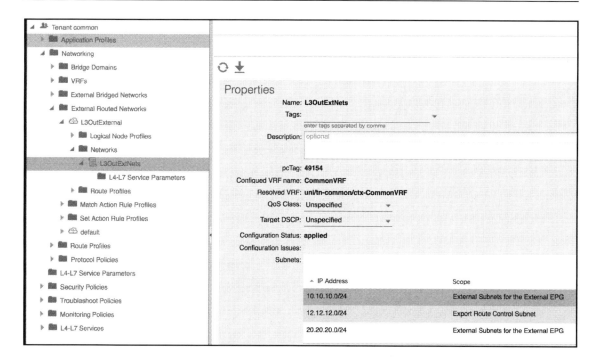

Notice that the `12.12.12.0/24` subnet has a scope of **Export Route Control Subnet**. This means that the route will be a transit route. The other routes are set as **External Subnets for the External EPG**. There is no control of the routing information coming in or going out of the fabric. If the subnet is not marked like this, then although the routes exported from one EPG will reach the EPG that is importing them (showing that the control plane is working), the actual traffic (data plane) will be dropped. This is due to the whitelisting behavior of the fabric, whereby the default is to drop traffic unless it is permitted by the relevant policy. Therefore, we would need to implement a contract between the two to permit the traffic.

There's more...

Refer to this link for more information on transit routing and the control flags for the subnet scope feature:

```
http://www.cisco.com/c/en/us/td/docs/switches/datacenter/aci/apic/sw/kb/b_KB_
Transit_Routing.html#id_30901
```

5
ACI Security

In this chapter, we will look at securing the ACI fabric using the following recipes:

- Creating local users
- Creating security domains
- Limiting users to tenants
- Connecting to a RADIUS server
- Connecting to an LDAP server
- Connecting to a TACACS+ server

Introduction

Given that there will be more than one person administering the ACI fabric, it makes sense that each have their own user account. This is a necessity for certifications such as PCI-DSS, and also just makes sense from an auditing perspective.

In this chapter, we will look at how we can connect to third-party authentication sources, such as RADIUS, TACACS+, and LDAP, and how we can limit the users down by a per-tenant or per-function basis.

AAA and multiple tenant support

ACI has been built with security in mind. Adding local users and connecting to external authentication services (such as RADIUS, TACACS+, and LDAP) is all very straightforward. Security is a constant theme throughout ACI--just look at contracts for an example.

Because of this focus on security, we can perform actions such as limiting the abilities of a user on a per-tenant basis and being very granular about the aspects of the fabric that they can and cannot read from or write to. The abilities of a user can be dictated in different ways; for example, a user can have full access to the entire fabric and the tenants within it, full access to one or more tenants, or even the ability to perform specific actions on one or more tenants.

This is referred to as **role-based access control** (**RBAC**).

Understanding ACI role-based access control (RBAC)

There are several preconfigured rules, and with these rules come different privileges. Here is a table listing the roles and a brief description of the different privileges that are contained within it:

Role	Description
AAA	For configuring authentication, authorization, and accounting as well as import and export policies
Admin	Full access to all fabric features
Access-Admin	Layer 1-3 configuration, including protocols for tenants, as well as fabric-wide settings (NTP, SNMP, and DNS)
Fabric-Admin	Layer 1-3 configuration, including protocols for the fabric
NW-SVC-Admin and NW-SVC-Params	Managing L4-L7 services
OPS	Monitoring and troubleshooting
Read-All	Read-all access (to everything)
Tenant-Admin	Administering all aspects of a tenant
Tenant-Ext-Admin	Externally-focused policy and configuration items (such as L3 and L2 Outs)
VMM-Admin	Virtual Machine Manager connectivity, inventory, and policies

You can also create custom roles if you need to.

 This table gives a very brief overview. For a full list with all of the role privileges, take a look at `http://www.cisco.com/c/en/us/td/docs/switches/datacenter/aci/apic/sw/kb/b_KB_AAA-RBAC-roles-privileges.html`.

Creating local users

Local users are the easiest way to start segregating users and leveraging some form of accountability. We will have a bigger administrative overhead, and clearly, this would not be the preferred solution. Instead, one would look to a centralized system, such as RADIUS or LDAP. However, local users are a good place for us to start.

How to do it...

1. Navigate to **Admin** | **AAA** | **Security Management** | **Local Users**.

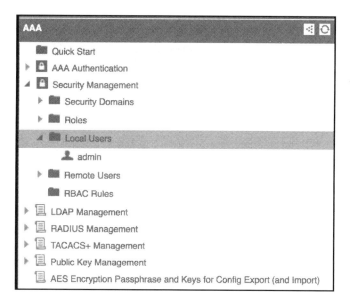

ACI Security

2. Click on **Actions** | **Create Local User**.
3. Select a **Security Domain**, or leave it at the default (all unticked).

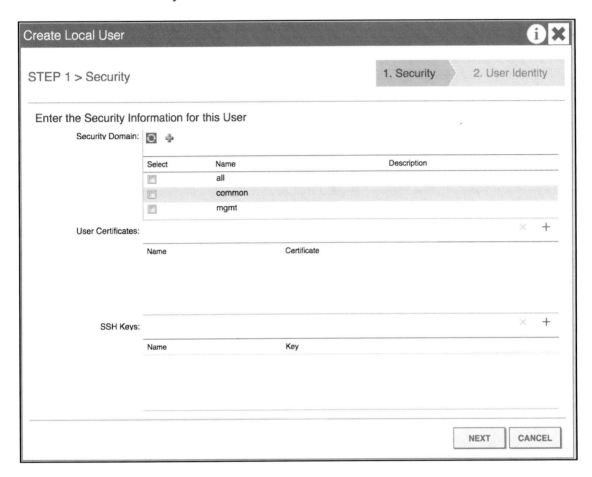

4. Click on **NEXT**.
5. Enter the **Login ID** and the **Password**, and fill in any other fields if desired.

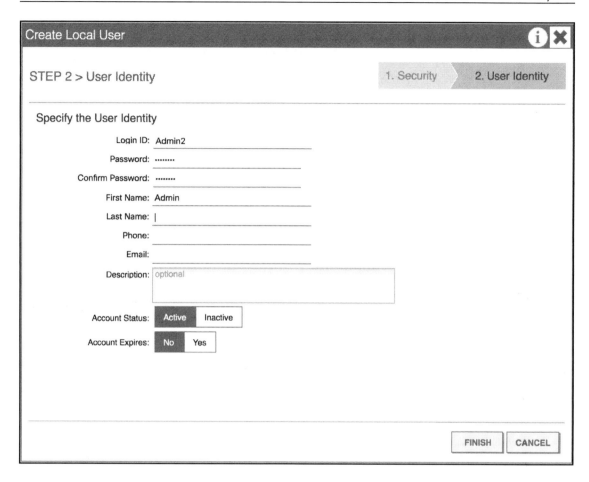

6. Click on **FINISH**.

How it works...

We can test the new user's access by connecting to the APIC with SSH:

```
Stuarts-MacBook-Pro:~ stuart$ ssh Admin2@192.168.1.205
Application Policy Infrastructure Controller
Admin2@192.168.1.205's password:
apic1#
```

The connection is successful. But what if need to limit access to a particular tenant? For that, we need to create a security domain.

Creating security domains

Security domains allow us to permit or deny administrators based on the tenants added as "associated objects" within the domain.

How to do it...

1. Navigate to **Admin** | **AAA** | **Security Management** | **Security Domains**.

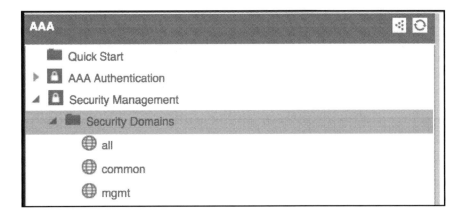

2. Click on **Actions**, then select **Create Security Domain**.
3. Name the new security domain. Here we will call the security domain `TenantA-SD`.

Chapter 5

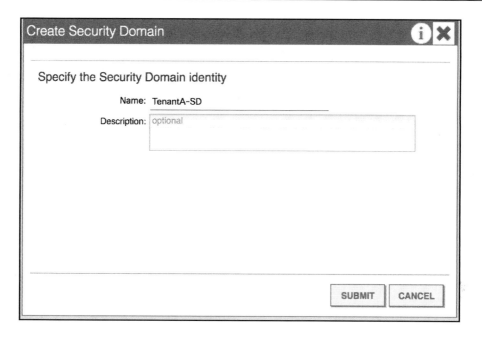

4. Click on **SUBMIT**.
5. The new security domain will be listed with the default ones.

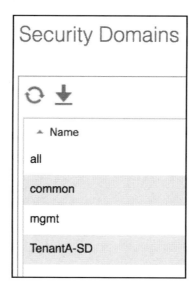

6. If you click on the security domain, you will see that there are no associated objects (tenants).

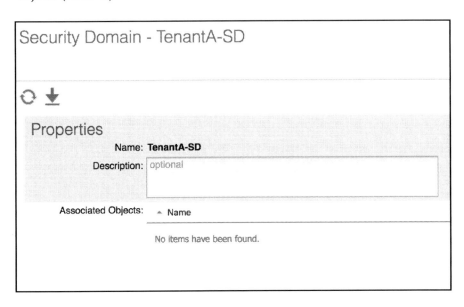

7. To associate a tenant to a security domain, navigate to the tenant (TenantA) and click on the **Policy** tab.

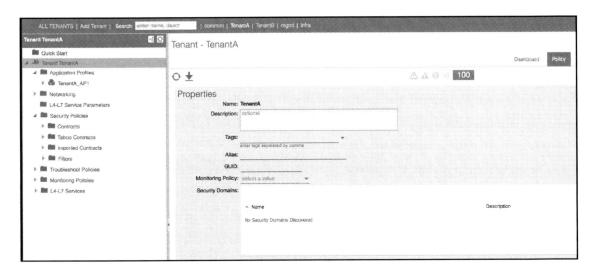

Chapter 5

8. Click on the plus sign next to **Security Domains**, and select **Tenant-SD** from the drop-down menu.

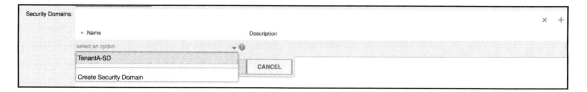

9. Click on **UPDATE**.

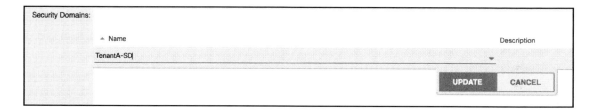

10. If you return to the TenantA-SD security domain in the AAA tab (step 1), you can see that TenantA is now listed under associated objects.

[253]

ACI Security

Limiting users to tenants

Now that we have a new security domain, let's set up the `Admin2` user to use it.

How to do it...

1. Navigate to **Admin** | **AAA** | **Security Management** | **Local Users**.
2. Select the **Admin2** user.

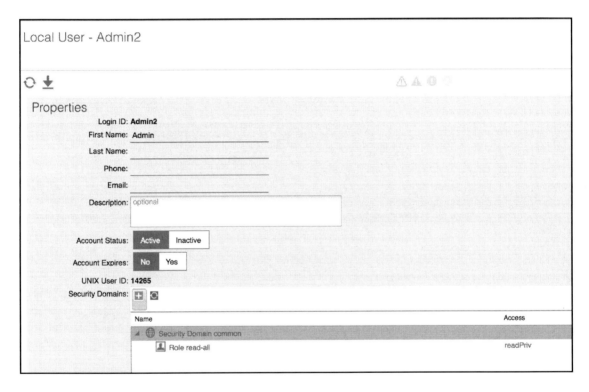

3. Click on the plus sign next to **Security Domains**.
4. Select **TenantA-SD** from the **Domain** dropdown.

Chapter 5

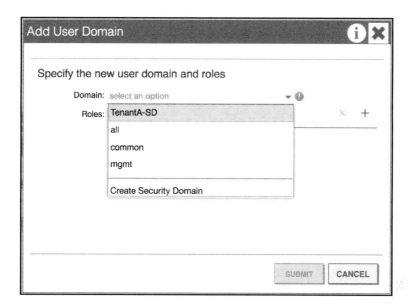

5. Select the required role and access type.

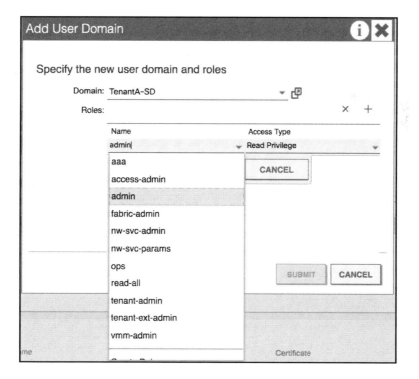

[255]

6. Click on **SUBMIT**.

Connecting to a RADIUS server

Using local authentication is not best practice. It presents a number of very legitimate security concerns and lacks any separation of duties. We can overcome this by using a centralized authentication system, to connect to an authentication system, such as Microsoft Active Directory.

The ACI fabric supports CHAP, MS-CHAP, and PAP as authorization protocols. In this recipe, we will use PAP to authenticate with a Windows 2008 server, running the RADIUS protocol. In order to achieve this, we will need to use the Management EPG, to provide authentication across the entire fabric.

How to do it...

1. Navigate to **Admin** | **AAA** | **RADIUS Management**. Select **RADIUS Providers**.

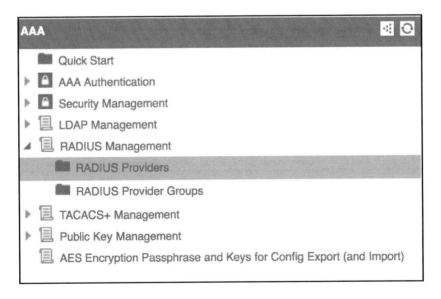

2. From the **Actions** menu, select **Create RADIUS Provider**.
3. Enter the IP address of the RADIUS server, choose the authorization protocol, and enter the key, along with the Management EPG.

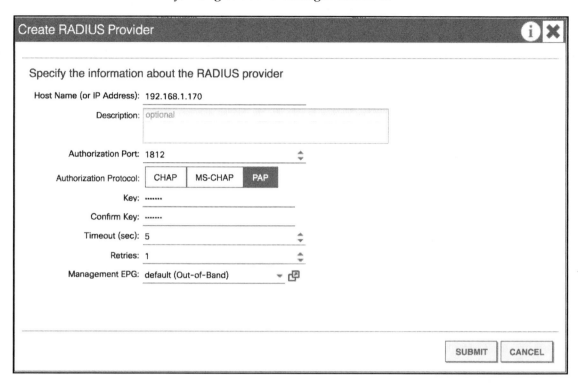

 If you use a management EPG other than the default one (Out-of-Band), make sure that it has access to the RADIUS, LDAP, or TACACS+ server!

4. Click on **SUBMIT**.

5. Go to **Admin** | **AAA** | **RADIUS Management** | **RADIUS Provider Groups**.

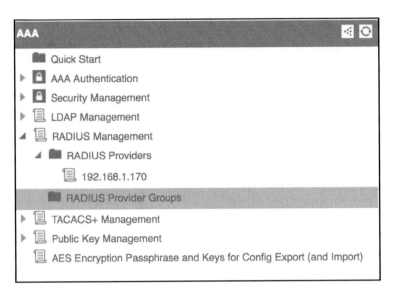

6. Click on **Actions** | **Create RADIUS Provider Group**.
7. Name the group, and select the provider created previously from the dropdown.

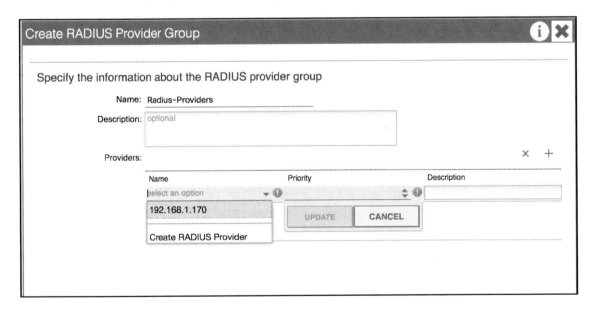

8. Set the priority and click on **UPDATE**.

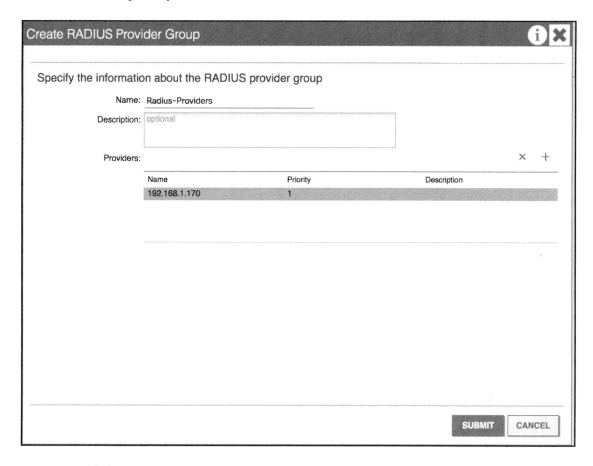

9. Click on **SUBMIT**.

10. From the main **AAA Authentication** menu, change the default authentication **Realm** to **RADIUS**.

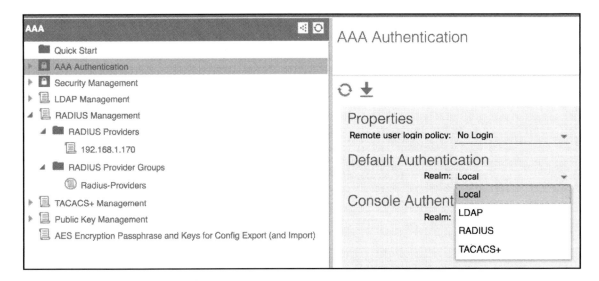

11. Select the **RADIUS Provider Group** created in step 7 from the drop-down list.

12. Optionally, you can set the console to use RADIUS authentication as well. It is wise to make sure that you can log in before setting console authentication.

How it works...

If we have a Windows 2008 server, we can use the **NPS** (**Network Policy Server**) role.

With this role installed and with two AD users (AdminA and AdminB), each in different AD groups (TenantA-Admins and TenantB-Admins, respectively), we can test RADIUS access.

Create a NAP client, specifying the IP address of the APIC, along with the password entered in step 3.

Create a network policy with the following settings:

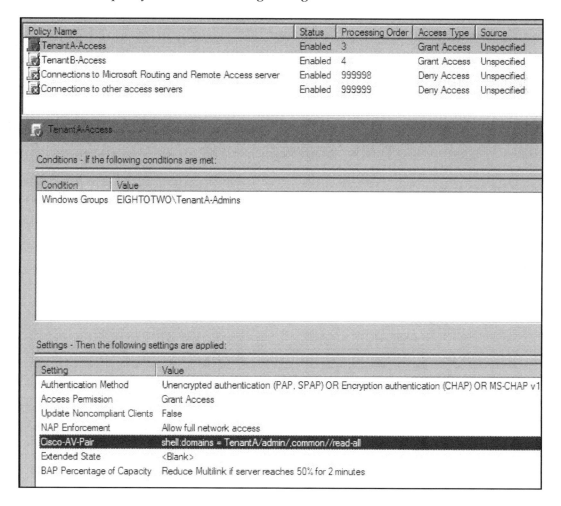

ACI Security

The Cisco AV-Pair setting controls what we have access to.

Let's try logging into the APIC:

```
Stuarts-MacBook-Pro:~ stuart$ ssh AdminA@192.168.1.205
Application Policy Infrastructure Controller
AdminA@192.168.1.205's password:
apic1#
```

We can log in to the APIC through SSH. Let's try the GUI.

> If you find that you are locked out, then you can get in by logging in to the GUI with the following method:
> Username: `apic:fallback<username>`
> Here, we can use our local user accounts (we would replace <username> with `admin`) because we are bypassing the RADIUS server using the `apic:fallback` prefix.

If we log in to the GUI, we can see the following:

Our abilities are significantly reduced, as you can see, because the **Fabric**, **VM Networking**, **L4-L7 Services**, and **Admin** tabs are all grayed out (or blued out, to be more precise).

We can look at our permissions from the drop-down arrow next to our username:

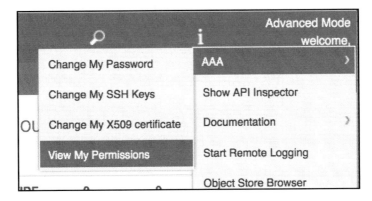

Clicking on **View My Permissions** shows us our permissions:

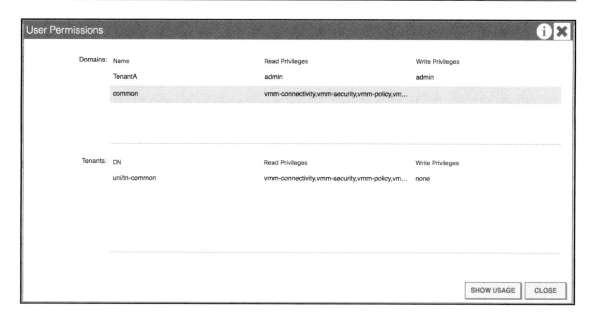

As you can see by clicking on the **Tenants** tab, we do not have access to the TenantA tenant:

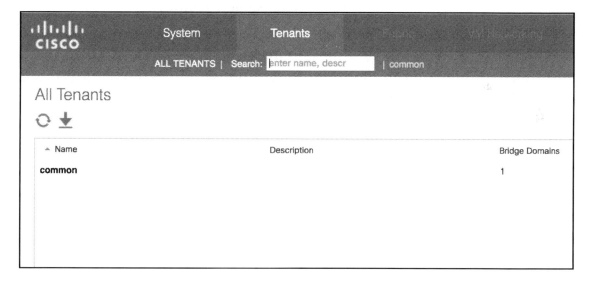

Syntax-wise, the AP-pair is correct. If we introduce an error into it (double slash instead of single), we are told that the AV pair is invalid when we try and log in:

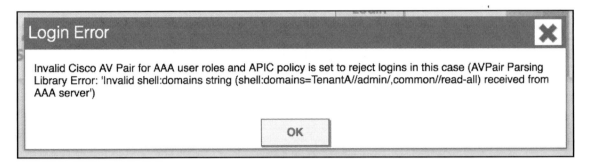

Let's try a different AV-pair.

Now can we see the tenant?

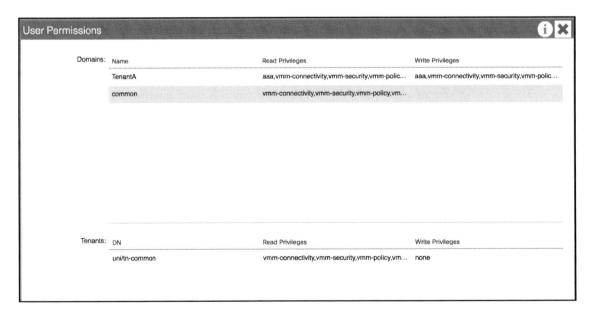

No, but let's step back and think about this logically. I have been adding a tenant in the domain, and not in the tenant area. Instead of referencing TenantA, I should have been referencing TenantA-SD:

Cisco-AV-Pair	shell:domains=TenantA-SD/tenant-admin/read-all,common//read-all

Does it work now?

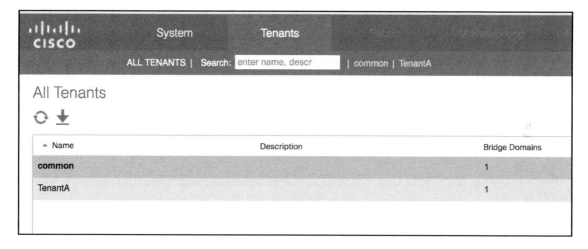

Bingo!

Getting the AV-Pair correct is probably the trickiest part of using an external authentication source, such as RADIUS. Setting up the providers is very similar, as we will see when we create an LDAP provider.

Connecting to an LDAP server

As well as RADIUS and TACACS+, we can connect to an LDAP server for authentication.

How to do it...

1. Navigate to **Admin** | **AAA** | **LDAP Management** | **LDAP Providers**.

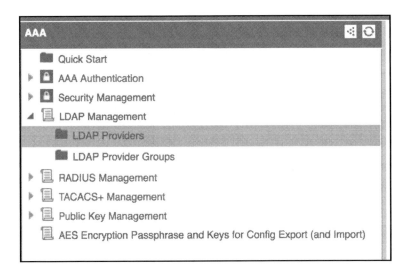

2. Go to **Actions** | **Create LDAP Provider**.
3. Enter the settings to connect to the AD server.

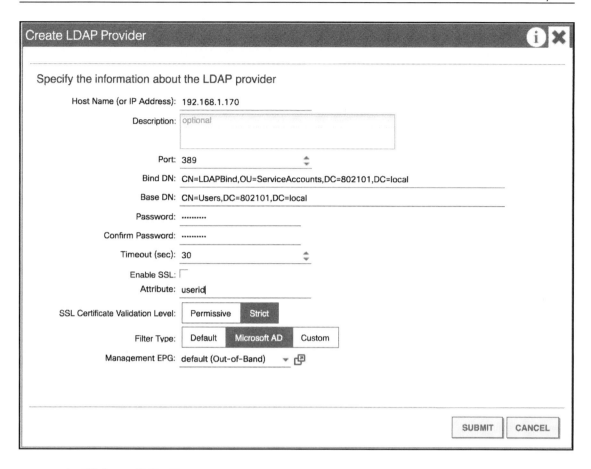

4. Click on **SUBMIT**.
5. Navigate to **Admin | AAA | LDAP Management | LDAP Provider Groups**.
6. Select **Actions | Create LDAP Provider Group**.
7. Add the server created in step 3 and set the priority.
8. Click on **SUBMIT**.
9. Select AAA Authentication, and set the default authentication to LDAP and the LDAP provider group to the provider group created in step 7.
10. Optionally, set the console authentication to LDAP.
11. Click on **SUBMIT**.

Connecting to a TACACS+ server

The steps for adding a TACACS+ server are similar to both RADIUS and LDAP.

How to do it...

1. Navigate to **Admin** | **AAA** | **TACACS+ Management** | **TACACS+ Providers**.
2. Select **Create TACACS+ Provider** from **Actions**.
3. Set the IP address, port (if different from the default of 49), the authorization protocol, and key, and select the management EPG.
4. Click on **SUBMIT**.
5. Navigate to **Admin** | **AAA** | **TACACS+ Management** | **TACACS+ Provider Groups**.
6. Select **Actions** | **Create TACACS+ Provider Group**.
7. Name it and add the provider created in step 3.
8. Click on **SUBMIT**.
9. Select AAA Authentication, and set the default authentication to TACACS+ and the TACACS+ provider group to the provider group created in step 7.
10. Optionally, set the console authentication to TACACS+.
11. Click on **SUBMIT**.

6
Implementing Quality of Service in ACI

In this chapter, we will be implementing **quality of service** (**QoS**) across the ACI fabric. The recipes we will cover in this chapter are:

- Preserving existing CoS settings
- Configuring user-defined classes
- Creating a basic QoS configuration
- Verifying QoS

Introduction

QoS allows us to prioritize traffic. This may be to give high priority treatment to the traffic coming from, or destined for, a business application, or to ensure that voice and video traffic are prioritized. Both voice and video traffic are sensitive to delay and jitter, so making sure that these receive priority is important for the user experience.

While ACI may not be designed with voice and video protocols in mind, there is no reason that the tenants are not running them or have other demands for QoS, such as preserving **class of service** (**CoS**) markings on traffic transiting through the fabric.

Preserving existing CoS settings

If traffic entering and exiting the fabric already has CoS markings (known as 802.1P, or dot1p), then we should either preserve them or modify them. In this recipe, we will instruct the fabric to preserve the settings.

How to do it...

1. Navigate to **Fabric | Access Policies**.
2. Expand **Global Policies** and select **QOS Class Policies**:

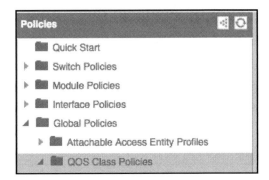

3. In the workspace, select the option to **Preserve COS**:

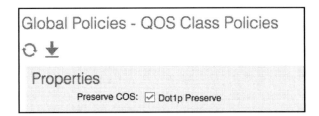

4. Click on **Submit** in the bottom right-hand corner.

How it works...

The ACI fabric will now preserve the 802.1P markings on traffic.

Beneath this setting, you can see three different levels, which are the user-defined classes which we will discuss next.

There's more...

We can enable CoS preservation from the CLI:

```
apic1# configure
apic1(config)# qos preserve cos
```

Configuring user-defined classes

There are three user-defined classes: **Level1**, **Level2**, and **Level3**.

We do not have the option to create any more, but we can edit the ones that are there.

How to do it...

1. Navigate to **Fabric | Access Policies | Global Policies | QOS Class Policies**.
2. Select **Level1** from the menu, or double-click on it in the workspace:

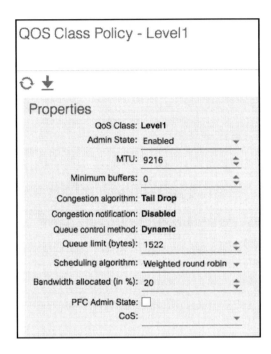

3. Change the bandwidth allocation to 25%, and set the **CoS** field to **cos 1**.
4. Tick **PFC Admin State**:

Chapter 6

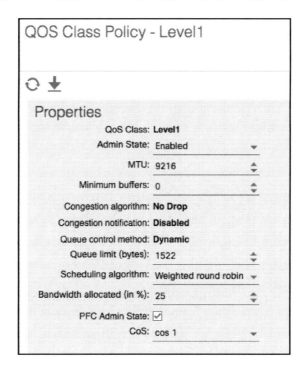

5. Click on **Submit**.

How it works...

Once we select a CoS marking, we must enable the **PFC Admin State**, which changes the congestion algorithm to **No Drop**. If we do no select the **PFC Admin State**, we will receive a warning when we click on **Submit**:

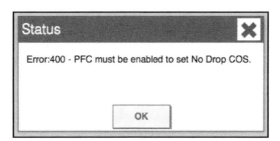

PFC stands for **priority flow control**: it prevents frame loss when there is congestion within the network and works on a per-CoS basis.

[273]

There's more...

Apart from the three user-defined classes, there are three reserved classes. The reserved classes are not configurable by the user, however.

The three reserved classes are:

- IFC
- Control
- SPAN

The IFC class classifies all traffic originating from or destined for the APIC. It is a strict priority class (whereby minimum and maximum bandwidth is guaranteed).

The control class is also a strict priority class and prioritizes control traffic, such as protocol packets, and all SUP traffic (supervisor engine).

The SPAN class is a best-effort class, utilizing **deficit weighted round robin** (**DWRR**). DWRR serves to equal out the amount of bandwidth used; an example would be that if on one "turn" the queue uses 25% of the bandwidth, bursting over its allotted 20% by 5%, on the next cycle DWRR will reduce the queue by 5% to 15%, so overall it keeps within its settings. All SPAN and ERSPAN traffic will be classified into the SPAN class.

Creating a basic QoS configuration

We will now create a basic QoS configuration for TenantA.

How to do it...

1. Navigate to **Tenants** | **TenantA** | **Application Profiles** | **TenantA_AP1** | **Application EPGs** | **EPG TenantA_EPG1**.
2. Click on the dropdown next to **Custom QoS** and select **Create Custom QOS Policy**.

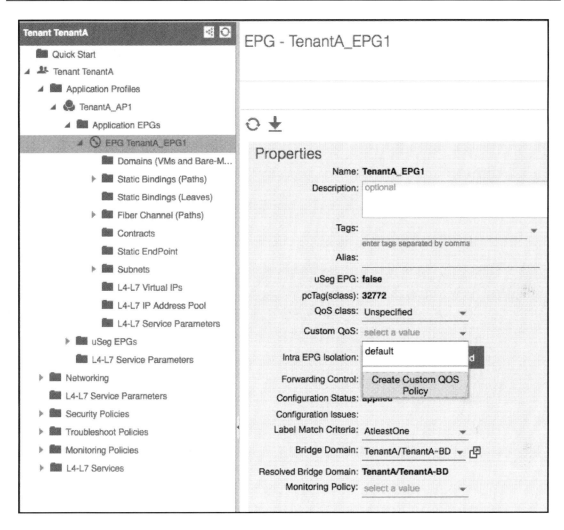

3. Name the policy.
4. Click on the plus sign next to **DSCP to priority map**.
5. From the **Priority** dropdown, select **Level1**.

Implementing Quality of Service in ACI

6. Select **AF13** from the **DSCP Range From** dropdown.
7. Select **AF22** from the **DSCP Range To** dropdown.
8. Select **AF31** as the **DSCP Target**.
9. Set the **Target CoS** to 5.

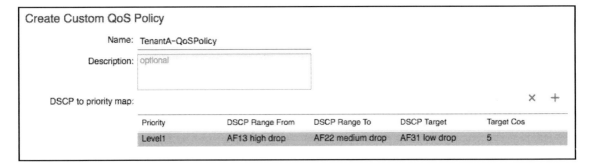

10. Click on **Update**.
11. Click on the plus sign next to **Dot1P Classifiers**.
12. Set the **Priority** to **Level1**, the **Dot1P Range From** to **1**, and the **Dot1P Range To** to **3**.
13. Set the **DSCP Target** to **CS1** and the **Target COS** to 1.

14. Click on **Submit**.
15. Click on **Submit** again on the main screen.

How it works...

Using these steps, we created some custom QoS translations. We translated the ingress QoS markings to our own egress markings.

There's more...

We can also create QoS policies by navigating to the tenant, selecting **Networking**, expanding **Protocol Policies**, right-clicking on **Custom QoS**, and selecting **Create Custom QOS Policy**:

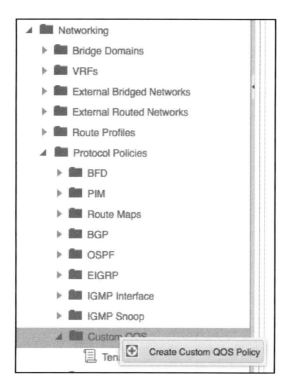

We would then need to repeat steps 1 and 2 from the recipe, selecting the new policy.

Verifying QoS

We can turn to the CLI to verify the QoS settings.

How to do it...

1. We can use the `show run tenant TenantA` command to list all of the configurations for a tenant (TenantA in this example). This can result in a lot of configurations being returned, so we can limit it down to be more precise in what we are looking for. We can reduce the scope down to an application profile, using the `show run tenant TenantA application TenantA_AP1` command to display the `TenantA_AP1` application profile and all of the EPGs defined within it. If we want to look at one particular EPG, we would add `epg TenantA_EPG1` to the end of the command. From the CLI, run the following command to see what QoS policy is assigned to the tenant:

   ```
   apic1# sh run tenant TenantA application TenantA_AP1 epg TenantA_EPG1
   # Command: show running-config tenant
   TenantA application TenantA_AP1 epg TenantA_EPG1
   tenant TenantA
     application TenantA_AP1
       epg TenantA_EPG1
         bridge-domain member TenantA-BD
         service-policy TenantA-QoSPolicy
       exit
         exit
           exit
   apic1#
   ```

2. Similarly, we can query the policy maps assigned to a tenant (using the type of either `data-plane` or `qos`). To see the policy settings, run this command:

   ```
   apic1# show run tenant TenantA policy-map type qos TenantA-QoSPolicy
   # Command: show running-config tenant
   TenantA policy-map type qos TenantA-QoSPolicy
   tenant TenantA
     policy-map type qos TenantA-QoSPolicy
       match dscp AF13 AF22 set-dscp AF31 set-class level1 set-cos 5
       match dot1p 1 3 set-dscp CS1 set-class level1 set-cos 1
     exit
       exit
   apic1#
   ```

Network Programmability with ACI

In this chapter, we will be looking at how to program the ACI fabric. We can program the fabric with XML or JSON using the REST API or use the Python SDK (known as Cobra). There is also the ACI toolkit, which we spoke about previously. We will be covering the following recipes:

- Browsing the object store using the Object Store Browser
- Programming the ACI through REST
- Authenticating through REST and XML
- Creating a tenant using REST and XML
- Deleting a tenant using REST and XML
- Creating an APN and an EPG using REST and XML
- Creating an application profile and EPG using REST
- Authenticating through REST and JSON
- Creating a tenant using REST and JSON
- Using the Python SDK
- Logging into the APIC using Cobra
- Creating a tenant using the SDK

Introduction

This is where DevOps really meets networking. As your ACI infrastructure grows, along with the tenant base, programming the fabric will save you so much time instead of having to repeat the same manual actions over and over again.

Browsing the object store using the Object Store Browser

The Object Store Browser is the easiest way of getting started with the object naming convention used within ACI.

How to do it...

1. To access the Object Store Browser, navigate to `https://<APIC>/visore.html`, where `<APIC>` is the IP address or DNS name of the APIC controller:

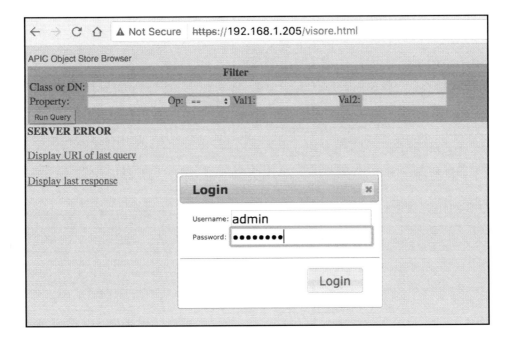

2. We are prompted to log in, and when we do, the window will change to list the components of the fabric (the spines, leaves, and controllers).

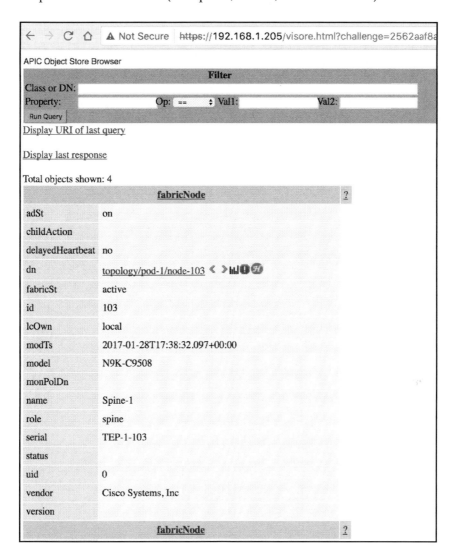

3. We can list objects, such as tenants, using their class. In this case, the class is `fvTenant`:

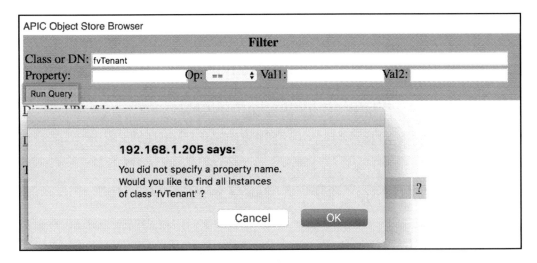

Because we have not entered any further filtering information, we are asked whether we want to return all of the records, which it does:

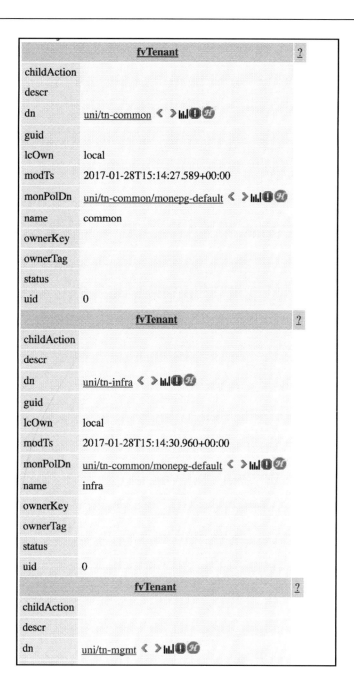

4. We can filter by any of the fields in green, though, to have more specific results returned:

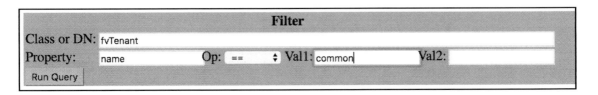

As you can see, we get the one result we were looking for.

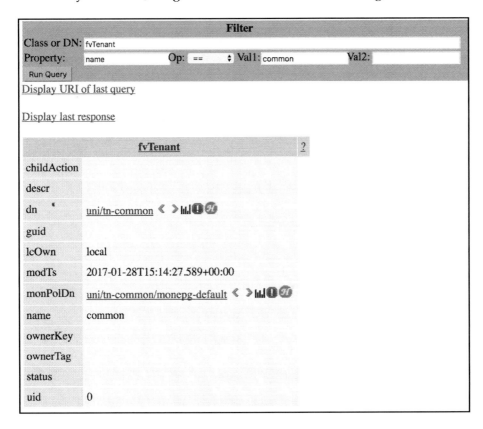

5. Next to the **dn** (Distinguished Name) field, we have a number of icons. In reverse order, we can see the health statistics; clicking on this shows a new box below the tenant:

6. Clicking on a fault's icon would show a similar box if there were any faults, but if there are none, no additional box will appear, and the same is true for the statistics. The arrow buttons will show us the child objects, of which there are many. Looking through this list is a good way of getting used to the object names, which we will need when we look at programming the fabric.

Programming the ACI through REST

Part of the issue with using the ACI simulator is that it does not save any changes. Rebooting the virtual machine results in a loss of work. A power cut results in a loss of work. Having the bathroom fitter turn off the power upstairs results in a...well, I am sure you get the idea.

Having to recreate everything through the GUI over and over again gets quite frustrating as you can imagine, but here we return to what we spoke about in the first chapter: the move from manual actions to programmability.

Getting ready

To perform the REST-based recipes in this chapter, you will need a REST client. Postman is a good one. You can download if from `https://www.getpostman.com/`.

How to do it...

1. Once you have downloaded and installed the client, we will need to turn off SSL certificate verification by clicking on the settings icon at the top right-hand corner (it looks like a wrench). Select **settings**, and from the **General tab**, turn off the second option.

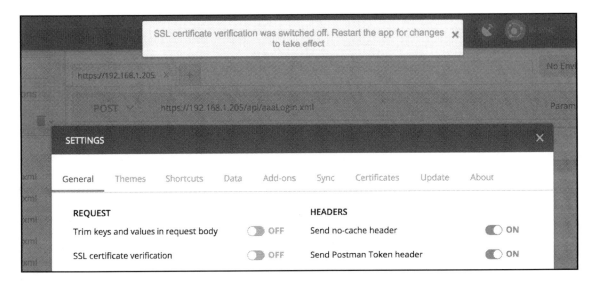

2. Restart the client and set the method to POST, switch to **Body**, and set the encoding type to **raw**:

We can now get started.

Authenticating through REST and XML

Without authenticating to the APIC first, we will not be able to run any subsequent commands.

How to do it...

1. Set the URL to https://192.168.1.205/api/aaaLogin.xml (obviously changing the IP address to the one of your APIC controller).
2. Enter the following on line 1:

   ```
   <aaaUser name="admin" pwd="admin123" />
   ```

3. Press **Send**.

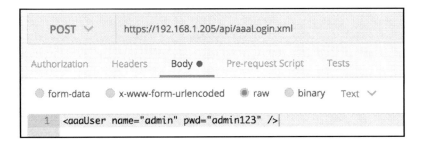

How it works...

The Postman application sends the raw XML to the `aaaLogin.xml` URL. In the results pane, we should see some XML returned and should have, on the left-hand side, a status code of **200** (meaning everything worked fine). The XML code should look like this:

```
<?xml version="1.0" encoding="UTF-8"?>
<imdata totalCount="1">
 <aaaLogin
token="8HoO9sU0o39ygQinBsHcrBD61hhXdr+JNiXaiETpZUz+5t+5C2ijW8JbTOCc/53dZP0M
9O4ByrbtNWknUwj0fkppYXPVEjPyGlkfP8JDOGV9THxEi28Dpcf0eDOBNlRNHlPAnsvXJ1B1cM+
aT+xk3ADfR4D9koFNT0VRTENzSux5uwKzjvScbRY1AIIN+Dor"
siteFingerprint="ROT0QumJdEhJzyqM" refreshTimeoutSeconds="600"
maximumLifetimeSeconds="86400" guiIdleTimeoutSeconds="1200"
restTimeoutSeconds="90" creationTime="1485709920"
firstLoginTime="1485709920" userName="admin" remoteUser="false"
unixUserId="15374" sessionId="nDZSNhXJSpiUq7+QmEgL1Q==" lastName=""
firstName="" version="2.1(0.36)" buildTime="Sat Jun 18 14:51:28 PDT 2016"
node="topology/pod-1/node-1">
 <aaaUserDomain name="all" rolesR="admin" rolesW="admin">
     <aaaReadRoles/>
     <aaaWriteRoles>
         <role name="admin"/>
     </aaaWriteRoles>
 </aaaUserDomain>
 <DnDomainMapEntry dn="uni/tn-common" readPrivileges="admin"
writePrivileges="admin"/>
 <DnDomainMapEntry dn="uni/tn-infra" readPrivileges="admin"
writePrivileges="admin"/>
 <DnDomainMapEntry dn="uni/tn-mgmt" readPrivileges="admin"
writePrivileges="admin"/>
 </aaaLogin>
</imdata>
```

Notice that we have entries (under `aaaUserDomain` and `DnDomainMapEntry`) showing the privileges available to us for the respective tenants.

We are now authenticated and can create a tenant.

Creating a tenant using REST and XML

When we created the TenantA tenant, way back in Chapter 2, *Configuring Policies and Tenants*, it was very straightforward. We named the new tenant, pressed **Submit,** and the tenant was created. Creating a tenant using the REST client is no harder.

How to do it...

1. From Postman, set the URL to `https://192.168.1.205/api/mo/uni.xml`.
2. On line one, enter the following:

   `<fvTenant name="TenantA"/>`

3. Press **Send**.

How it works...

You may need to reauthenticate if you get a status of **403 Forbidden** and the following returned:

```
<?xml version="1.0" encoding="UTF-8"?>
<imdata totalCount="1">
 <error code="403" text="Token was invalid (Error: Token timeout)"/>
</imdata>
```

If this is the case, then you can repeat commands from the list on the left-hand side.

If all worked well, in the result, you should get a status of **200 OK** and the following code:

```
<?xml version="1.0" encoding="UTF-8"?>
<imdata totalCount="0"></imdata>
```

Here is the tenant from the object browser:

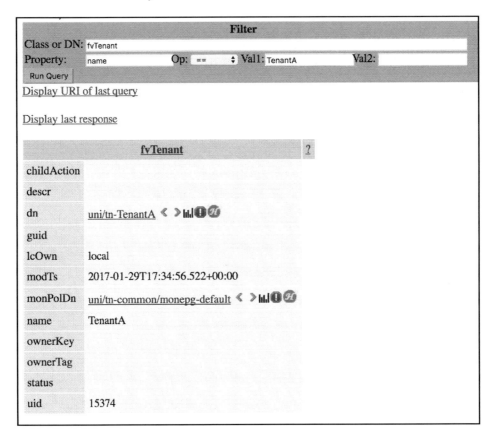

Now that we have a tenant, let's delete it!

Deleting a tenant using REST and XML

Deleting a tenant is also a one-line affair.

How to do it...

1. Set the URL to `https://192.168.1.205/api/mo/uni.xml`.
2. Use the following XML code:

   `<fvTenant name="TenantA" status="deleted"/>`

3. Press **Send**.

How it works...

If we check the object browser now, we will not get any objects returned:

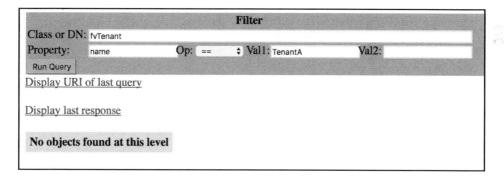

Creating an APN and an EPG using REST and XML

One of the cool things about using the REST client is that we can run more than one command at a time. We created a tenant and then deleted it. Now we want to create a bridge domain, but need a tenant to go with it. We do not need to create the tenant separately; we can create it at the same time as creating the bridge domain.

How to do it...

1. Keep the URL the same as before.
2. Enter the following:

   ```
   <fvTenant name="TenantA">
   <fvCtx name="TenantA_VRF"/>
   <fvBD name="TenantA-BD">
   <fvSubnet ip="10.0.0.1/24"/>
      <fvRsCtx tnFvCtxName="TenantA_VRF"/>
   </fvBD>
   </fvTenant>
   ```

3. Press **Send**.

How it works...

This creates the tenant, the VRF (context), the bridge domain, and the subnet:

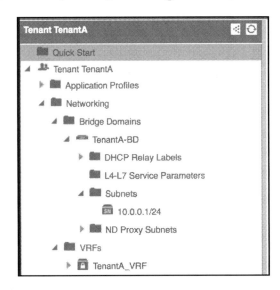

The code also associates the VRF to the bridge domain:

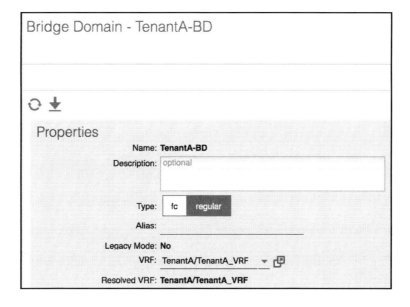

Creating an application profile and EPG using REST

We'll use the same process as before.

How to do it...

1. Use the same URL as the previous recipes.
2. Use the following code:

   ```
   <fvTenant name="TenantA">
   <fvAp name="TenantA_AP1">
   <fvAEPg name="TenantA_EPG1">
   <fvRsBd tnFvBDName="TenantA-BD"/>
   </fvAEPg>
   </fvAp>
   </fvTenant>
   ```

3. Press Send.

How it works...

From the APIC GUI, we should see the (new) application profile, along with the EPG:

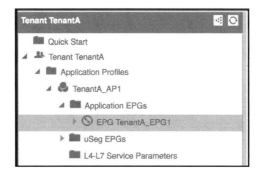

We can also put all of this in one code segment:

```
<fvTenant name="TenantA">
<fvCtx name="TenantA_VRF"/>
<fvBD name="TenantA-BD">
<fvSubnet ip="10.0.0.1/24"/>
<fvRsCtx tnFvCtxName="TenantA_VRF"/>
</fvBD>
<fvAp name="TenantA_AP1">
<fvAEPg name="TenantA_EPG1">
<fvRsBd tnFvBDName="TenantA-BD"/>
</fvAEPg>
</fvAp>
```

Authenticating through REST and JSON

We can also use JSON to achieve the same results. First, we need to log in.

How to do it...

1. Change the URL to `https://192.168.1.205/api/aaaLogin.json`.
2. Use the following code:

   ```
   {
     "aaaUser" : {
       "attributes" : {
   ```

```
            "name" : "admin"
            "pwd" : "admin123"
                }
        }
    }
```

3. Press **Send**.

How it works...

You should get a response of **200 OK**. In the results pane, you'll see something like this:

Creating a tenant using REST and JSON

Once you get used to the syntax, it is pretty easy to switch from XML to JSON. We can create a tenant using a few lines.

How to do it...

1. Use the URL `https://192.168.1.205/api/mo/uni.json`.
2. Use the following code:

```
{
   "fvTenant" : {
     "attributes" : {
     "name" : "TenantB"
      }
    }
}
```

3. Press **Send**.

How it works...

In the same way that we created a tenant through the GUI and through XML, we can create one through JSON. If we run the command and look at the GUI, we can see the new tenant listed:

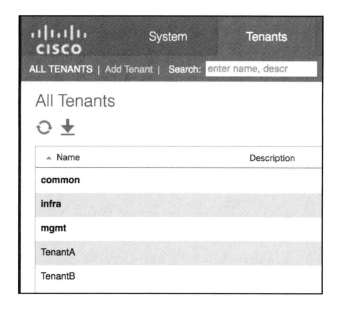

Using the Python SDK

Python is a great language and you can do so much with it. While not every network engineer wants to know a programming language, knowing the basics of Python will make life easier, especially as the current trend of opening up API access to physical hardware progresses.

Getting ready

We have a couple of requirements:

- Python 2.7
- `easy_install`
- `pip`

How to do it...

1. Once we have these installed, we start by installing the SDK. We need two egg files, which can be downloaded from https://<APIC address>/cobra/_downloads/.
2. Download the two egg files (acicobra-1.1_1j-py2.7.egg and acimodel-1.1_1j-py2.7.egg).
3. Install the two files:

   ```
   easy_install -Z /path/to/acicobra-1.1_1j-py2.7.egg
   easy_install -Z /path/to/acimodel-1.1_1j-py2.7.egg
   ```

Logging into the APIC using Cobra

Once we have set up our, environment we can log in.

How to do it...

1. Create a new Python file (on Linux, this can be done using the command vi aciLogin.py.
2. In the VI editor, switch to insert mode by pressing *i* on the keyboard.
3. Enter the following:

   ```
   import cobra.mit.access
   import cobra.mit.session
   apicUri = 'https://192.168.1.205'
   apicUser = 'admin'
   apicPassword = 'admin123'
   ls = cobra.mit.session.LoginSession(apicUri, apicUser, apicPassword)
   md = cobra.mit.access.MoDirectory(ls)
   md.login()
   ```

4. Save the file by pressing the *Esc* key and then typing :wq!.
5. Make the file executable, using the command chmod a+x aciLogin.py.
6. Run the file using the command python ./aciLogin.py.

Creating a tenant using the SDK

We have the tools, and we can log in. Let's now add a tenant using the SDK.

How to do it...

1. Create a new Python file (on Linux, this can be done using the command `vi aciNewTenant.py`).
2. In the VI editor, switch to insert mode by pressing *i* on the keyboard
3. Enter the following:

   ```
   import cobra.model.pol
   import cobra.model.fv
   import cobra.mit.request
   polUniMo = cobra.model.pol.Uni('')
   tenantMo = cobra.model.fv.Tenant(polUniMo, 'TenantC')
   config = cobra.mit.request.ConfigRequest()
   config.addMo(tenantMo)
   md.commit(config)
   ```

4. Save the file by pressing the *Esc* key and then pressing `:wq!`.
5. Make the file executable using the command `chmod a+x aciLogin.py`.
6. Run the file using the command `python ./aciLogin.py`.

8
Monitoring ACI

In this chapter, we will cover:

- Finding faults
- Viewing events
- Navigating the audit logs
- Setting up Call Home
- Configuring SNMP
- Configuring Syslog
- Configuring NetFlow

Introduction

Monitoring ACI, as with anything, will be a mixture of reactive and proactive steps. We can be reactive, looking for faults and events that may explain some unexpected behavior--we may need to look through audit logs to find who did what--or we can be proactive. We can set up Call Home (or CallHome, as it is sometimes written) to send us (and Cisco TAC) alerts, and we can also pull data out of ACI, giving us metrics for utilization and uptime through SNMP. We can retain logs for compliance reasons, and lastly, we can export our flow data (the conversation between two endpoints) using NetFlow.

We will do all of that in this chapter.

Finding faults

No one likes faults, but this is where we should start the chapter.

Looking at the dashboard, we can see that there are a number of faults in the system. These are separated into counts by domain and by type.

Fault Counts By Domain will list the sum of faults by severity, from critical to informational at the top and, underneath that, by the individual domain:

Fault Counts By Domain				
Fault Level:	⚠	⚠	❗	❗
SYSTEM WIDE	2	3	21	238
Access	0	0	0	3
External	0	0	0	0
Framework	0	0	0	0
Infra	2	3	6	235
Management	0	0	0	0
Security	0	0	12	0
Tenant	0	0	3	0

Fault Counts By Type shows the faults of the communications, configuration, environmental, and operational types.

Fault Counts By Type				
Fault Level:	⚠	⚠	❗	❗
Communicati…	0	0	0	0
Config	0	0	9	0
Environmental	0	3	0	0
Operational	2	0	12	238

Looking at these screenshots, we have a number of faults. Let's find out what they are.

How to do it...

1. Navigate to **System** | **Faults**.

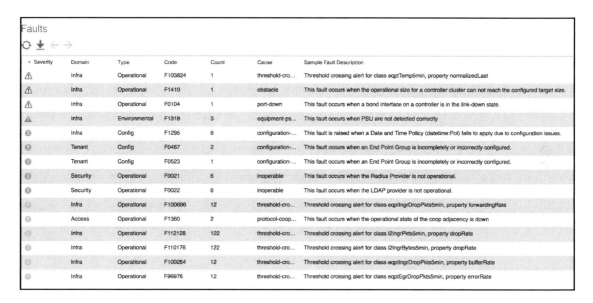

2. The listed faults (which are samples in this instance) are listed in order of severity. Double-clicking on one of them will open a fault detail page:

3. Faults will display a severity on the left-hand side. If the icon is a green circle with a tick in it, then the fault has cleared. We can acknowledge the fault by ticking the checkbox.

4. Double-clicking on the fault will open another window. Clicking on the down arrow next to **Details** will show more information, such as the change set and the number of occurrences of the fault:

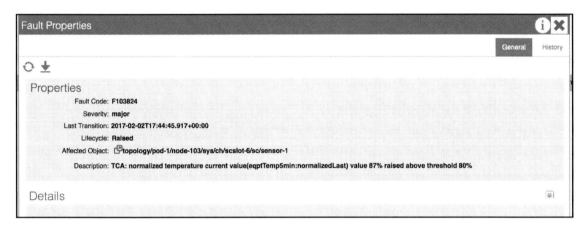

5. Clicking on the **History** tab will show us a timeline of the fault:

6. We have a few icons at the top:

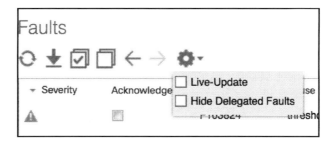

These icons offer us the ability to (from left to right):

- Refresh the screen
- Save the table as either XML or JSON
- Acknowledge all the items on the screen
- Un-acknowledge the items
- Move to the previous view or the next view
- Enable live update or hide the delegated faults

Delegated faults are where a fault that may have been missed for one reason or another creates a secondary fault in a different and more visible area.

There's more...

We can look at faults on a per-tenant basis by navigating to the tenant and selecting **Faults** from the right-hand side to see the current faults:

We can also see the historical faults by clicking on **History** and then selecting **Faults**.

 For more information on faults, including the fault lifecycle, check out this page:
http://www.cisco.com/c/en/us/td/docs/switches/datacenter/aci/apic/sw/1-x/faults/guide/b_APIC_Faults_Errors/b_IFC_Faults_Errors_chapter_01.html

Viewing events

Events are not centrally collated, unlike faults. We need to go and find them. We need to keep an eye out for a **History** tab, like the one shown before.

How to do it...

Let's look at how we can view events.

Tenant events

1. From the tenant, select **History** and then **Events**:

There is nothing to see here:

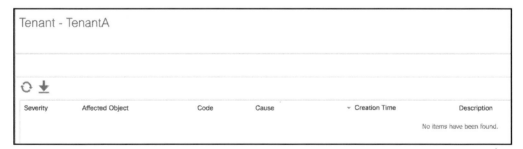

Fabric events

Let's look at the fabric.

1. From the **Fabric** menu, select the pod, select **History**, and then select **Events**:

Chapter 8

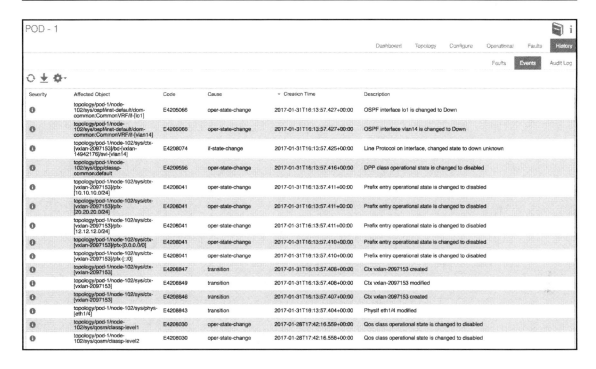

Here, we have some data.

2. Double-clicking on an event will bring up another window with more information:

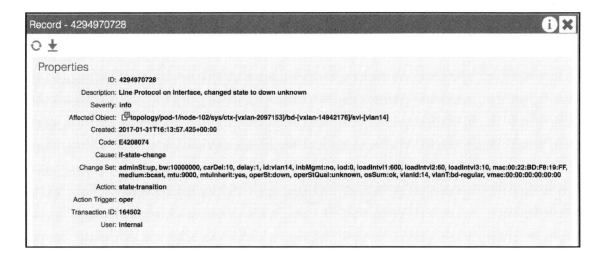

[307]

AAA events

We can see what changes have been made to AAA by following these steps:

1. Go to **Admin | AAA | AAA Authentication**, then select the **History** tab, and then select **Events**:

Here, we can see the changes we made in `Chapter 5`, *ACI Security*, when we set up AAA authentication on the fabric. The cause is listed as a **transition** (because we made a change to an existing property), and we have a brief description. Double-clicking on an entry brings up more information, but does not include what we transitioned from and what we transitioned to.

To see what we changed from and what we went to, we need to use look at the audit logs.

Navigating the audit logs

The audit logs will show what changes have been made to objects. Staying with AAA, if we switch to the **Audit Log** tab, we can see a list of the changes that have been made:

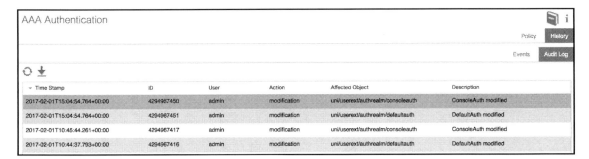

How to do it...

1. Double-clicking on an entry shows the changes (in the **Change Set** field):

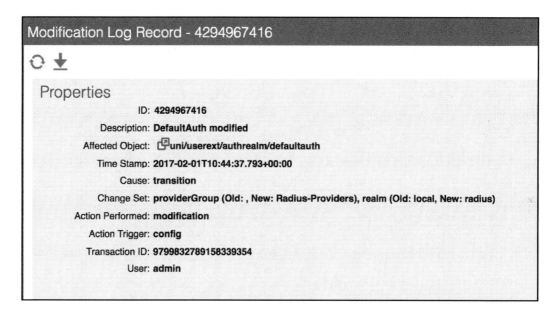

Here, we can see that the default authentication method was modified, and we switched from local authentication to RADIUS authentication.

Monitoring ACI

Earlier, we saw that there were no historical events for the tenant. We do, however, have lots of audit logs:

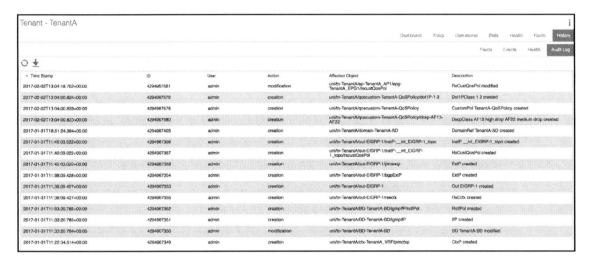

2. Again, clicking on an entry will bring up a new window with the details:

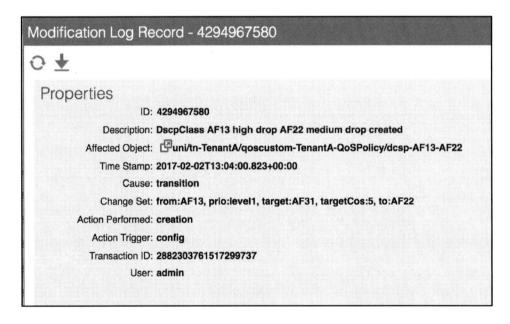

Here, we can see the QoS changes we made in `Chapter 6`, *Implementing Quality of Service in ACI.*

[310]

Setting up Call Home

Cisco's Call Home allows you to react quicker and more efficiently to issues. It will also send the logs directly to Cisco, creating cases directly with **Technical Assistance Center (TAC)**. We can send these Call Home messages on a regular basis or on an ad hoc basis in the event of an issue. The regular ones are useful for keeping track of systems and any patches that may be relevant, which is the first type we will create.

How to do it...

We start by creating a regular schedule.

1. Navigate to **Admin** | **Schedulers**.
2. Click on **Create a Scheduler** in the **Quick Start** menu.
3. Name the schedule, and click on the plus sign (+) next to **Schedule Windows**.
4. Select **Recurring**, and set the schedule to be every Sunday at 1 a.m. Accept the defaults for the other fields.
5. Click on **Submit**:

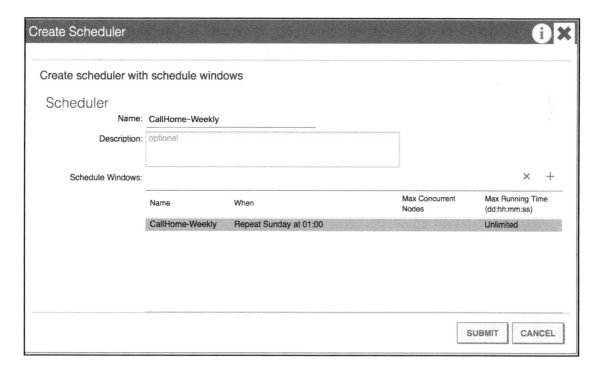

Monitoring ACI

6. Click on **Submit** again.

 Max Concurrent Nodes refers to the number of tasks that can be processed concurrently.

6. Next, navigate to **Admin | External Data Collectors**.
7. Click on **Create a Query Group**.
8. Name the query group and click on the plus sign.
9. Name the query, and set the **Type** to **class**, the **Target** to **subtree**, and the **Response Subtree** to **full**. Click on the **Check All** checkbox.
10. We will not be able to click on **OK** until we enter a class or DN. Recall from Chapter 7, *Network Programmability with ACI*, recipe *Browsing the Object Store using the Object Store Browser*, that we could use the object browser to query this, and using fvTenant gave us some good results, so let's use the query type of **class** and the class name of fvTenant, and click **OK**.
11. Click on **Submit**.
12. The new entry will be listed under the **Callhome Query Group** list on the left-hand side:

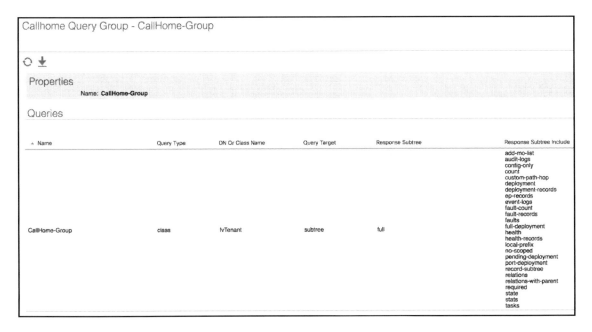

Chapter 8

13. Staying within the **Admin | External Data Collectors** menu, right-click on **Monitoring Destinations** and select **Create Callhome Destination Group**:

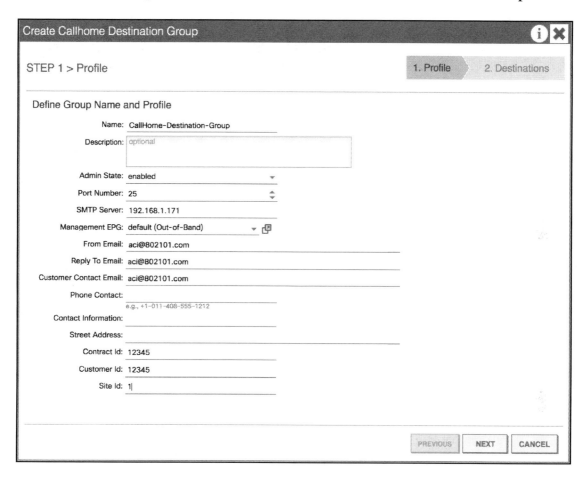

Monitoring ACI

14. Click on **Next**.
15. Add the destinations:

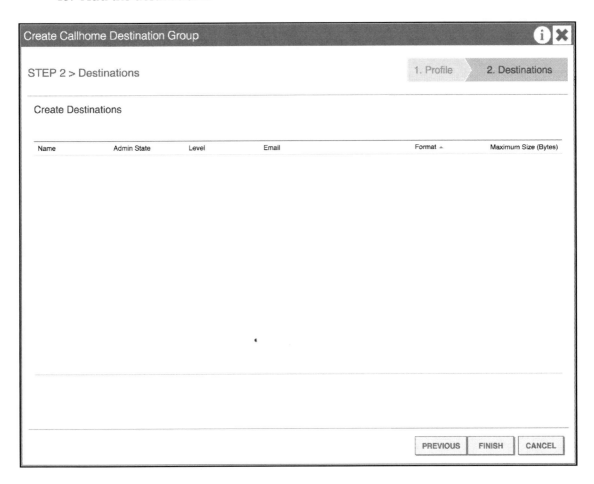

16. Click on **Finish**:
17. If you cannot add the destinations (as in the previous screenshot), then navigate to the monitoring destination, right-click on the newly created group, and select **Create Callhome Destination**, or click on **Actions** and select **Create CallHome Destination Group**:

18. Enter the name and destination e-mail address:

Monitoring ACI

19. Click on **Submit**.
20. Navigate to **Fabric** | **Fabric Policies** | **Monitoring Policies** | **default**.
21. Click on the plus sign and enter the details, choosing the destination group and query groups created earlier:

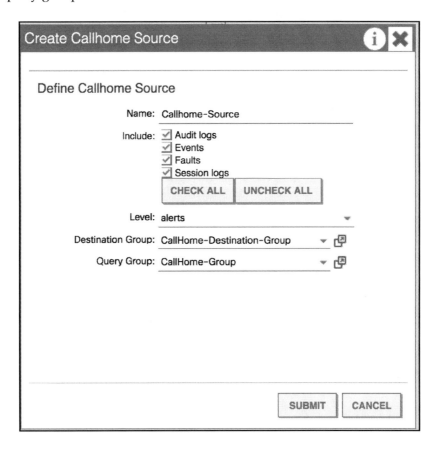

22. Click on **Submit**.
23. Repeat the previous tasks for the **Common Policy**:

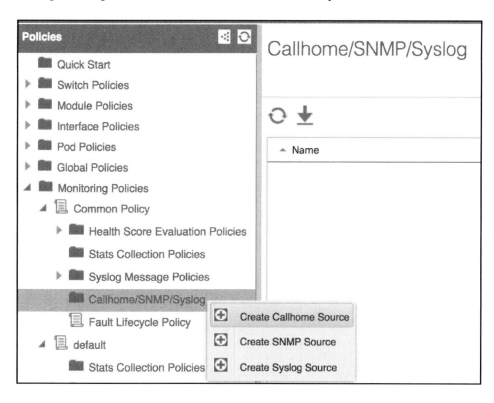

Monitoring ACI

24. Navigate to **Fabric** | **Access Policies** | **Monitoring Policies** | **default** | **Callhome/SNMP/Syslog**.
25. Click on the plus sign in the work pane and create a source:

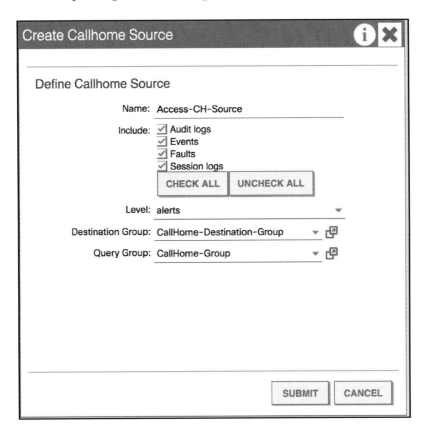

How it works...

According to the schedule (every Sunday at 1 a.m.), we should receive a Call Home e-mail from the ACI fabric. Queued messages will try to be sent again until they are successful:

```
[root]
NOQUEUE: reject: RCPT from unknown[192.168.1.83]:
451 4.3.5 Server configuration problem;
from=<aci@802101.com>
to=<callhome-alerts@802101.com>
proto=ESMTP
helo=<spine1>
```

In the screenshot, we can see that the Call Home message has been sent to the mail server. While it shows that there was an issue (the mail was rejected by the server), it does prove that the Call Home system works, and this will work much better for you if you spend longer than 5 minutes throwing together an e-mail server just to test with!

There's more...

We can also create Call Home policies for the switches. These will be the ad hoc alerts in the event of an issue.

1. Navigate to **Fabric** | **Fabric Policies** | **Switch Policies** | **Policies** | **Callhome Inventory Policies**.
2. There may be a default policy listed; if not, create a new one. Select the default policy by double-clicking on it.
3. Select the destination group created earlier:

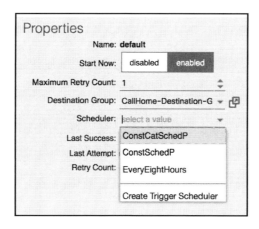

Monitoring ACI

4. We cannot select the scheduler created earlier as it is a recurring one. We need to create a new "trigger" one or use one of the existing ones:

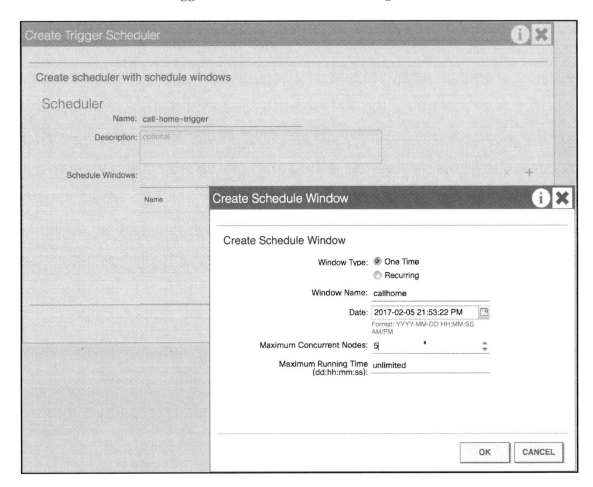

5. Click on **OK** and then **Submit**.
6. Expand **Switch Policies**, right-click on **Policy Groups**, and select **Create Spine Switch Policy Group**. Alternatively, select **Policy Groups**, click on the **Actions** menu and select **Create Spine Switch Policy Group**:

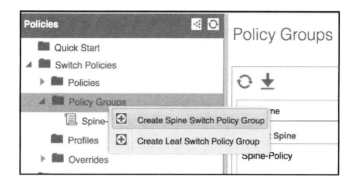

7. Name the policy group, click on the drop-down box next to **Inventory Policy**, and select **Create Callhome Inventory Policy**.
8. Name the policy and select the destination group and the scheduler created in step 4:

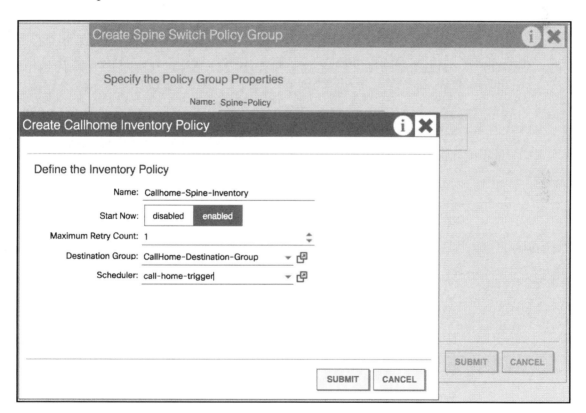

Monitoring ACI

9. Click on **Submit** and then **Submit** again.
10. Repeat the process and create a **Leaf Switch Profile Group**.
11. Next, create a **Spine Switch Profile** by going to **Policies** | **Switch Policies** and right-clicking on **Profiles**:

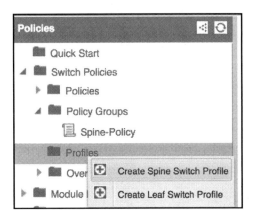

12. Select the policy created in step 8 in the **Switch Associations** field. Select the module associations and interface associations:

Chapter 8

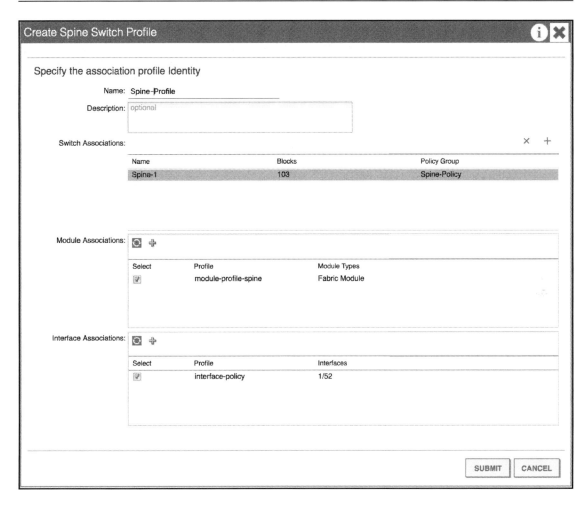

13. Repeat the process to create a leaf switch profile.

Configuring SNMP

So far in this chapter, we have looked at the GUI to get information on faults and events. These do, however, require someone to be watching and actively looking for them. We should be a little more proactive and have such details sent to a centralized monitoring platform. We will start by configuring **Simple Network Management Protocol (SNMP)**, which when combined with a suitable **Network Management Station (NMS)**, such as Zabbix or Nagios, will allow us to receive alerts by e-mail, SMS, or any other number of methods.

Try to keep the community string simple. Originally, I used the community string ACI-Community. After many hours trying to troubleshoot the lack of SNMP output, I asked on the Cisco support forums and Tomas De Leon suggested changing it. Once I set it to cisco123, everything started to work.

Getting ready

We do need a couple of things set up before SNMP will workL

- An out-of-band contract in the mgmt tenancy, permitting SNMP traffic (UDP/161). This should already be set up as part of the *Using Contracts between Tenants* recipe from Chapter 2, *Configuring Policies and Tenants*.
- APIC out-of-band IP addresses to be configured in the mgmt tenant. While these IP addresses are configured during the initial setup, they must be *explicitly* set for the OOB contract to take effect. Refer to the *Switch Diagnostics* recipe in Chapter 9, *Troubleshooting ACI*, for how to set this up.

How to do it...

1. Navigate to **Admin | External Data Collectors | Monitoring Destinations**.
2. Right-click on **SNMP** and select **Create SNMP Monitoring Destination Group**. Enter the details for your SNMP server, following the wizard:

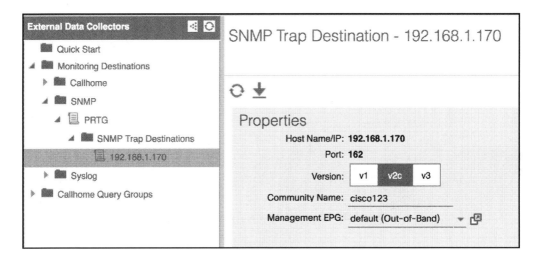

3. From the **Fabric** menu, select **Fabric Policies**.
4. Select **Create an SNMP Policy** from the `Quick Start` menu.
5. Name the policy and set the state to **Enabled**.
6. Click on the plus sign next to **Community Policies**.
7. Enter a name for the policy.
8. Click on **Update**.

9. Optionally, create an SNMP v3 user (if you elected to use SNMP in step 2).
10. Click on the plus sign next to **Client Group Policies**.
11. Name the client and set the IP address and the management EPG:

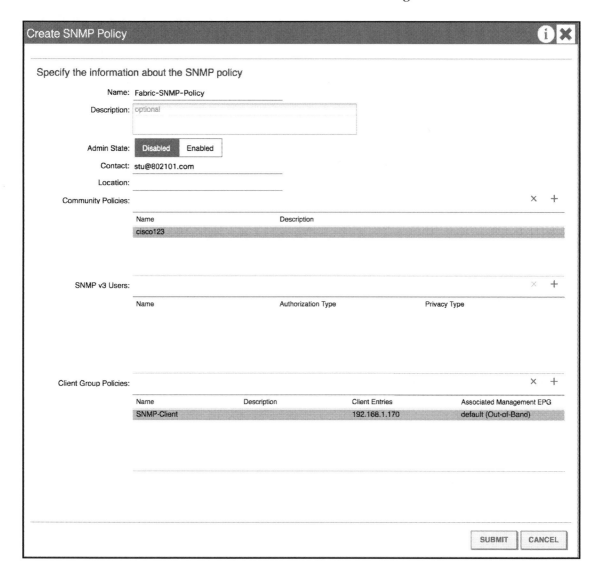

12. Click on **Submit**.
13. Go down to the **Policy Groups** and set the existing **PoD-Policy** to use the **Fabric-SNMP-Policy**:

Chapter 8

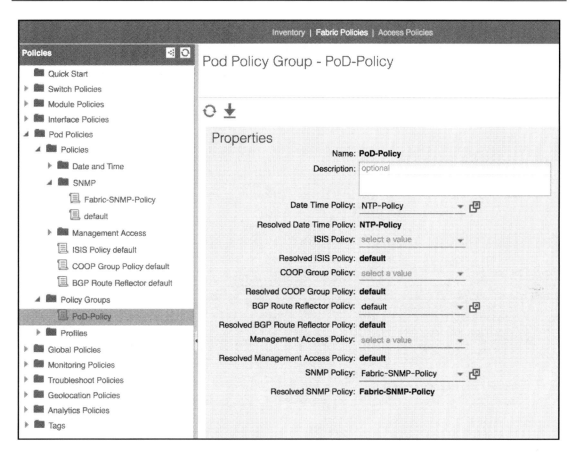

14. Click on **Submit**.
15. Navigate to **Fabric | Fabric Policies | Monitoring Policies** and for all the policies you have (**Common, default**, and any custom ones), create a policy for SNMP by clicking on the SNMP source type in the work pane and clicking on the plus sign. Select the destination group to be the one created in step 2.
16. Do the same for **Fabric | Access Policies | Monitoring Policies**.
17. Switch to the **Tenants** menu and select the mgmt tenant.
18. Navigate to **Networking | VRFs**. Right-click on **oob**, and select **Create SNMP Context**.
19. Add the community name (or user if using SNMP v3) and click on **Submit**.

20. Select **External Management Network Instance Profiles** from the left-hand menu, right-click on it, and select **Create External Management Network Instance Profile**.
21. Name the new profile `oob-mgmt-ext`.
22. Set the consumed contract to be **OOB-SNMP** (created in `Chapter 2`, *Configuring Policies and Tenants*), and add the subnet of `192.168.1.0/24` in the **Subnets** table.
23. Click on **Submit**:

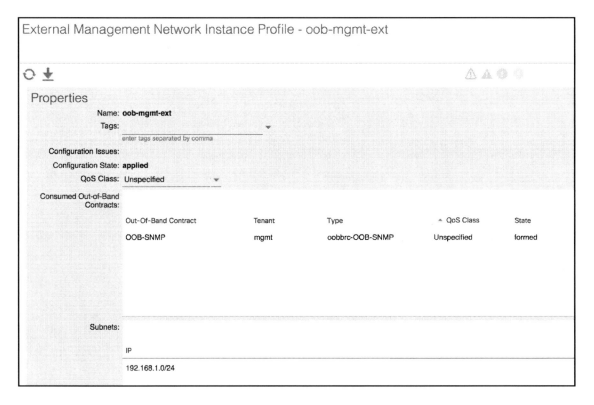

24. Under **Node Management EPGs**, select **Out-of-Band EPG - default**, and set the provided contract to be **OOB-SNMP**.
25. Click on **Submit**.

26. Under **Networking** | **VRFs** | **oob**, enter the context name and the community profile (which is the community string `cisco123`).
27. Click on **Submit**:

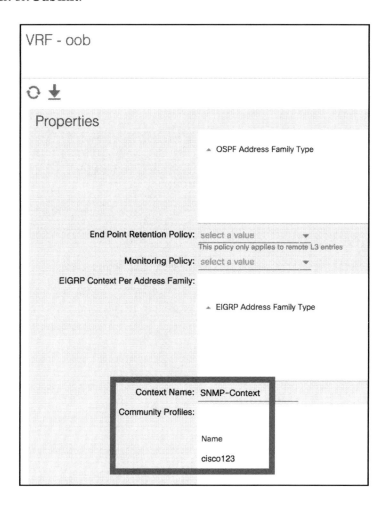

Monitoring ACI

How it works...

In this recipe, which is the longest one we have covered, we joined a number of different recipes together. So many that you could be forgiven for thinking that SNMP actually stands for "Surely, No More Policies!"

Firstly, with newer versions of ACI, the contract is required (it was not required in earlier versions), so we finally got around to using that. This permitted traffic between the ACI fabric and the SNMP client, which we set up as an external data collector. We then created policies and enabled the fabric to be polled by the entire 192.168.1.0/24 subnet.

In relation to everything else in ACI, this is actually one of the more convoluted processes. ACI is easy to pick up quickly, but this would be one of the more advanced areas, due to the dependencies on other areas (such as the filters, contracts, and out-of-band configuration required), though this is by no means a bad thing!

There's more...

We can check the SNMP configuration from the command line:

```
apic1# show snmp clientgroups
 SNMP Policy          Name           Description      Client Entries
Associated Management EPG
 ------------         --------       --------------   ----------------    --------
------------------
 default              PRTG-Server                     192.168.1.170       default
(Out-Of-Band)
 Fabric-SNMP-Policy SNMP-Client                       192.168.1.170       default
(Out-Of-Band)
apic1#
apic1# show snmp community
 SNMP Policy              Community Name     Description
 --------------------     ------------------ -----------------------------
 default                  ACI-Community
 Fabric-SNMP-Policy       ACI-Community
apic1# show snmp hosts
 IP-Address              Version    Security Level Community
 --------------------    ---------- -------------- --------------------
 192.168.1.170           v2c        noauth         ACI-Community
apic1# show snmp policy default
 Name                    Admin State Location               Contact
Description
 --------------------    ---------- --------------------   --------------------
------------------
 default                 enabled
```

```
apic1# show snmp policy Fabric-SNMP-Policy
 Name                   Admin State Location             Contact
Description
 ---------------------  ----------  ------------------- -------------------
 ---------------------
 Fabric-SNMP-Policy     enabled                         stuart@802101.com
apic1# show snmp summary

Active Policy: Fabric-SNMP-Policy, Admin State: enabled

Local SNMP engineID: [Hex] 0x800000098094ab6e6f42b58c5800000000

---------------------------------------
Community               Description
---------------------------------------
ACI-Community

---------------------------------------------------------------
User                    Authentication         Privacy
---------------------------------------------------------------


---------------------------------------------------------------
Client-Group           Mgmt-Epg               Clients
---------------------------------------------------------------
SNMP-Client            default (Out-Of-Band)  192.168.1.170

---------------------------------------------------------------
Host           Port   Version Level   SecName
---------------------------------------------------------------
192.168.1.170  162    v2c     noauth  ACI-Community

apic1# show snmp users
 SNMP Policy Name Authorization Type Privacy Type
 ----------------- ------------------ ------------------ ----------
 ---------

apic1#
```

We can see the result in PRTG:

Pos ▼	Sensor	Status	Message	Graph		Priority	
1.	PING	Up	OK	Ping Time	0 msec	★★★★★	
2.	SSL Security Check (Port 443)	Up	OK	Security Rating	Only Strong Prot	★★★☆☆	
3.	HTTPS	Up	OK	Loading time	13 msec	★★★☆☆	
4.	SNMP Trap Receiver	Up	OK	Messages	0 #/s	★★★☆☆	
5.	SNMP System Uptime	Up	OK	System Uptime	13 d	★★★☆☆	

Monitoring ACI

 To get a list of the MIBs supported by ACI, go to `http://www.cisco.com/c/dam/en/us/td/docs/switches/datacenter/aci/apic/sw/1-x/mib/list/mib-support.html`.

Configuring Syslog

While the GUI does a great job of showing us the issues and events in the fabric, many people use third-party tools to aggregate data. Setting up a Syslog server is very beneficial for the aggregation of logs.

How to do it...

Setting up Syslog is very similar to setting up Call Home and SNMP, but with fewer steps required.

1. Create a new external data collector (**Admin | External Data Collectors | Monitoring Destinations**) by right-clicking on **Syslog** and selecting **Create Syslog Monitoring Destination Group**:

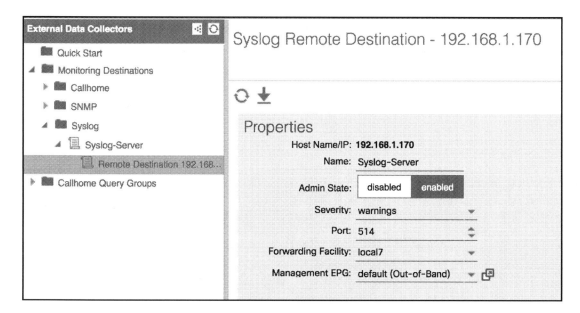

[332]

2. Navigate to **Fabric** | **Fabric Policies** | **Monitoring Policies** | **Default**.
3. Create a Syslog entry for the **default** and **Common** policies, by clicking on **CallHome/SNMP/Syslog**, selecting **Syslog** as the source type in the work pane, and clicking on the plus sign. Select the data collector created in step 1:

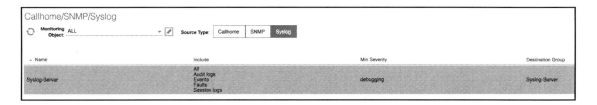

4. Repeat the process for the **Access Policies**, creating the Syslog object in the default policy.

How it works...

The logs should start to come into the Syslog server (in this case, Kiwi Syslog).

Configuring NetFlow

Cisco ACI supports NetFlow version 9 and can be configured at two levels, infra or tenant. In this recipe, we will walk through the steps needed to configure it under a tenant.

 NetFlow is supported on ACI version 2.2 and above.

How to do it...

1. Select the tenant from the **Tenants** menu.
2. Expand **Analytics**.
3. Right-click on **NetFlow Monitors** and select **Create Flow Monitor**.
4. Fill in the details for the monitor and click on **Submit**.
5. From the tenant, go to **Analytics** | **NetFlow Records**.

6. Right-click on **NetFlow Monitors** and select **Create Flow Record**.
7. Select the desired parameters from the **Collect Parameters** field.
8. Choose the match parameters.
9. Click on **Submit**.
10. Right-click on **NetFlow Exporters** and select **Create External Collector Reachability**.
11. Create the exporter and click on **Submit**.
12. Within the tenant, select **Networking | Bridge Domains**.
13. In the work pane, select **Policy | Advanced Troubleshooting**.
14. From the **NetFlow Monitor Policies** table, select the filter type and the policy created earlier, and click on **Update**.
15. Click on **Submit**.

There's more...

There are a couple of very good videos on how to implement NetFlow in ACI on the **Cisco ACI** YouTube channel, titled **NetFlow Configuration**:

- `https://www.youtube.com/watch?v=6Yl_GelaS7g`(**part 1**)
- `https://www.youtube.com/watch?v=LQCZdf9Sux0` (**part 2**)

9
Troubleshooting ACI

In this chapter, we will look at some troubleshooting steps, along with how we can back up and restore the fabric.

These are the recipes we will cover:

- Layer 2 troubleshooting
- FEX troubleshooting
- SSL troubleshooting
- Switch diagnostics
- APIC troubleshooting
- Upgrading the ACI software
- VMM troubleshooting
- Routing verifications
- Troubleshooting external connectivity
- Multicast troubleshooting
- QoS troubleshooting

Introduction

Although the recipes have, more often than not, been relatively painless and trouble free (the exception being configuring SNMP), we should cover some basic troubleshooting steps.

We will start from the ground up, working from layer 2 upward before we get to the APIC and then on to troubleshooting VMM domains, routing and multicast, and QoS.

Because of the fast pace at which ACI is growing, the command set is also increasing. The commands listed in the following recipes are by no means the only ones available. Be sure to check the most recent command reference guides at http://www.cisco.com/c/en/us/support/cloud-systems-management/application-policy-infrastructure-controller-apic/tsd-products-support-series-home.html.

Layer 2 troubleshooting

Layer 2 troubleshooting starts with checking the cables. This may seem obvious but is a step that many hardened engineers can miss, making the assumption that everything is cabled correctly.

Assuming that everything *is* connected correctly, we can move on to some basic checks.

How to do it...

1. We can check that we can see the neighboring devices using some `show` commands:

   ```
   show cdp neighbors
   show lldp neighbors
   ```

   > **Link Layer Discovery Protocol (LLDP)** is vendor neutral, whereas **Cisco Discovery Protocol (CDP)** is proprietary to Cisco, so depending on the makeup of the fabric, one will be more applicable at times then the other.

2. We can check the status of a particular interface from the GUI by navigating to **Fabric | Inventory | Pod 1 | Leaf-1 | Interfaces | Physical Interfaces**, selecting the interface, and looking at the **LLDP Neighbor** field.

Chapter 9

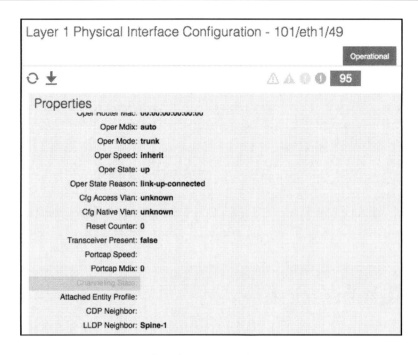

3. This does not give us much information, though, and we need to know which interface to select (there may be lots of them in your fabric), so to get a better overview, go to **Fabric | Inventory | Pod 1 | Leaf-1 | Protocols | LLDP neighbors**.

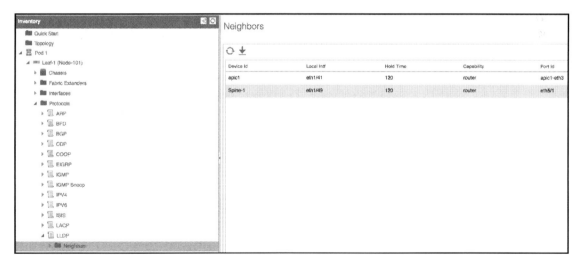

Here we can see all of our neighbors and the port we are connecting to.

[337]

We should be able to see the connected nodes and other devices, such as VMWare servers, routers, and fabric extenders (assuming they support and are running either CDP or LLDP).

4. From the command line, we can get the same level of detail, using commands such as `show lldp entry` followed by the system name of the peer (which we would get from the `show lldp neighbor` command and choosing one of the device IDs listed).
5. We can also use `show lldp neighbors detail` to get the information for all of our neighbors, including their management IP addresses, which we can then use to connect to them.
6. If we are using CDP, we can achieve the same level of output, using the commands `show cdp entry` and `show cdp neighbors detail`.

FEX troubleshooting

If you have extended your fabric with a **Fabric Extender** (**FEX**), you can check the connectivity and status from the leaf node.

How to do it...

1. Once you have connected to the leaf that the FEX attaches to, you can run these commands:

   ```
   sh fex
   sh fex detail
   ```

   The first command will show the state, model, and serial number. The second command will show the same information, along with the port states.

2. If we wanted to dig deeper, we could check the link between the FEX and the leaf, using the `show fex transceiver` command, which will show us the hardware properties of the transceiver. We can also look at the environmental data (such as temperature and CPU usage) using the `show environment fex` command. While we would hope that the same information would be readable through SNMP and already available to us in our monitoring platform, we may be in a situation where that information is not flowing (such as the CPU being overworked).

There's more...

Other useful commands are `show logging level fex` to make sure that we are sending the logs that we need (at the correct severity), `show system reset-reason fex` to tell us why the FEX may have rebooted, and `show fex version` in case there are any issues with strange behavior arising due to a version difference.

Now that we have confirmed that we can see our nodes, we need to make sure that they are communicating properly with the fabric.

SSL troubleshooting

The communication between the nodes occurs through SSL encrypted channels; without this, our spine and leaf nodes will not be able to register with the controller(s), so once we have checked that our cables are connected and we can see everything on layer 2, we should check whether we are communicating in the right manner with the nodes.

How to do it...

We can check that the nodes have a valid SSL certificate.

1. Navigate to **Fabric** | **Inventory** | **Fabric Membership**.
2. Check that the nodes all have an SSL certificate.

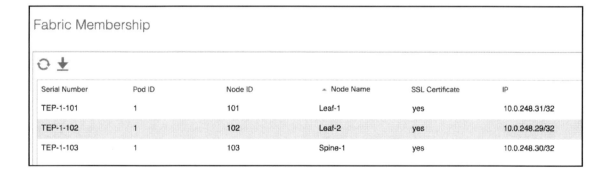

There's more...

We can also check that the communication is working using the following command on the APIC:

```
netstat -ant | grep :12
```

Check that the output lists the connections as ESTABLISHED:

```
apic1# netstat -ant | grep :12
tcp        0      0 10.0.0.1:12151          0.0.0.0:*               LISTEN
<truncated>
tcp        0      0 10.0.0.1:12567          10.0.248.29:49187       ESTABLISHED
tcp        0      0 10.0.0.1:12343          10.0.248.30:45965       ESTABLISHED
tcp        0      0 10.0.0.1:12343          10.0.248.31:47784       ESTABLISHED
tcp        0      0 10.0.0.1:12343          10.0.248.29:49942       ESTABLISHED
tcp        0      0 10.0.0.1:12343          10.0.248.30:42946       ESTABLISHED
tcp        0      0 10.0.0.1:50820          10.0.248.31:12439       ESTABLISHED
<truncated>
apic1#
```

We will have some rows in the LISTEN state (so new devices can connect), but the nodes (the 10.0.248. addresses) should be established. A state of ESTABLISHED shows that **Inter-Fabric Messaging (IFM)** is working between the nodes and the APIC. We can also use the `acidiag fnvread` command (where `fnv` stands for "fabric node vector") to confirm this:

```
apic1# acidiag fnvread
     ID   Pod ID              Name      Serial Number            IP Address     Role          State LastUpdMsgId
-----------------------------------------------------------------------------------------------
                                        101         1                           Leaf-1
TEP-1-101    10.0.248.31/32    leaf                 active     0
     102   1                   Leaf-2    TEP-1-102                10.0.248.29/32
leaf          active     0
     103   1                   Spine-1   TEP-1-103                10.0.248.30/32
spine         active     0
Total 3 nodes
apic1#
```

All looks well here.

We can look at the certificates by connecting using OpenSSL:

```
openssl s_client -state -connect 10.0.0.1:12567
```

The output will show the full details of the certificate, which must have a valid start date and end date. The current date must be within that period. Otherwise, the certificate will not be valid yet, or its validity will have expired. The certificate should also be signed by the **Cisco Manufacturing Certificate Authority (CMCA)**.

If we have an issue with one (or more) of the nodes, we can right-click on it in the GUI and decommission the device. Once the device reboots, it should attempt to rejoin the fabric (using the same process).

Switch diagnostics

We have a couple of nodes in our ACI fabric (Spine-1, Leaf-1, and Leaf-2). These switches will inherit the policies we create, and these policies will be pushed down to them by the APIC. Unlike traditional networking, we will rarely need to connect to them on a day-to-day basis; however, from time to time, we will need to connect to them through SSH. Being the proactive people we are, we should also make sure that we can monitor them. To do this, we will need them to have out-of-band IP addresses.

How to do it...

1. Navigate to **Tenants** | **mgmt** | **Node Management Addresses**.
2. Right-click on **Static Node Management Addresses** and select **Create Static Node Management Addresses**.
3. Enter the node range (`101-103`).
4. Select **Out-of-Band Addresses** and **In-Band Addresses**.
5. Select the OOB management EPG (**default**) and enter the starting IP address and subnet mask in CIDR format (`192.168.1.81/24`).
6. Enter the IPv6 addresses (if required).
7. Do the same for the in-band addresses, creating the management EPG if necessary (which I named `InBand-Mgmt`). I have used the addresses `4.4.4.81` to `4.4.4.83`.

Troubleshooting ACI

8. Click on **Submit**.

Node	Type	EPG	IPV4 Address	IPV4 Gateway
pod-1/node-101	Out-Of-Band	default	192.168.1.81/24	192.168.1.1
pod-1/node-102	Out-Of-Band	default	192.168.1.82/24	192.168.1.1
pod-1/node-103	Out-Of-Band	default	192.168.1.83/24	192.168.1.1
pod-1/node-101	In-Band	InBand-Mgmt	4.4.4.81/24	4.4.4.1
pod-1/node-102	In-Band	InBand-Mgmt	4.4.4.82/24	4.4.4.1
pod-1/node-103	In-Band	InBand-Mgmt	4.4.4.83/24	4.4.4.1

Static Node Management Addresses

9. Navigate to **IP Address Pools**, right-click on it, and select **Create IP Address Pool**.
10. Name this address pool `oob-address-pool`, and enter the gateway IP in CIDR format (`192.168.1.1/24`). Untick the gateway validation option if the gateway is not reachable. Set the IP address range.
11. Click on **Update**. If you are unable to click on **Submit** when setting the range, then leave the range empty, and set ranges from the work pane window.

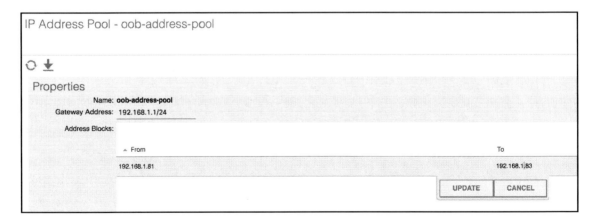

[342]

12. Click on **Submit**.
13. Create a second IP address pool (`inb-address-pool`) for the in-band addresses.

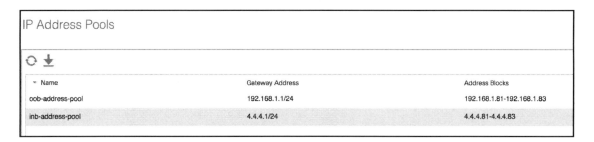

14. Managed Node Connectivity Groups - right-click and select **Create Managed Node Connectivity Group**.
15. Name the group and select both the tick boxes.
16. Choose the **default** EPG and the **oob-address-pool** for out-of-band management, and select the **InBand-Mgmt** EPG (created in step 7) and the **inb-address-pool** (created in step 13).

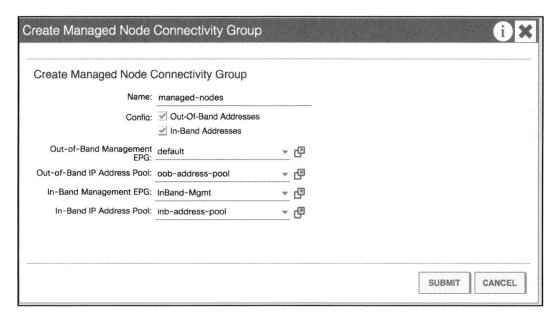

Troubleshooting ACI

17. We now need to navigate to **Node Management Addresses | default**.
18. Select type **ALL** and set the **Managed Node Connectivity Group** to the **managed-nodes** group created in step 16.

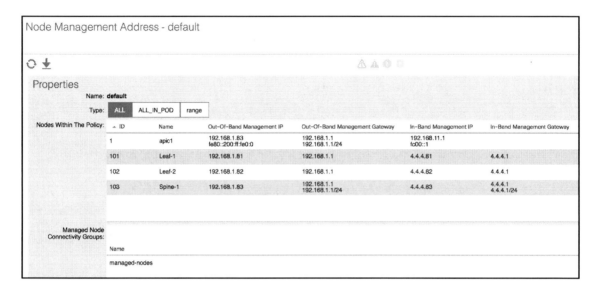

How it works...

We now have out-of-band IP addresses for the nodes as well as in-band ones using a different IP address range. This means that we should be able to access the nodes through SSH and be able to pull data out using SNMP.

We can check the addresses using the `show switch` APIC command.

I have removed the IPv6 columns for the sake of formatting.

```
apic1# show switch
ID     Pod    Address           In-Band IPv4   OOB IPv4         Version
Flags  Serial Number    Name    ----           ---              -------------  ------------  -
-----------    --------------   -----          -------------    ------------   --------
101    1      10.0.248.31       4.4.4.81       192.168.1.81     simsw-2.1(0.36)
aliv   TEP-1-101        Leaf-1
102    1      10.0.248.29       4.4.4.82       192.168.1.82     simsw-2.1(0.36)
aliv   TEP-1-102        Leaf-2
```

[344]

```
103      1       10.0.248.30    4.4.4.83        192.168.1.83    simsw-2.1(0.36)
asiv     TEP-1-103          Spine-1
Flags - a:Active | l/s:Leaf/Spine | v:Valid Certificate | i:In-Service
apic1#
```

So, we have covered layer 2, we have covered node communication with the fabric, and we have covered switch communication. Most of this does require a working APIC, so let's look at that next.

APIC troubleshooting

We have already covered a lot about troubleshooting within the APIC, but so far, we have missed one very vital piece of detail: how to backup and restore our configuration. We will look at that now.

How to do it...

1. Navigate to **Admin** | **Config Rollbacks**.

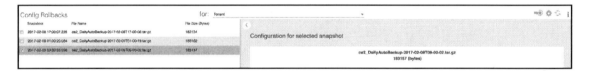

We can see that we have a few automatically generated config backups listed.

2. Right-click on the most recent one.

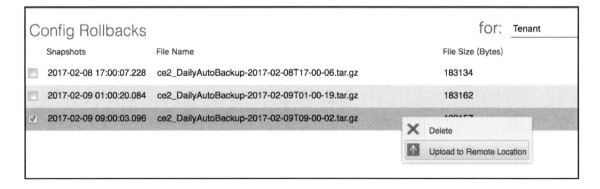

Troubleshooting ACI

3. Select **Upload to Remote Location**.
4. In the new window, tick the box next to **Or create a new one:**.

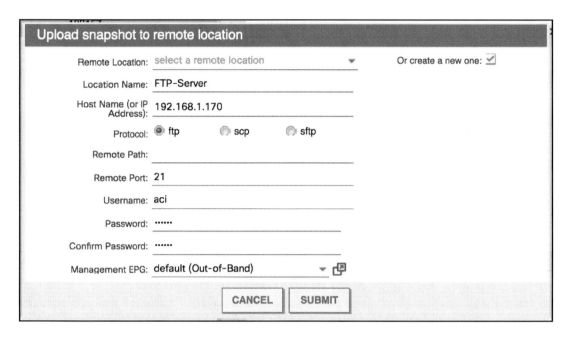

5. Give the location a name, enter the IP address, and select the protocol.
6. Enter any path details; the port (if different from the protocol default); and the username, password, and management EPG.
7. Click on **Submit**.
8. The backup file will be uploaded to the destination specified.

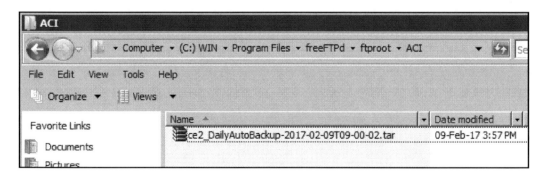

Chapter 9

Now, if we have to roll back, we can. To do this, we perform the following steps:

9. From the **Admin** | **Config Rollbacks** menu, click on the icon that shows an arrow and a circle.
10. In the window that pops up, enter the filename to upload (which must match the file name in the import source) and select and import the source from the drop-down menu (if one has been created previously; otherwise, create a new one).

11. Click on **Submit** to upload the backup config back to the APIC.
12. Select the newly imported file in the left-hand window.
13. You can compare two snapshots by selecting one from the drop-down list. Any differences will be shown in the work pane.
14. Click on **Rollback to this Configuration** to perform the rollback.
15. Click on **Yes** to confirm.

Troubleshooting ACI

There's more...

We can have configurations automatically exported by navigating to
Admin | Import/Export, right-clicking on **Export Policies**, and selecting **Create Configuration Export Policy**. I have created one here using the existing **EveryEightHours** schedule and set it to export to the FTP server created in this recipe:

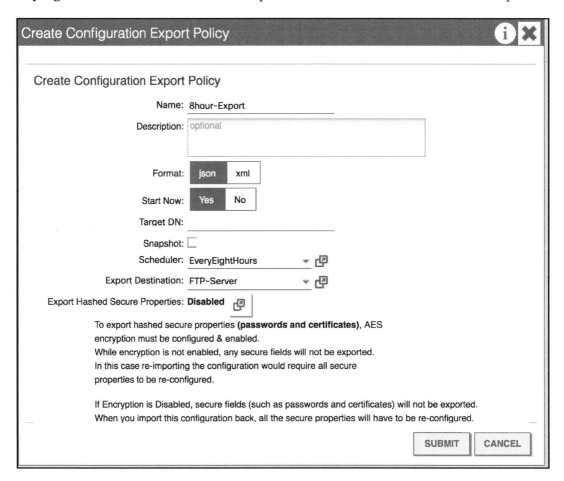

There is already a daily export, which is set as a snapshot, meaning that it cannot be exported. This also runs every 8 hours.

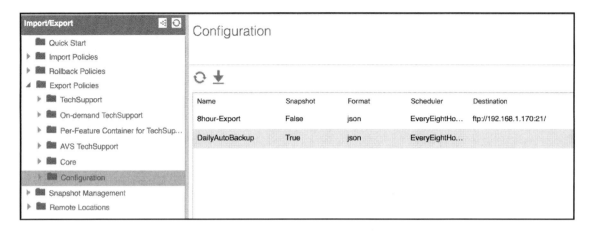

Now, if we make an error, we can roll back to a working version.

Sometimes, however, we may find an issue that is not of our making and can only be resolved by performing an upgrade.

Upgrading the ACI software

Upgrades can be required to gain new features or to resolve an issue. Before we can upgrade the software, we need to create a source (similar to the way we created a remote location for backing up and restoring our configurations).

Getting ready

Before we can upgrade the ACI fabric, we need to tell it what to download (which ISO image) and where to download it from. We do this by creating a download task.

1. Navigate to **Admin** | **Firmware** | **Download Tasks**.
2. From the actions menu, select **Create Firmware Download Task**.

Troubleshooting ACI

3. Enter the details for the image to be downloaded to the APIC.

4. Click on **Submit**.
5. This creates a download task, and the APIC will attempt to download the software specified. To check the status, click on **Operational** (on the right-hand side) and wait till the download percent reaches 100%.

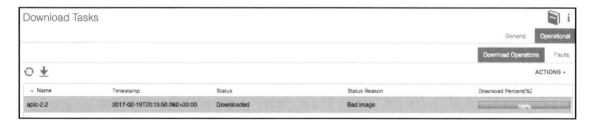

6. Navigate to **Firmware Repository** to check that that the new firmware has been successfully added to the system.

From the **Firmware Repository**, you can also click on the **Actions** menu and select **Upload Firmware to APIC**.

How to do it...

1. Navigate to **Admin** | **Firmware** | **Controller Firmware**.
2. From the **Actions** menu, select **Controller Upgrade**.
3. Select the new firmware version from the dropdown and choose when to apply the new policy (either **Apply Now** or **Apply Later**).
4. Click on **Submit**. Once you do, the status window will show the progress. Controllers will be upgraded serially so that the fabric will be fully operational during the upgrade procedure. Each APIC will take around 10 minutes to upgrade, and each will reboot during the procedure. After the upgraded controller reboots, it will rejoin the cluster and the next controller will start to upgrade.

There's more...

Once the controllers have been upgraded (and are **Fully Fit**), we can upgrade the switches. To do this, we need to create a firmware group and a maintenance group. We can do this by right-clicking on the relevant menu option under **Fabric Node Firmware** and selecting the **Create...** option, or we can create them using the firmware upgrade wizard, which is what we will do.

1. Navigate to **Admin** | **Firmware** | **Fabric Node Firmware**.
2. Right-click on it and select **Firmware Upgrade Wizard**.

3. Select all the nodes you want to add to the firmware group.

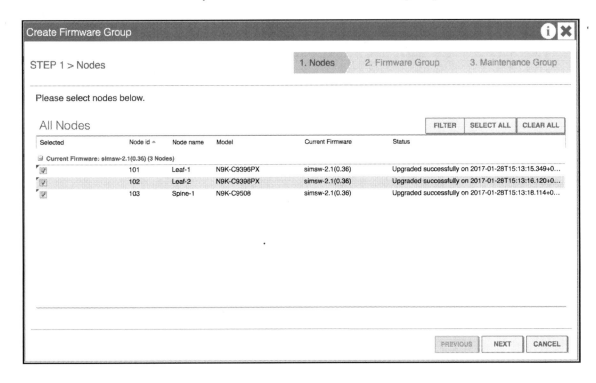

Chapter 9

4. Click on **Next**.
5. Name the firmware group and select a target firmware version.

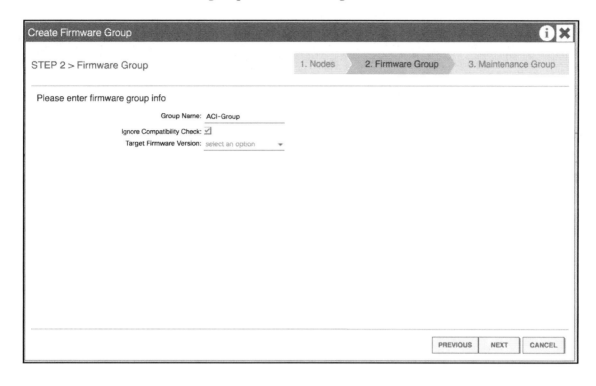

Troubleshooting ACI

6. Click on **Next**.
7. In this third step, select the nodes to add to the maintenance group.

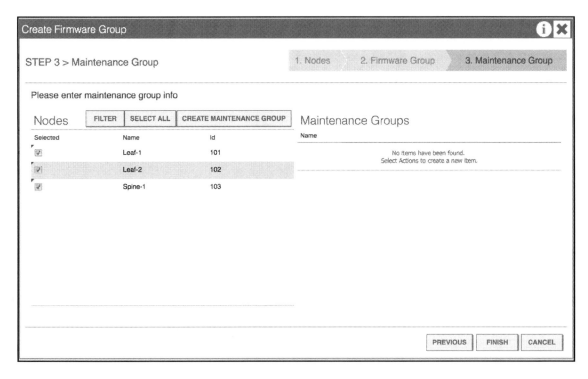

8. Click on the option to **Create Maintenance Group**.
9. Name the maintenance group and select a schedule from the drop-down menu.

Chapter 9

10. Click on **Submit**.

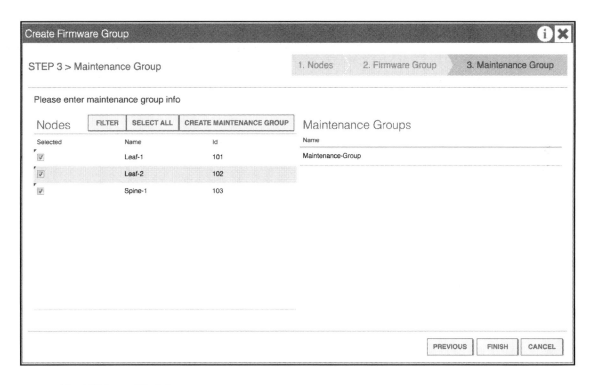

11. Click on **Finish**.

[355]

12. To check the progress of the upgrade, click on the maintenance group that was created from the list on the left-hand side.

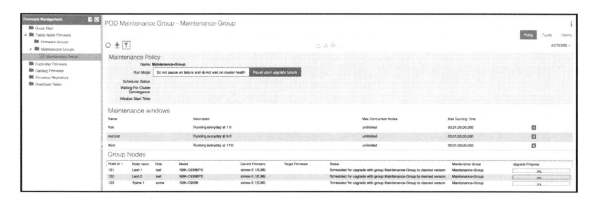

 You can also right-click on the maintenance group and select **Upgrade Now** to force the upgrade.

VMM troubleshooting

While VMM covers three different vendors (Microsoft, VMWare, and OpenStack), there is still a basic troubleshooting methodology appropriate to all three. The first step would be to make sure that we have connectivity between the APIC and the target system.

How to do it...

1. Firstly, we can make sure that the hypervisor connectivity is working, using the `show <hypervisor> domain` command, where the hypervisor is either `vmware` or `microsoft`:

```
apic1# show vmware domain
Faults: Grouped by severity (Critical, Major, Minor, Warning)

 Domain                       Type          Encap    EPGs   Faults
 ---------------------------  ------------  -------  -----  ---------------
 ACI-VMWare-vSwitch           VMware vDS    vlan     0      0,0,0,0
apic1#
```

[356]

2. We can drill into the domain by specifying it in the same command:

```
apic1# show vmware domain name ACI-VMWare-vSwitch
Domain Name                    : ACI-VMWare-vSwitch
Virtual Switch Mode            : VMware Distributed Switch
Switching Encap Mode           : vlan
Vlan Domain                    : ACI-VMWare-vSwitch (10-20)
Physical Interfaces            :
Number of EPGs                 : 1
Faults by Severity             : 0, 0, 0, 0
LLDP override                  : RX: enabled, TX: enabled
CDP override                   : no
Channel Mode override          : no

vCenters:
Faults: Grouped by severity (Critical, Major, Minor, Warning)
  vCenter              Type      Datacenter              Status    ESXs   VMs
Faults
  ----------------------------------------------------------------------------
  --------------
  192.168.1.18         vCenter   802101.local            online    3      16
0,0,0,0

Trunk Portgroups:
  Name                                                 VLANs
  ----------------------------------------------------------------------------
  ------------------
apic1#
```

3. We can see what virtual machines there are, using the show <hypervisor> vm command:

```
apic1# show vmware vm
vCenter 192.168.1.18, Domain ACI-VMWare-vSwitch:
  VM Name                VM State  Interface  VNic MAC           VNic IP
DVS      Port Group      Nic State
  ------------------------------ ------ ---------- ----------------- ------------
---      ----------      -----------
  acisim-0.0-0.1a        UP        adapter 1  00:0C:29:2E:54:BE  0.0.0.0
--                       up
  acisim-0.0-0.1a        UP        adapter 2  00:0C:29:2E:54:C8  0.0.0.0
--                       up
  flawless-server_2.5    UP        adapter 1  00:0C:29:39:84:48  0.0.0.0
--                       up
  ISE 1.4                DOWN      adapter 1  00:0C:29:3D:4C:83  0.0.0.0
--                       down
  ISE 2.0                DOWN      adapter 1  00:0C:29:44:2E:5E  0.0.0.0
```

Troubleshooting ACI

```
    --                      down
    mailserver              UP      adapter 1   00:50:56:83:24:AB   0.0.0.0
    --                      up
    management-server       DOWN    adapter 1   00:50:56:83:85:E7   0.0.0.0
    --                      down
    openstack-template      DOWN    adapter 1   00:50:56:83:ED:AB   0.0.0.0
    --                      down
    Tiny-ACI                DOWN    adapter 1   00:50:56:83:78:6E   0.0.0.0
    --                      down
    UNL v9                  DOWN    adapter 1   00:50:56:80:A2:DB   0.0.0.0
    --                      down
    UNL v9                  DOWN    adapter 2   00:50:56:80:2A:6E   0.0.0.0
    --                      down
    UNL v9                  DOWN    adapter 3   00:0C:29:E7:F7:D6   0.0.0.0
    --                      down
    vCenter                 UP      adapter 1   00:0C:29:7F:8D:8A   192.168.1.18
    --                      up
    VIRL.1.2.83             DOWN    adapter 1   00:0C:29:37:15:90   0.0.0.0
    --                      down
    VIRL.1.2.83             DOWN    adapter 2   00:0C:29:37:15:9A   0.0.0.0
    --                      down
    VIRL.1.2.83             DOWN    adapter 3   00:0C:29:37:15:A4   0.0.0.0
    --                      down
    VIRL.1.2.83             DOWN    adapter 4   00:0C:29:37:15:AE   0.0.0.0
    --                      down
    VIRL.1.2.83             DOWN    adapter 5   00:0C:29:37:15:B8   0.0.0.0
    --                      down
    Win2008Server           UP      adapter 1   00:50:56:83:43:BD   0.0.0.0
    --                      up
    WSA-9                   DOWN    adapter 1   00:0C:29:5E:24:15   0.0.0.0
    --                      down
    WSA-9                   DOWN    adapter 2   00:0C:29:5E:24:1F   0.0.0.0
    --                      down
    WSA-9                   DOWN    adapter 3   00:0C:29:5E:24:29   0.0.0.0
    --                      down
    WSA-9                   DOWN    adapter 4   00:0C:29:5E:24:33   0.0.0.0
    --                      down
    WSA-9                   DOWN    adapter 5   00:0C:29:5E:24:3D   0.0.0.0
    --                      down
apic1#
```

We can also look at the same information, but limit it down to a particular virtual machine:

```
apic1# show vmware vm name Win2008Server
VM Name         VM State       Domain Name     Interface VNic MAC          VNic
IP      Port Group Encap Nic State
-------------   ------------   -------------   --------- ----------------  ------
----    ---------- ----- ---------
Win2008Server UP                ACI-VMWare-    adapter 1 00:50:56:83:43:BD
0.0.0.0    --             --    up
                                vSwitch
apic1#
```

Routing verifications

If you have ever tried troubleshooting a routing issue on a different platform, such as IOS, you'll find that verifying routing within the ACI fabric is not much different. We need to remember that we are dealing with VRFs, more than we might normally do, but this is where the context-sensitive help comes into play.

How to do it...

1. Taking OSPF as the example, we can look at the neighbors for a particular VRF using the `show ip ospf neighbors vrf <vrf-name>` command or all of the neighbors using `show ip ospf neighbors vrf all`.
2. Similarly, we can look at the OSPF routes using `show ip ospf route vrf <vrf-name>` or `show ip ospf route vrf all`.

Troubleshooting external connectivity

Verifying external connectivity is done using the `show external-l3` or `show external-l2` command. From here, we can see the layer 3 adjacencies, and the ports through which these adjacencies have formed, or the layer 2 connectivity (such as to an FEX).

Troubleshooting ACI

How to do it...

1. The context-sensitive help becomes very useful here (as it does everywhere else).

```
apic1# show external-l3 ?
bgp            Show command for BGP peers
eigrp          Show command for external-l3 eigrp
epg            Show command for external-l3 epgs
interfaces     Show command for external-l3 interfaces
ospf           Show command for external-l3 ospf
route-map      Show command for external-l3 route-map
static-route   Show command for external-l3 static routes
apic1#
```

2. We can look at our interfaces and see which node, tenant, tenant VRFs and interfaces, and IP addresses are used for form the adjacencies:

```
apic1# show external-l3 interfaces
Node   Tenant       VRF          Interface         IP Address
-----  -----------  -----------  ---------------   ----------------
102    common       CommonVRF    lo/2.2.2.2        2.2.2.2
102    common       CommonVRF    vlan-1212 eth1/4  12.12.12.254/24
apic1#
```

This command lists all of the layer 3 interfaces, no matter which routing protocol is used by it.

3. To look at the protocol information, we could use `show external-l3 ospf`, for instance:

```
apic1# show external-l3 ospf
Area Id : 0.0.0.100
Tenant : common
Vrf : CommonVRF
User Config :

Node ID Area Properties
----    ------------------------------------------------
102 Type: nssa, Cost: 1, Control: redistribute,summary

    Configuration :

 Node ID Route Map
 ----    ----------------
 102     L3OutExternal_out
Interfaces :
```

```
    Configuration :

Node ID Interface   IP Address
----  ------------  ---------------
102   vlan1212      12.12.12.254/24
      eth1/4
apic1#
```

Here, we can see that we are calling a route map called `L3OutExternal_out`.

4. We can look at this further:

```
apic1# show external-l3 route-map
Tenant : common VRF: CommonVRF
         Table1: Route Map Configuration

 Node  Routemap           Type      Name            Match            Set
Attributes
-----  ------------------  -------  ---------------  ---------------  --------
---------
 102   L3OutExternal_out  PfxList  L3OutExtNets     12.12.12.0/24
apic1#
```

Multicast troubleshooting

Like routing troubleshooting, the commands for multicast are no different to other operating systems.

How to do it...

1. From the switch, use the `show ip mroute vrf <vrf|all>` command, either specifying a VRF or using the `all` command to list all of the multicast routes.
2. Because we use PIM within ACI, you can use commands such as `show ip pim neighbor vrf <vrf-name>` and `show ip pim route vrf <vrf|all>` to list the neighbors and routes, respectively.

3. From the GUI, we can look at our leaf nodes through the **Fabric | Inventory** menu and ensure that PIM is enable.

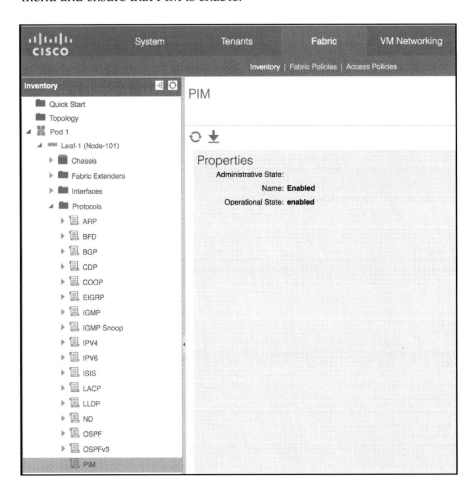

QoS troubleshooting

We covered verifying QoS in *Chapter 6*, using the `show run tenant TenantA application TenantA_AP1 epg TenantA_EPG1` command to find which QoS policy map is applied to the tenant and then `show run tenant TenantA policy-map type qos TenantA-QoSPolicy` to look at the policy settings. In this recipe, we will look at a couple more commands.

How to do it...

We can also check from the GUI whether the QoS policy has been applied.

1. Navigate to **Tenants** | **TenantA** | **Application Profiles** | **TenantA_AP1** | **Application EPGs** | **TenantA_EPG1**.
2. Confirm that the correct QoS policy is set under **Custom QOS**.

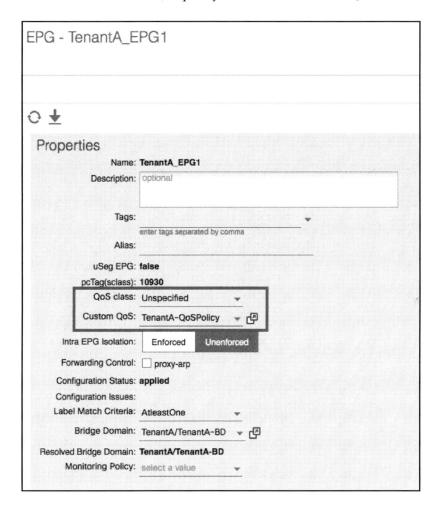

There's more...

Other commands that may come in useful are as follows:

- `show copp policy`

    This command will show the **Control Plane Policing (CoPP)** settings:

```
ACI-leaf1# show copp policy
COPP Class              COPP proto              COPP Rate           COPP Burst
ifc                     ifc                     5000                5000
igmp                    igmp                    1500                1500
cdp                     cdp                     1000                1000
pim                     pim                     500                 500
dhcp                    dhcp                    1360                340
lacp                    lacp                    1000                1000
ospf                    ospf                    2000                2000
arp                     arp                     1360                340
lldp                    lldp                    1000                1000
acllog                  acllog                  500                 500
stp                     stp                     1000                1000
coop                    coop                    5000                5000
traceroute              traceroute              500                 500
isis                    isis                    1500                5000
icmp                    icmp                    500                 500
bgp                     bgp                     5000                5000
```

- `show system internal qos classes`

    This command will show all of the possible system default QoS settings:

```
ACI-leaf1# show system internal qos classes
----------------------------------------------------
QOS Class
----------------------------------------------------
Id: span
Mtu: 9216
Buffer: min 0
Cong: algo 0 ecn 0
Sched: bw 1 meth WRR
Queue: limit 1500 meth Dynamic
----------------------------------------------------
QOS Class
----------------------------------------------------
Id: control-plane
Mtu: 9216
Buffer: min 0
```

```
         Cong: algo 0 ecn 0
         Sched: bw 0 meth SP
         Queue: limit 1500 meth Dynamic
         ----------------------------------------------------
         QOS Class
         ----------------------------------------------------
         Id: level3
         Mtu: 9216
         Buffer: min 0
         Cong: algo 1 ecn 0
         Sched: bw 20 meth WRR
         Queue: limit 1522 meth Dynamic
         ----------------------------------------------------
         QOS Class
         ----------------------------------------------------
         Id: level2
         Mtu: 9216
         Buffer: min 3
         Cong: algo 1 ecn 0
         Sched: bw 20 meth WRR
         Queue: limit 1522 meth Dynamic
         ----------------------------------------------------
         QOS Class
         ----------------------------------------------------
         Id: level1
         Mtu: 9216
         Buffer: min 0
         Cong: algo 1 ecn 0
         Sched: bw 10 meth SP
         Queue: limit 1522 meth Dynamic
```

We can confirm this in the GUI by navigating to **Fabric | Access Policies | Global Policies | QOS Class Policies**:

Name	Admin State	Priority Flow Control Admin State	MTU	Minimum Buffers	Congestion Algorithm	Congestion Notification	Queue Control	Queue Limit (Bytes)	Scheduling Algorithm	Bandwidth Allocated (in %)
Level1	Enabled	false	9216	0	Tail drop	Disabled	Dynamic	1522	Strict priority	n/a
Level2	Enabled	false	9216	3	Tail drop	Disabled	Dynamic	1522	Weighted round robin	20
Level3	Enabled	false	9216	0	Tail drop	Disabled	Dynamic	1522	Weighted round robin	20

- `show system internal qos vlan all`

This command will show the QoS settings applied to the VLANs on the system:

```
ACI-leaf1# show system internal qos vlan all
Requested VLAN ALL
----------------------------------------------------------------
Vlan
----------------------------------------------------------------
PI id: 10 (0xe2aeeac, 0xe2b3354) flags 0x0
Type: VLAN     Encap: 1011
refcnt: 1 pinst: 87032487 def_nodeid: 87032487
Default Qos Group = 1
Vlan list for this EPG (PI ids): 10
Policies
------------
DSCP name: (null)
      qos_grp: 3 from: 48 to: 48 markDscp: 64
```

An End-to-End Example Using the NX-OS CLI

In this final chapter, we will create a full end-to-end configuration comprising a tenant, connecting to a VMWare VMM domain, and with one EPG providing a simple service to another. This simple service will be offered through a contract and secured through an ASA firewall.

So that we don't just rehash old ground, we will use the NX-OS CLI a lot more (which will save us from having too many repetitive screenshots). While the goal of this chapter is to stick to the CLI for configuration, some elements are better configured through the GUI, and this will also highlight any pitfalls along the way.

The steps we will cover are:

- Setting up in-band and out-of-band access to the nodes
- Creating the security domain
- Creating the VLAN domain
- Creating the VMWare domain
- Creating the tenant
- Creating the VRF
- Creating the bridge domains
- Creating the applications and EPGs
- Creating the contract
- Creating an L4-L7 device
- Creating service templates
- Setting up the client VMs

Introduction

The recipes so far have been without context, so it will be nice to be able to see a "proper" environment, supplying a service (of some description).

While this chapter will cover the same content as the earlier recipes, we will be putting everything into a more realistic scenario and will be able to see how everything comes together, and we will look at the problems that come in the course of this process.

Background

ACME Corp has two distinct departments, **finance** and **marketing**. The finance team hosts a web application that enables the marketing department to keep track of their budget and update it accordingly.

Due to security requirements, the two departments are separated by an ASA firewall:

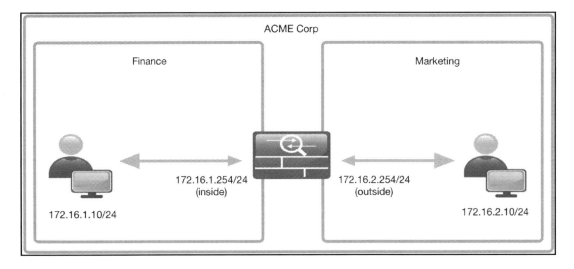

Before you start...

To make things cleaner, I have reset the ACI appliance. This has removed the tenancies already created to make the recipe easier to read, and it will make the code at the end much more succinct.

Some parts have already been set up:

- The ASA package has already been imported
- The ASAv, Finance, and Marketing VMs have been imported into vCenter

There are a number of steps in this recipe, so they have been separated into smaller recipes. Because this is a new setup, we should set up the in-band and out-of-band access.

Setting up in-band and out-of-band access to the nodes

Before we start, we should set up the switches.

How to do it...

We will be using the same settings as we did in the *Switch diagnostics* recipe in Chapter 9, *Troubleshooting ACI*.

1. Log into the controller with the credentials defined during installation.
2. First, we need to name our switches:

   ```
   apic1(config)# system switch-id TEP-1-101 101 Leaf-1 pod 1
   apic1(config)# system switch-id TEP-1-102 102 Leaf-2 pod 1
   apic1(config)# system switch-id TEP-1-103 103 Spine-1
   ```

   These commands select the nodes as seen by the fabric (the "TEPs"). We give each one a switch ID, so TEP-1-101 gets the switch ID 101. We then name the switches and select the pod to which they are assigned. By default, the system will use pod 1, so we do not have to add this ourselves, as you can see with Spine-1.

3. The next step is to set up the in-band and out-of-band management IP addresses. We do this for both the mgmt0 and inband-mgmt0 interfaces, specifying the EPG as well:

   ```
   apic1(config)# switch 102
   apic1(config-switch)# interface mgmt0
   apic1(config-switch-if)#
   ip address 192.168.1.82/24 gateway 192.168.1.1
   apic1(config-switch-if)# oob-mgmt epg default
   apic1(config-switch-if)# exit
   ```

An End-to-End Example Using the NX-OS CLI

```
apic1(config-switch)# interface inband-mgmt0
apic1(config-switch-if)#
ip address 4.4.4.82/24 gateway 4.4.4.1
apic1(config-switch-if)# inband-mgmt epg InBand-Mgmt
apic1(config-switch-if)# exit
apic1(config-switch)# exit
apic1(config)# switch 103
apic1(config-switch)# interface mgmt0
apic1(config-switch-if)#
ip address 192.168.1.83/24 gateway 192.168.1.1
apic1(config-switch-if)# oob-mgmt epg default
apic1(config-switch-if)# exit
apic1(config-switch)# interface inband-mgmt0
apic1(config-switch-if)#
ip address 4.4.4.83/24 gateway 4.4.4.1
apic1(config-switch-if)# inband-mgmt epg InBand-Mgmt
apic1(config-switch-if)# exit
apic1(config-switch)# exit
apic1(config)# switch 101
apic1(config-switch)# interface mgmt0
apic1(config-switch-if)#
ip address 192.168.1.81/24 gateway 192.168.1.1
apic1(config-switch-if)# oob-mgmt epg default
apic1(config-switch-if)# exit
apic1(config-switch)# interface inband-mgmt0
apic1(config-switch-if)#
ip address 4.4.4.81/24 gateway 4.4.4.1
apic1(config-switch-if)# inband-mgmt epg InBand-Mgmt
apic1(config-switch-if)# exit
apic1(config-switch)# exit
apic1(config)#
```

How it works...

We can confirm from the GUI that we have in-band and out-of-band addresses on our nodes (Tenants | mgmt | Node Management Addresses | Static Node Management Addresses):

Node	Type	EPG	IPV4 Address	IPV4 Gateway
pod-1/node-101	Out-Of-Band	default	192.168.1.81/24	192.168.1.1
pod-1/node-102	Out-Of-Band	default	192.168.1.82/24	192.168.1.1
pod-1/node-103	Out-Of-Band	default	192.168.1.83/24	192.168.1.1
pod-1/node-101	In-Band	InBand-Mgmt	4.4.4.81/24	4.4.4.1
pod-1/node-102	In-Band	InBand-Mgmt	4.4.4.82/24	4.4.4.1
pod-1/node-103	In-Band	InBand-Mgmt	4.4.4.83/24	4.4.4.1

Static Node Management Addresses

Now that we have configured our switches, we can start with the fabric services (the VMWare environment).

Creating the security domain

The security domain will be applied to both the VMWare environment and the tenant. So it makes for a good place to start.

How to do it...

1. From the CLI, enter the command `rbac security-domain`, followed by the name in quotes:

   ```
   apic1(config)# rbac security-domain "ACME-SD"
   apic1(config-security-domain)# exit
   apic1(config)#
   ```

2. Next, we can create the VMWare environment, but before that, we need a VLAN domain.

Creating the VLAN domain

We need the VLAN domain so that we have a range of VLANs that the VMWare domain can use.

How to do it...

1. We will create a range of VLANs from 30 to 60, in a VLAN domain called `ACI-vSwitch`. These will be dynamic and designed for VMWare environments:

   ```
   apic1(config)# vlan-domain ACI-vSwitch dynamic type vmware
   apic1(config-vlan)# vlan-pool ACME-VLANs
   apic1(config-vlan)# vlan 30-60 dynamic
   apic1(config-vlan)# exit
   apic1(config)#
   ```

How it works...

From **Fabric** | **Access Policies** | **Pools** | **VLAN**, we can see the new pool.

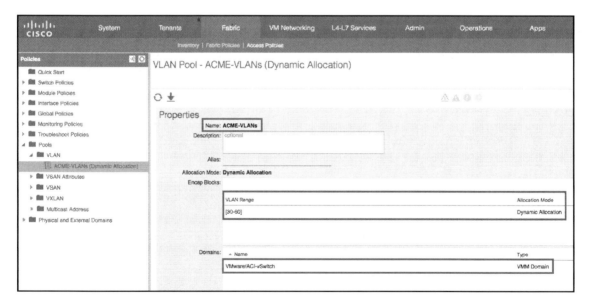

Next, we can create the VMWare domain.

Creating the VMWare domain

The VMWare domain will allow our tenant to use the virtual machines hosted within vCenter.

How to do it...

1. We start by creating the VMWare domain, adding it to the VLAN domain created previously as well as the security domain.
2. We then specify the credentials needed to connect to it and then create the distributed virtual switch:

```
apic1(config)# vmware-domain ACI-vSwitch
apic1(config-vmware)# vlan-domain member ACI-vSwitch type vmware
apic1(config-vmware)# security-domain ACME-SD
apic1(config-vmware)# vcenter 192.168.1.18 datacenter 802101.local dvs-version 6.0
apic1(config-vmware-vc)# username administrator@802101.local
Password: Password123
Retype password: Password123
apic1(config-vmware-vc)# exit
apic1(config-vmware)# configure-dvs
apic1(config-vmware-dvs)# cdp enable
apic1(config-vmware-dvs)# channel-mode on
apic1(config-vmware-dvs)# exit
apic1(config-vmware)# exit
apic1(config)#
```

How it works...

We have created a VMWare domain (`ACI-vSwitch`), making it a member of the VLAN domain and security domain created earlier. We can check in the GUI (**VM Networking | Inventory**):

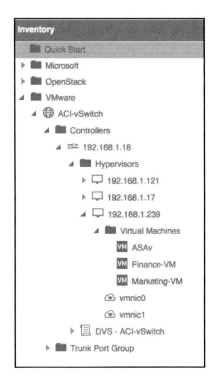

We can also see that the switch is created in vSphere:

Chapter 10

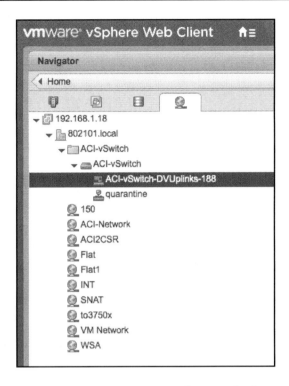

Now, we need to add the host (`192.168.1.239`) to this. To do that, we right-click on **ACI-vSwitch** and select the option to add a host and follow the prompts:

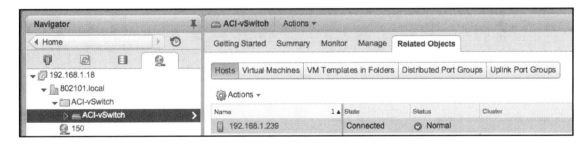

With these components in place, we can create the tenant.

Creating the tenant

We start by creating the ACME Corp tenant.

How to do it...

1. Creating the tenant requires one command, `tenant`, followed by the name of the tenant. We also make it a member of the same security domain as the VMWare domain.

   ```
   apic1(config)# tenant ACMECorp
   apic1(config-tenant)# security domain ACME-SD
   apic1(config-tenant)#
   ```

How it works...

The tenant, ACMECorp, is visible in the GUI under the Tenants menu.

Next, we can move on to creating the VRF for the tenant.

Creating the VRF

We will only be using one VRF in this recipe.

How to do it...

We create the VRF using the command `vrf context`, followed by the name of the VRF:

```
apic1(config-tenant)# vrf context ACME-VRF
apic1(config-tenant-vrf)# exit
apic1(config-tenant)#
```

How it works...

The VRF has been created (**Tenants** | **ACMECorp** | **Networking** | **VRFs**):

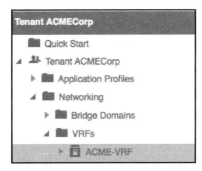

We can move on to creating the bridge domains.

Creating the bridge domains

Each EPG will need a bridge domain, but they can share the same VRF.

How to do it...

1. We will create two bridge domains (`Finance-BD` and `Marketing-BD`); they will use the same VRF we created a moment ago, and we will enable ARP flooding and layer-2 unknown unicast flooding, which is required when using an ASA in `GoTo` mode:

```
apic1(config-tenant)# bridge-domain Finance-BD
apic1(config-tenant-bd)# arp flooding
apic1(config-tenant-bd)# l2-unknown-unicast flood
apic1(config-tenant-bd)# vrf member ACME-VRF
apic1(config-tenant-bd)# exit
apic1(config-tenant)# bridge-domain Marketing-BD
apic1(config-tenant-bd)# arp flooding
apic1(config-tenant-bd)# l2-unknown-unicast flood
apic1(config-tenant-bd)# vrf member ACME-VRF
apic1(config-tenant-bd)# exit
apic1(config-tenant)#
```

How it works...

The bridge domains have been created with the flooding options and are members of the VRF (Tenants | ACMECorp | Networking | Bridge Domains):

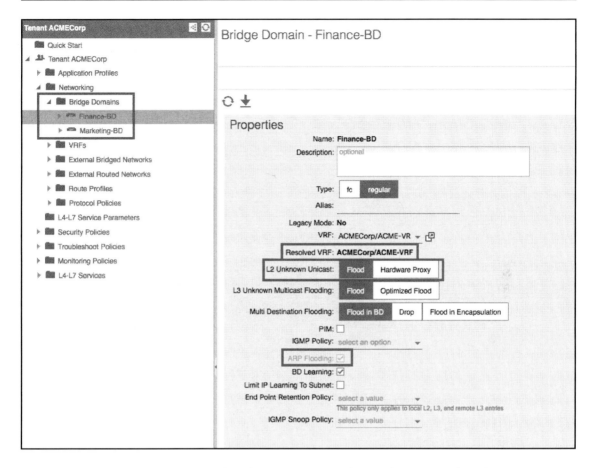

Now that we have this part completed, we can create the application and EPGs.

Creating the applications and EPGs

We will create one application network profile called ACME-AP and two EPGs: one for Finance and one for Marketing.

How to do it...

1. Like the tenant creation, we need to enter the command `application` followed by the name of the application.
2. We then create the EPGs, add them to the bridge domains, and make them members of the VMWare domain:

```
apic1(config-tenant)# application ACME-AP
apic1(config-tenant-app)# epg Finance
apic1(config-tenant-app-epg)# bridge-domain member Finance-BD
apic1(config-tenant-app-epg)#
vmware-domain member ACI-vSwitch push on-demand
apic1(config-tenant-app-epg-domain)# exit
apic1(config-tenant-app-epg)# exit
apic1(config-tenant-app)#
apic1(config-tenant-app)# epg Marketing
apic1(config-tenant-app-epg)# bridge-domain member Marketing-BD
apic1(config-tenant-app-epg)#
vmware-domain member ACI-vSwitch push on-demand
apic1(config-tenant-app-epg-domain)# exit
apic1(config-tenant-app-epg)# exit
apic1(config-tenant-app)# exit
apic1(config-tenant)#
```

How it works...

We can see the two applications--Finance and Marketing--within the tenant (Tenants | ACMECorp | Application Profiles | ACME-AP | Application EPGs):

Chapter 10

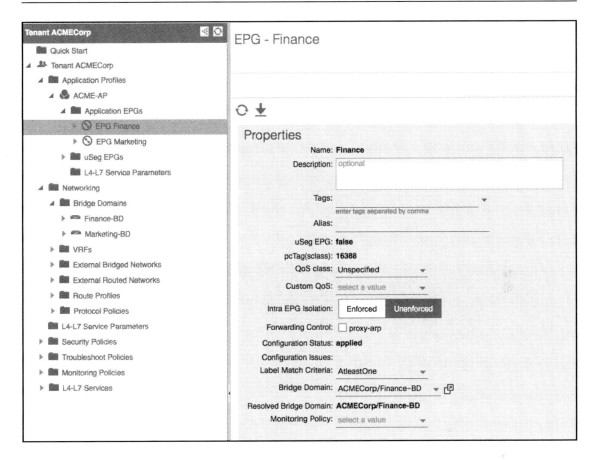

If we return to vSphere, we can see two new distributed port groups:

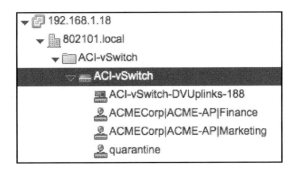

Creating the contract

When we create a contract, we need to create the scope (where the contract can be applied) and a subject, which contains the access-group and the service template graph.

How to do it...

1. We start by creating the contract:

    ```
    apic1(config-tenant)# contract ACME-Contract
    apic1(config-tenant-contract)# scope tenant
    apic1(config-tenant-contract)# subject Subject
    apic1(config-tenant-contract-subj)# access-group default both
    apic1(config-tenant-contract-subj)# 1417 graph ACME-SGT
    apic1(config-tenant-contract-subj)# exit
    apic1(config-tenant-contract)# exit
    apic1(config-tenant)#
    ```

2. The next part of creating the contracts is to assign the provider and consumer roles:

    ```
    apic1(config-tenant)# application ACME-AP
    apic1(config-tenant-app)# epg Finance
    apic1(config-tenant-app-epg)# contract provider ACME-Contract
    apic1(config-tenant-app-epg)# exit
    apic1(config-tenant-app)# epg Marketing
    apic1(config-tenant-app-epg)# contract consumer ACME-Contract
    apic1(config-tenant-app-epg)# exit
    apic1(config-tenant-app)# exit
    apic1(config-tenant)#
    ```

Chapter 10

How it works...

We are borrowing the default filter from the common tenant. This is useful if you need to use one of the shared filters, but you can also create custom filters in the common tenant if they need to be applied to more than one tenant:

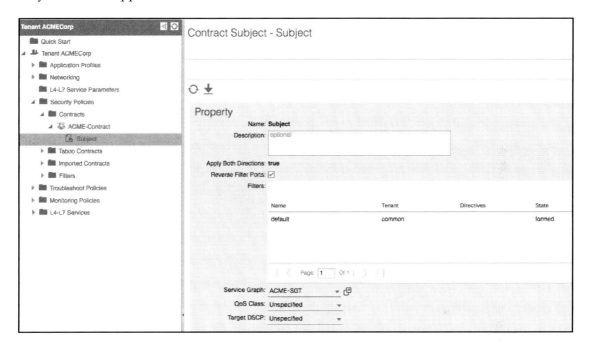

From the GUI, we can also see the relationship between the two EPGs (Tenants | ACMECorp | Application Profiles | ACME-AP):

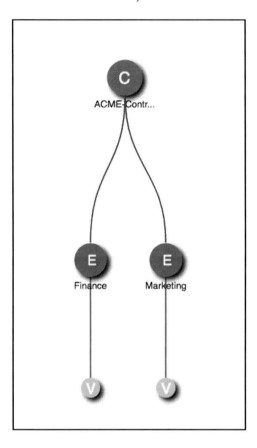

Now that we have a contract, we should have something to use it.

Creating an L4-L7 device

When creating an L4-L7 device, the GUI is most useful.

The ASA device package, like other packages, has some required entries, and the NX-OS cannot be re-written to account for all the required fields from all the different vendors. So, while scripting may be quicker, the GUI wins here.

How to do it...

1. First of all, we need to set up the ASA's management interface for DHCP and allow HTTPS access:

    ```
    ASAv# sh run int management 0/0
    !
    interface Management0/0
      management-only
      nameif management
      security-level 0
      ip address dhcp
    ASAv# sh run | i http
    http server enable
    http 0.0.0.0 0.0.0.0 management
    ASAv#
    ```

2. You will also need an administrative account for the APIC to be able to connect to and manage the firewall.

An End-to-End Example Using the NX-OS CLI

While we do not have to do this next step, it's useful as it highlights the control over the VMWare environment that the APIC can have. So, assign the ASA interfaces to the **Finance** and **Marketing** port groups:

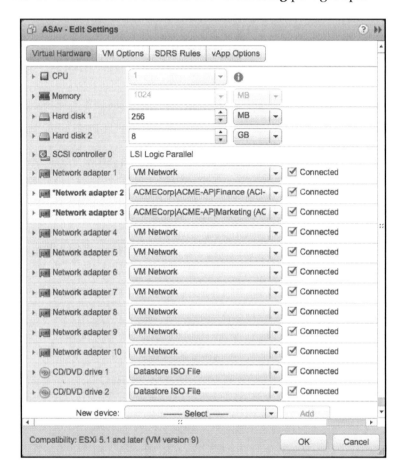

3. Let's set the ASAv in ACI now.

> From **Tenants** | **ACMECorp** | **L4-L7 Services**, right-click on **L4-L7 Devices** and select **Create L4-L7 Device**. In the **General** window, set the name, service type, device type, VMM domain, the device package, and model. We will be using a **GoTo** function type, as this will mean we are using a firewall in routed mode (whereas **GoThrough** would be used if we were setting up a transparent firewall).

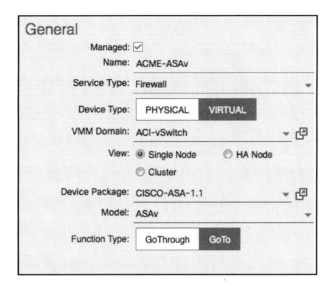

4. Next, enter the connectivity (**Out-Of-Band**) and the credentials of the account set up on the firewall.

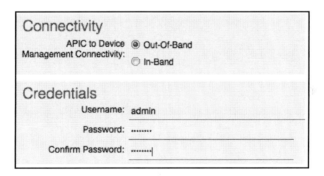

5. In the Device 1 details, we need to assign the management IP address, which would be the IP address assigned to the **Management 0/0** interface. We also need to set the access method (the management port) to **HTTPS**.

An End-to-End Example Using the NX-OS CLI

6. Under the **Device Interfaces** area, we need to set the mapping between the interfaces on the device in the ACI fabric and the virtual device running on vSphere. It is important to remember to leave the first network adapter and start from network adapter 2. The first network adapter would be the **Management 0/0** interface on the ASAv and would not be usable within ACI.

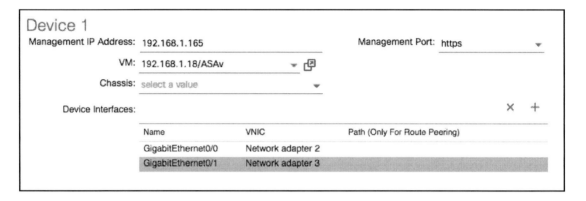

7. The **Cluster** settings are used to map the different roles to the specific interfaces.

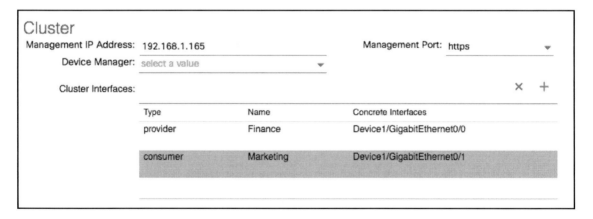

When the settings have been entered, click on **Next**, and then click on **Finish**.

How it works...

The ASA is now visible in the APIC. It may take a few moments for the device to stabilize, but make sure that the **Configuration State** shows **stable**:

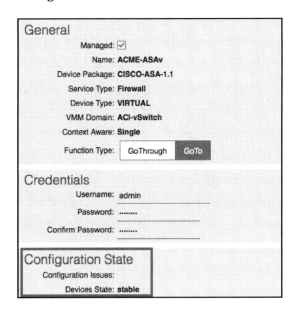

There's more...

This can be scripted; however, to do so, we need to use XML rather than the NX-OS CLI.

You can see how to do this using the following link:

http://www.cisco.com/c/en/us/td/docs/security/asa/apic/api-reference/guide/apic-xml127.html#pgfId-773842

Creating service templates

The service template creates a service graph, linking the contract to the bridge domains and setting one EPG as the provider and the other as the consumer.

How to do it...

1. Navigate to **Tenants | ACMECorp | L4-L7 Services**. Right-click on **L4-L7 Service Graph Templates** and select C**reate L4-L7 Service Graph Template**.
2. Name the template, and drag the ASAv object from the left-hand side to be between the consumer and provider EPGs. Set the firewall to be routed and use a routed profile.

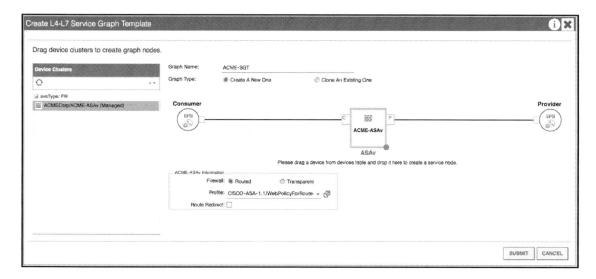

3. Click on **Submit**.
4. Right-click on the new template and select **Apply L4-L7 Service Graph Template**.

Chapter 10

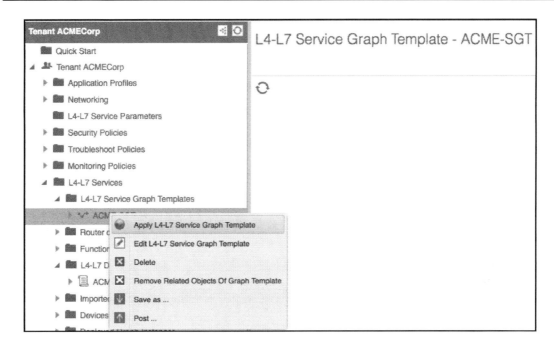

5. Here, we select the consumer and provider EPGs. We also either create a contract or use an existing one.

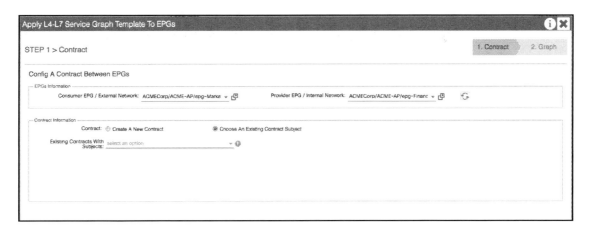

[391]

An End-to-End Example Using the NX-OS CLI

6. Here, I am unable to select the contract created earlier. It does not appear in the dropdown, so I need to create a new one.

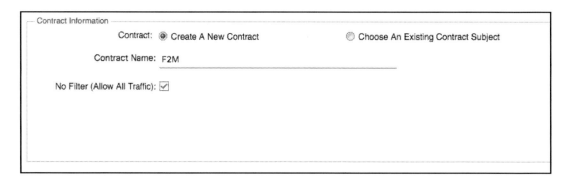

7. Again, this goes to show that using the GUI can get you further. Click on **Next**.

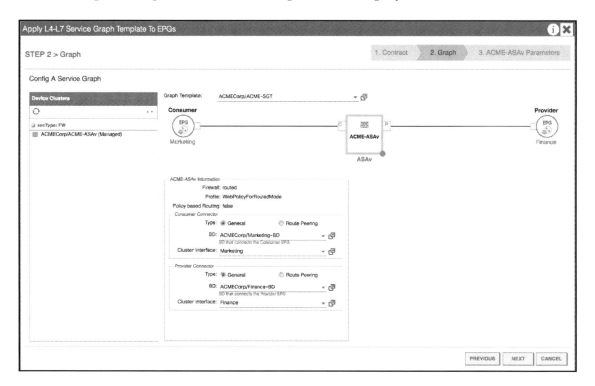

8. These settings should be prefilled, so here we just click on N**ext**.

Chapter 10

9. This next window is where we configure the ASAv. There will be some defaults, so we can edit, add, and modify as required. Select **All Parameters**, then select **Access Lists**. We have a default access list called **access-list-inbound**, which permits HTTP and HTTPS access. Click on the plus sign next to the first **Access Control Entry** line, and add a new entry for **IP**. We only need to name it (`permit-ip`), set the action (`permit`), and number it (`10`).

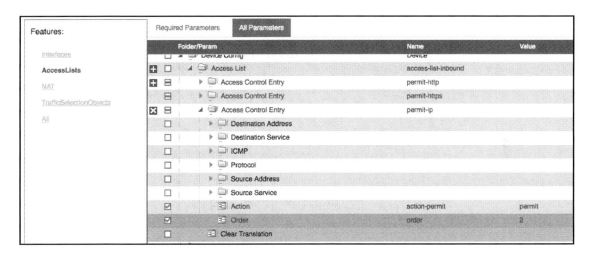

10. Next, select **Interfaces** and set the interface IP addresses--first, for the internal interface (the one in the finance department).

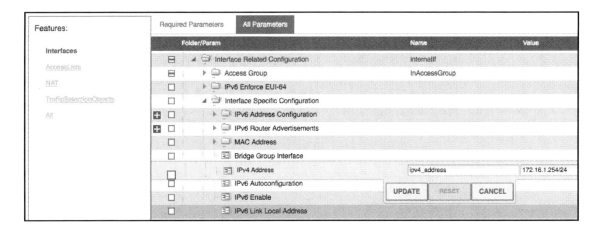

An End-to-End Example Using the NX-OS CLI

11. Repeat the process for the external interface (the marketing interface).

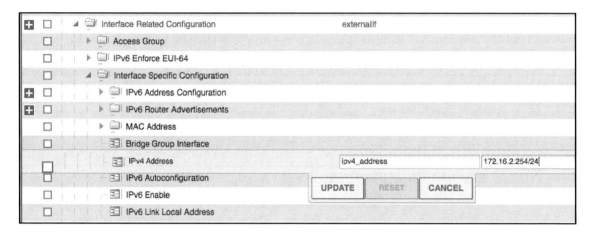

12. Click on **Finish**.

How it works...

If we look at vSphere, we can see new port groups, which contain the name of the VRF and the bridge domain:

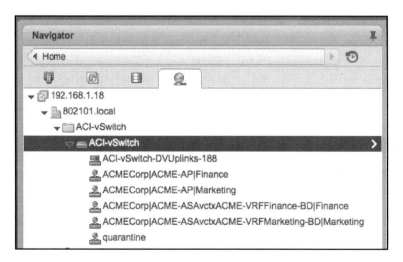

[394]

Earlier, we placed the interfaces of the ASA into the first set of port groups that were created when we joined the tenant to the VMWare domain. Now if we check on the ASA, we can see that they have changed:

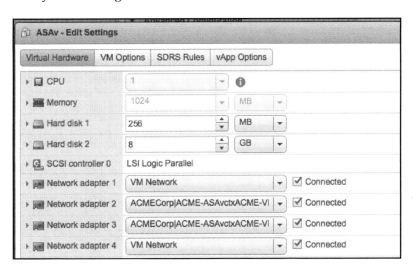

If we look at the ASA's configuration, we can see the **access-list-inbound** access list, containing the extra entry we added:

```
ASAv# show access-list
access-list cached ACL log flows: total 0, denied 0 (deny-flow-max 4096)
 alert-interval 300
access-list access-list-inbound; 3 elements; name hash: 0xcb5bd6c7
access-list access-list-inbound line 1 extended permit ip any any
(hitcnt=0) 0x7e90fe9a
access-list access-list-inbound line 2 extended permit tcp any any eq www
(hitcnt=0) 0xc873a747
access-list access-list-inbound line 3 extended permit tcp any any eq https
(hitcnt=0) 0x48bedbdd
ASAv#
```

If we look at the interfaces, we can see that they have the names set by the service graph template (`internalIf` and `externalIf`), but they do not have the IP addresses:

```
ASAv# sh run int gi 0/0
!
interface GigabitEthernet0/0
  nameif internalIf
  security-level 0
  no ip address
```

An End-to-End Example Using the NX-OS CLI

```
ASAv# sh run int gi 0/1
!
interface GigabitEthernet0/1
  nameif externalIf
  security-level 0
  no ip address
ASAv#
```

From the GUI, we can look at the errors (from Tenants | ACMECorp and then selecting Faults from the right-hand side):

Description
Graph configuration resulted in "Major script error : Configuration error : ip address 172.16.2.254 24 ^ ERROR: % Invalid Hostname " for ipv4_address in context ACME-VRF on cluster ACME-ASAv in tenant ACMECorp
Graph configuration resulted in "Major script error : Configuration error : ip address 172.16.1.254 24 ^ ERROR: % Invalid Hostname " for ipv4_address in context ACME-VRF on cluster ACME-ASAv in tenant ACMECorp

Perhaps the IP address needs to be entered in the `<IP address> <subnet mask>` format, instead of the CIDR format used here. In later releases of the ASA package, the CIDR format works fine, but this will not stop us working as we can enter the addresses manually:

```
ASAv(config)# int gi0/0
ASAv(config-if)# ip add 172.16.1.254 255.255.255.0
ASAv(config-if)# exit
ASAv(config)# int gi0/1
ASAv(config-if)# ip add 172.16.2.254 255.255.255.0
ASAv(config-if)# exit
ASAv(config)#
```

Can we get the two VMs to talk to each other?

Setting up the client VMs

I am using the Tiny Linux distro here, because of the small footprint. They are both running on the same host as the ASAv and therefore have access to the same EPGs as the ASA does.

How to do it...

1. You can download the same VM from here: `https://communities.vmware.com/docs/DOC-21621`.
2. The OVA file should be imported into vCenter and named **Finance-VM**. Set the network interface to use the **ACME-ASAvctxACME-VRFFinance-BD** port group.

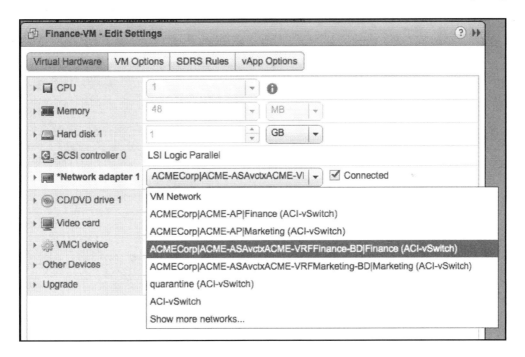

3. Repeat the process for the second VM, calling it **Marketing-VM** and making sure that it is connected to the **Marketing** EPG.

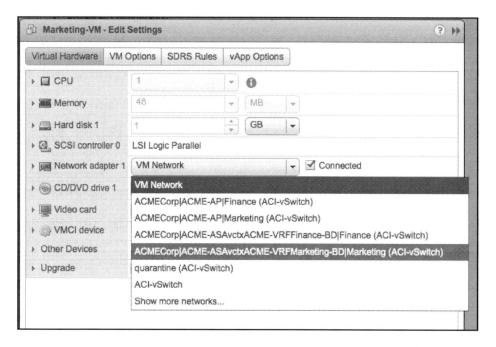

4. Following the topology diagram at the start of this chapter, the **Finance** VM has an IP address of `172.16.1.10/24`, and the **Marketing** VM has an IP address of `172.16.2.10/24`. Both have their default gateways set to the ASAv's respective interface, and both can ping their default gateways. Here is the **Finance** VM pinging the ASA:

```
tc@Finance-VM:~$ ping 172.16.1.254
PING 172.16.1.254 (172.16.1.254): 56 data bytes
64 bytes from 172.16.1.254: seq=0 ttl=255 time=5.940 ms
64 bytes from 172.16.1.254: seq=1 ttl=255 time=1.058 ms
64 bytes from 172.16.1.254: seq=2 ttl=255 time=0.682 ms
64 bytes from 172.16.1.254: seq=3 ttl=255 time=0.826 ms
^C
--- 172.16.1.254 ping statistics ---
4 packets transmitted, 4 packets received, 0% packet loss
round-trip min/avg/max = 0.682/2.126/5.940 ms
tc@Finance-VM:~$
tc@Finance-VM:~$
```

Chapter 10

5. Here we can see the **Marketing** VM pinging the ASA:

```
tc@Marketing-VM:~$ ping 172.16.2.254
PING 172.16.2.254 (172.16.2.254): 56 data bytes
64 bytes from 172.16.2.254: seq=0 ttl=255 time=6.102 ms
64 bytes from 172.16.2.254: seq=1 ttl=255 time=0.746 ms
64 bytes from 172.16.2.254: seq=2 ttl=255 time=0.710 ms
64 bytes from 172.16.2.254: seq=3 ttl=255 time=0.745 ms
^C
--- 172.16.2.254 ping statistics ---
4 packets transmitted, 4 packets received, 0% packet loss
round-trip min/avg/max = 0.710/2.075/6.102 ms
tc@Marketing-VM:~$
```

6. Because we permitted IP traffic through the firewalls, the two VMs can reach each other. We can now ping from one VM to the other.

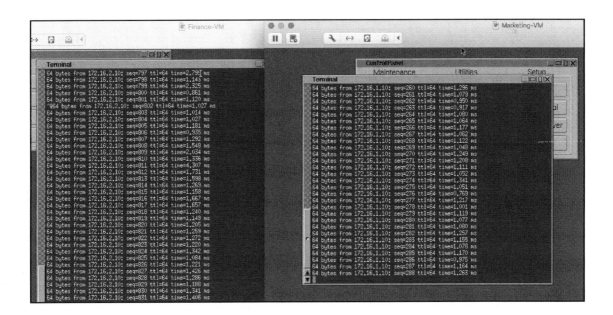

[399]

7. We can see the hits on the ACL increasing as we stop and start the pings:

   ```
   ASAv(config)# sh access-list
   access-list access-list-inbound line 1 extended permit ip any any
   (hitcnt=3) 0x7e90fe9a
   access-list access-list-inbound line 2 extended permit tcp any any
   eq www (hitcnt=0) 0xc873a747
   access-list access-list-inbound line 3 extended permit tcp any any
   eq https (hitcnt=0) 0x48bedbdd
   ASAv(config)# sh access-list
   access-list access-list-inbound line 1 extended permit ip any any
   (hitcnt=4) 0x7e90fe9a
   access-list access-list-inbound line 2 extended permit tcp any any
   eq www (hitcnt=0) 0xc873a747
   access-list access-list-inbound line 3 extended permit tcp any any
   eq https (hitcnt=0) 0x48bedbdd
   ASAv(config)#
   ```

The goal of this chapter was to use the NX-OS CLI as much as possible, which has been achieved to some extent. Some aspects of the configuration are beyond the capabilities of the CLI because Cisco cannot be expected to account for every different vendor's requirements. We could mix and match our approach by using the CLI and XML to perform all of the tasks or even keep to a purely XML-based approach, but this depends on your preferred approach.

In some ways, this is the beauty of ACI. ACI is actually very easy to get to grips with, and quite fun. While getting hands-on experience with the physical equipment may be difficult (due to the cost), there are the free Cisco DevNet labs which will enable you to practice most of the recipes in this book. There are also the full hardware labs available, but (as I said earlier in the book) these do get booked up months in advance. You can access the labs at `https://developer.cisco.com/site/devnet/sandbox/`.

Index

A

A10
  integrating 156, 157, 158, 162, 164, 165, 166, 167, 168
  reference link 168
  URL, for downloading 159
AAA (Authentication, Authorization, and Accounting)
  about 42
  events, viewing 308
  multiple tenant support 245
access policies
  CDP, turning off 70, 75, 76
  creating 60, 62, 64, 66, 67, 68, 70
ACI endpoints
  tracking 154
ACI fabric
  overlay 24, 26, 27, 28
  overview 14
ACI image
  uploading, with SCP 21
  uploading, with SCP from another SCP server 22
  uploading, with USB drive 22
ACI mode
  Cisco Nexus NX-OS mode, converting to 20
ACI plugin for vCenter
  about 142
  URL 142
ACI software
  switches, upgrading 351, 354, 356
  upgrading 349, 350
ACI Toolkit virtual machine
  URL 155, 156
APIC (Application Policy Infrastructure Controller)
  about 9, 10, 12, 13, 14
  logging into, with Cobra 298
  troubleshooting 345, 346, 347
APIC-EM (Application Policy Infrastructure Controller Enterprise Module) 10
APN
  creating, with REST and XML 291
Application Centric Infrastructure (ACI)
  about 7, 10, 12, 13, 14
  hardware 14, 15, 16, 18
  monitoring 301
  programming, through REST 286, 287
  third-party integration 18, 19, 20
application network profiles
  creating 95, 96, 97, 98
application profiles (APs)
  about 95
  creating, with REST 293
Application Virtual Switch (AVS)
  about 147
  deploying 147, 148, 149, 150
  reference 147, 150
ASAv
  deploying 169, 171
  reference link 172
ASICs (application-specific integrated circuitry) 14
attachable entity profile (AEP) 131
audit logs
  navigating 308, 309, 310

B

BIGIP-13.0.0.0.0.1645.ALL-scsi.ova 174
Border Gateway Protocol (BGP)
  about 185
  reference link 210
  routing 201, 202, 206, 207, 208
bridge domains (BDs)
  about 79
  associating, with external network 215, 216, 218

configuring 79, 80, 81, 82, 83, 84, 85, 88
multicast, configuring 238

C

Call Home
  policies, creating 319, 320, 321, 322
  setting up 311, 312, 314, 315, 317, 318
Cisco DevNet labs
  URL 400
Cisco Discovery Protocol (CDP) 46, 336
Cisco Manufacturing Certificate Authority (CMCA) 24, 341
Cisco Nexus NX-OS mode
  ACI image, upgrading 22
  ACI image, uploading 21
  converting, to ACI mode 20
  logging in 22
  reverting to 23
Citrix NetScaler
  integrating 183
  URL 183
class of service (CoS)
  about 269
  existing CoS settings, preserving 270, 271
client VM
  URL, for downloading 397
Cobra
  used, for logging into APIC 298
configuration export policy
  creating 348, 349
contexts
  configuring 88, 90, 91, 92, 93, 94
contracts
  creating, within tenants 118, 119, 120
  references 102
  used, between tenants 102, 103, 104, 105, 106, 108, 109, 110, 112, 113, 115
control class 274
Control Plane Policing (CoPP) 364
controller 131

D

deficit weighted round-robin (DWRR) 274
device packages
  about 125
  installing 128, 129, 130
  reference link 128, 131
Devnet
  URL 36
DHCP (Dynamic Host Configuration Protocol) 26
DHCP relay
  creating 186
  creating, with Common tenant 187, 188, 191
  global DHCP relay, creating 192, 195, 196
distributed virtual switch (DVS) 135
DMZ (demilitarized zone) 11
DNS
  utilizing 196, 197, 198, 201

E

electronic programmable logic device (EPLD) 21
end-to-end example
  applications, creating 379
  background 368
  bridge domain, creating 377
  client VMs, setting up 397, 399, 400
  contract, creating 382
  creating, with NX-OS CLI 367
  EPGs, creating 379
  in-band and out-of-band access, setting up to nodes 369, 371
  L4-L7 device, creating 385, 386, 389
  preparation 368
  reference 389
  security domain, creating 371
  service templates, creating 389, 391, 393, 395, 396
  tenant, creating 375
  VLAN domain, creating 372
  VMWare domain, creating 373, 375
  VRF, creating 376
endpoint groups (EPGs)
  about 95
  creating 98, 99, 100
  creating, with REST 293
  creating, with REST and XML 291
Enhanced Interior Gateway Routing Protocol (EIGRP)
  about 185
  routing with 230, 231, 232

equal-cost multipathing (ECMP) 13
events
  AAA events, viewing 308
  fabric events, viewing 306
  tenant events, viewing 306
  viewing 306
existing CoS settings
  preserving 270, 271
external connectivity
  troubleshooting 359, 361
external SVI
  configuring 213, 214

F

F5
  integrating with 174, 175, 176, 177, 178, 180, 181, 182
  references 183
  URL 174
Fabric Extender (FEX)
  troubleshooting 338
fabric
  about 14
  events, viewing 306
  policies, creating 47, 48, 50, 51, 52, 54, 58
faults
  checking, on per-tenant basis 305
  reference 305
  searching 302, 303, 304, 305
filters
  creating 115, 116
FUEL plugin
  URL 172
Fully Qualified Domain Name (FQDN) 51

G

GUI
  about 29, 30
  Admin 42
  Fabric menu 37, 38, 40
  L4-L7 Services 41
  Operations 42
  System menu 30, 32, 33, 34, 35, 36
  Tenants menu 36
  VM Networking 41

H

Head-End Replication (HER) 14

I

IFC class 274
inter-fabric messaging (IFM) 24, 340
interfaces
  multicast, configuring 238
IPv6
  using, within ACI 233
iWorkflow-2.1.0.0.0.10285-scsi.ova 174

J

JSON
  and REST, authenticating through 294
  and REST, used for creating tenant 296

L

layer 2
  troubleshooting 336, 338
layer-3 outside interface
  configuring, for tenant networks 210
  external SVI, configuring 213, 214
  routed interface, creating 210, 212
  routed sub-interfaces, configuring 215
LDAP server
  connecting to 265, 266
leaf switch 14
Link Layer Discovery Protocol (LLDP) 8, 26, 336
local users
  creating 247, 248

M

managed object (MO) 20
management contracts
  creating 121, 122, 123
management information tree (MIT) 46
MIB (Management Information Base)
  about 19
  reference 331
Mirantis OpenStack
  URL 172
multicast
  configuring, on bridge domain 238

configuring, on interfaces 238
setting up, for tenants 236
troubleshooting 361

N

NetFlow
  configuring 333
  reference, for configuration 334
Network Management Station (NMS) 324
northbound protocols 10
NPS (Network Policy Server) 261
NTP (Network Time Protocol) 46
NX-OS CLI
  used, for creating end-to-end example 367

O

Object Store Browser
  used, for browsing object store 280, 282, 285
Open Shortest Path First (OSPF)
  about 185
  routing with 223, 228, 230
OpenStack
  integrating with 172
  references 173
OpFlex
  about 18
  references 20

P

Postman
  URL 286
Promise theory 19
Protocol Independent Multicast(PIM) 236
Python SDK
  using 297

Q

quality of service (QoS)
  about 95
  basic configuration, creating 274, 276
  commands 364, 366
  policy, creating 277
  troubleshooting 362, 364
  verifying 277

R

RADIUS server
  connecting to 256, 257, 258, 259, 260, 261, 264, 265
reserved classes
  control class 274
  IFC class 274
  SPAN class 274
REST
  ACI, programming 286, 287
  and JSON, authenticating through 294
  and JSON, used for creating tenant 296
  and XML, used for creating APN 291
  and XML, used for creating EPG 291
  and XML, used for creating tenant 289
  and XML, used for deleting tenant 290
  authenticating through 287, 289
role-based access control (RBAC) 246
roles
  AAA 246
  Access-Admin 246
  Admin 246
  Fabric-Admin 246
  NW-SVC-Admin 246
  NW-SVC-Params 246
  OPS 246
  Read-all 246
  reference link 247
  Tenant-Admin 246
  Tenant-Ext-Admin 246
  VMM-Admin 246
route peering 240, 242
route reflectors
  using 219, 223
route targets (RTs) 12
routed interfaces
  creating 210, 212
routed sub-interfaces
  configuring 215

S

SDK
  used, for creating tenant 299
security domains

creating 250, 252
service insertion 125
service-level agreements (SLAs) 95
Simple Network Management Protocol (SNMP)
  about 8, 19, 324
  configuration, checking from command line 330
  configuring 324, 325, 326, 328, 330
software-defined networking (SDN) 9
southbound protocol 10
SPAN class 274
spine switch 14
SSL
  communication, checking 340, 341
  troubleshooting 339
switches
  monitoring 341, 343, 344
Syslog
  configuring 332, 333

T

TACACS+ server
  connecting to 268
TCAM (ternary content-addressable memory) 14
Technical Assistance Center (TAC) 311
tenant
  creating, with REST and JSON 296
  creating, with REST and XML 289
  creating, with SDK 299
  deleting, with REST and XML 290
  events, viewing 306
TenantA_EPG1 (consumer) 182
TenantA_EPG3 (provider) 182
tenants
  contracts, creating within 118, 119, 120
  contracts, using between 102, 103, 104, 105, 106, 108, 109, 110, 112, 113, 115
  creating 77, 78
  multicast, setting up 236
  users, limiting 254
  vCenter domains, associating 143, 144, 146
  virtual machines, adding 152, 153, 154

TEPs (tunnel endpoints) 26
transit routing
  about 240, 242
  reference link 243

U

user-defined classes
  configuring 271, 273
users
  limiting, to tenants 254

V

vCenter domains
  associating, with tenants 143, 144, 146
verifications
  routing 359
Virtual Machine Manager (VMM) domains
  creating 131, 132, 134, 135, 136, 137, 138, 139, 140, 142
virtual machines
  adding, to tenants 152, 153, 154
VMM
  troubleshooting 356, 359
VMWare endpoints
  discovering 150, 151, 152
VMWare
  integrating 131, 132, 134, 135, 136, 137, 138, 139, 141, 142
VRF (Virtual Routing and Forwarding) 12, 88
vSphere Distributed Switch (VDS) 147
vThunder device package
  URL, for downloading 159
VXLAN Tunnel Endpoints (VTEPs) 14

X

XML
  and REST, used for creating APN 291
  and REST, used for creating EPG 291
  and REST, used for creating tenant 289
  and REST, used for deleting tenant 291
  authenticating through 287, 289

Made in the USA
Columbia, SC
10 August 2017